Birding in Ohio

Birding
in Ohio

TOM THOMSON

Indiana University Press *Bloomington*

Manufactured in the United States of America

Library of Congress Cataloging in Publication Data

Thomson, Tom, 1924–
    Birding in Ohio.

    Bibliography: p.
    Includes index.
    1. Bird watching—Ohio.   I. Title.
QL684.O3T48   1983   598'.07'234771   82-49012
ISBN 0-253-10735-0
1 2 3 4 5 87 86 85 84 83

On the previous page: Gray-cheeked Thrush.
Shown on the title pages for Parts I, II, III, and IV are, respectively,
Double-crested Cormorants, Yellow-bellied Sapsucker, Hooded Warbler, and shorebirds in flight.

Contents

Maps

Preface

It is hoped that this book will serve as a guide and reference to the wonderful variety of birdlife found in Ohio and add to the enjoyment of all those who come within its spell.

While this book is the result of many years of personal fieldwork, it was nevertheless through the generous contributions of many individuals and organizations that the enterprise was a success. I am especially grateful for materials and data made available by the Wheaton Club, the Columbus Audubon Society, the Cleveland Audubon Society, the Kirtland Bird Club, the Cleveland Natural Science Club, the Columbus and Franklin County Metropolitan Parks, the Dayton-Montgomery County Park District, the Cleveland Metropolitan Park District, the Akron Metropolitan Park District, the Cincinnati Board of Park Commissioners; the Toledo Metropolitan Park District, and naturalists of Glen Helen Nature Preserve, the Aullwood Audubon Center, the Ohio Historical Society, and the Ohio Department of Natural Resources.

Companions in the field and lab who contributed their knowledge and encouragement include Carl Albrecht, Kirk Alexander, Burt Anderson, Bruce Armstrong, Frank Bader, the late Floyd Bartley, C. F. Bateman, Ann Bingaman, David Blyth, Harold and the late Helen Boecher, Harold Bolin, Mike Bolton, Mary Boren, Donald Borror, A. S. Bradshaw, Ann Buhr, Harold Burtt, Lou Campbell, Jerry Cairo, Lynn Champney, Clarence Chrisp, Audrey Claugus, Bob Conlon, Rick Counts, the late Robert Crofts, Lois Day, Cloyd Dawson, Cornelius Franz, James Fry, Charles Gambill, Maurice Giltz, Eugene Good, Evelyn Gordon, Fritz Griffith, Jan Hall, Lee Hall, Dave Henderson, Mrs. James Hengst, the late Lawrence E. Hicks, Chuck Hocevar, Ed Hutchins, Emmajane James, Lee Johnson, Kelly Jones, Charles King, Ernie Limes, the late Irv Kassoy, Robert Kavanagh, the late Arthur Kiefer, Steve Kress, Randy Little, Mrs. M. C. Markham, Ruth Melvin, Richard and Sue Meyer, Gordon Mitchell, Jean and Carl Nielsen, Ruth Osborne, Jan Palmer, Bruce Peterjohn, John Pogacnik, Peter Post, Ralph Ramey, the late Gene and Helen Rea, Carl and Katheryn Reese, Esther Reichelderfer, the late Irv Rickley, Richard Roederer, David, Charles, and the late Henry Schuer, Bill Schultz, Don Smith, Granville Smith, Al Staffan, Frank Jr. and Penny Starr, Jim and Jean Stahl, Bruce Stehling, William Stull, the late Marian Thomas, John Thomas, Cris Toops, Milton B. and Mary Trautman, K. Roger Trautman, Charles Triplehorn, Walter Tucker, Jeff White, Laurel Van Camp, Charles Wheeler, and George S. Wolfram.

A special word has to be said for my long-time friend and mentor, the late Dr. Edward S. Thomas. His never-failing interest in birds and natural science and his wonderful personal warmth and charm were an inspiration to me through the years.

I also owe a debt of gratitude to my brother, David D. Thomson, for his invaluable editorial assistance; to my children, Jan, Jeff, and James, who persevered through many a tedious field trip as youngsters; to Jeanne Thomson, their mother, and to my mother, Mrs. Lucille Page Thomson.

Introduction

Over 200 good birding sites in every corner of Ohio are described in these pages with directions on how to get to each one. Many are extensive natural areas of many square miles, some are renowned for large concentrations of birds or rare breeding species, and others are out-of-the-way spots relatively uninvestigated ornithologically where opportunities abound for adding to our knowledge of the distribution and breeding ranges of Ohio birds. Some sites, because they are representative of the regions in which they are located, are discussed in greater detail than others, and it can be assumed there are often similar birds in nearby areas not treated as thoroughly in the text.

Part I directs the birder to sites in the northern tier of counties, in many of which birding is influenced by Lake Erie. Part II investigates the west-central counties, and Part III explores the unglaciated Allegheny Plateau counties of southern and eastern Ohio. In each part, the sites are presented in alphabetical order and keyed to section maps. In the site descriptions, the birds and seasons of the year discussed in the greatest detail are those considered most important ornithologically at that particular location.

Part IV is an expanded annotated checklist of the birds of Ohio. This represents the first statewide review of Ohio's bird records in many years. Records were obtained from a variety of sources, including many personal observations, and those of other observers reported to the author, and from published periodicals and books which are denoted by an asterisk in the bibliography.

In this book, I have attempted to open up new vistas for those who love to take to the field in search of birds, new and old. Ohio with its wide diversity of habitats is ideally situated for such high adventure.

Birding in Ohio

PART I

The Northern Tier of Counties

NORTHERN OHIO is blessed with both a diversity and a plenitude of favorable bird habitats. Its riches include the oak openings of Lucas County, the great complex of marshes that stretches from Toledo to Sandusky, the many fine lookout points along the Erie shore from Huron to Cleveland and on east to Ashtabula, the flat farmland and woodlots of northwestern Ohio, and the rolling, often rugged terrain of the northeastern counties with their many reservoirs and large lakes.

Fortunately, significant portions of these natural areas are being saved for future generations—not only of people, but of birds, animals, plants, and all the other life forms that cohabit the earth with us. State and metropolitan parks, national refuges, state wildlife areas, nature preserves, and sanctuaries all contribute to this life-saving process.

Part I describes 83 birding sites in the 31 counties of the northern tier. The westernmost counties, shown on Map A,* are Allen, Ashland, Crawford, Defiance, Erie, Fulton, Hancock, Henry, Huron, Lucas, Ottawa, Paulding, Putnam, Richland, Sandusky, Seneca, Van Wert, Williams, Wood, and Wyandot counties. The northeastern section, shown on Map B, includes Ashtabula, Cuyahoga, Geauga, Lake, Lorain, Mahoning, Medina, Portage, Summit, Trumbull, and Wayne counties. Descriptions of, and directions to, the birding spots are presented in alphabetical order.

Amann Reservoir *Take U.S. 61 south from Galion to the County Line Road. (Map A–1)*

In March and April, this 156-acre park and reservoir is always worth checking for Mallards, American Black Ducks, Blue-winged Teals, American Wigeons, Redheads, Ring-necked Ducks, Lesser Scaups, and Hooded Mergansers. Trails through the surrounding beech woods can aid in compiling a good list of land birds.

Aurora Pond and Bog *Take Ohio 14 south of Cleveland to Twinsburg, then Ohio 82 east to Aurora, and Ohio 43 north to the pond. (Map B–2)*

In addition to migratory waterbirds in the spring and fall, this unique

* All maps and map outlines by the Ohio Department of Natural Resources and the Ohio Department of Transportation.

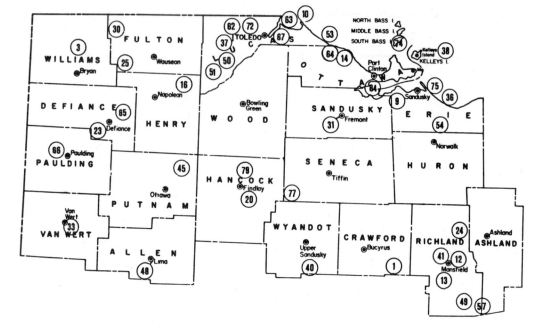

MAP A

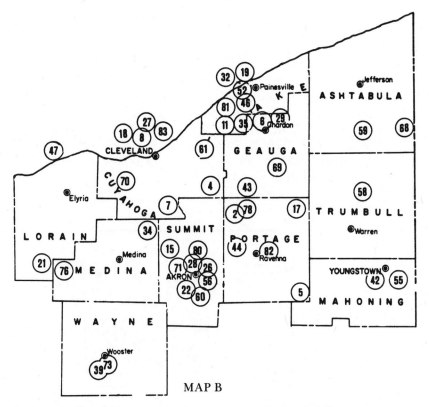

MAP B

spot boasts an impressive list of nesting birds. Summer visitors and breeding birds include Great Blue and Green-backed herons, Great Egret, Least and American bitterns, Mallard, American Black and Wood ducks, Sharp-shinned Hawk, Virginia Rail, Sora, Common Moorhen, Black Tern, Brown Creeper, Marsh and Sedge wrens, Veery, Yellow-throated Vireo, Prothonotary and Yellow warblers, Northern Waterthrush, and Scarlet Tanager.

Bay Shore Power Plant   *See Oregon Power Plant.*

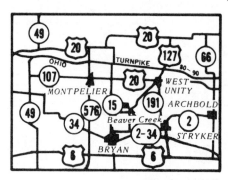

Beaver Creek   *On Ohio 15 six miles north of Bryan,*
State Wildlife Area   *in Williams County. (Map A–3)*

If you want to find a representative sample of the birds that breed in extreme northwestern Ohio, this 153-acre wildlife tract can be extremely rewarding. There is a 40-acre beech-maple woods, the creek, brushy areas, and fields.

Near the entrance, look for Eastern Kingbirds, Indigo Buntings, and Field Sparrows. A Belted Kingfisher is often present along the creek; in the woods there are Eastern Wood-Pewees, Tufted Titmice, House Wrens, Gray Catbirds, Brown Thrashers, Red-eyed Vireos, Cerulean Warblers, Ovenbirds, and Rufous-sided Towhees. Red-tailed Hawks can be seen in the vicinity, and Barred Owls nest in the woods.

Bedford Reservation and   *Take Ohio 14 south of Cleveland to*
Tinkers Creek Gorge   *Egbert Road. (Map B–4)*

This 1,335-acre tract is an important part of Cleveland's Emerald Necklace system of metropolitan parks. Rugged hiking trails, a deep gorge, and beautiful scenery make this a delightful place to visit any time of the year. Upland forests are beech-maple, oak, hickory, and ash, while mountain maple, yellow birch, and hemlock are found in the floodplain. There are bridle paths and several picnic areas.

Rewards of a hike into the gorge area during the breeding season will include the discovery of the Winter Wren, Solitary Vireo, Magnolia, and Canada warblers. Other breeding birds found on the reservation include the Broad-winged Hawk, Great Horned Owl, Pileated Woodpecker, Acadian and Least flycatchers, Cerulean Warbler, Ovenbird, Louisiana Waterthrush, American Redstart, and Scarlet Tanager.

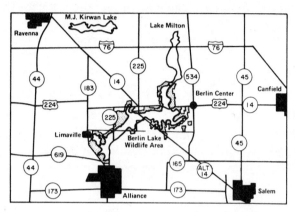

Berlin Reservoir
State Wildlife Area

Located midway between Youngstown, Akron, and Canton, the area can best be reached on U.S. 224, which crosses the reservoir. (Map B–5)

This 6,763-acre impoundment attracts large numbers of waterbirds in March and the first two weeks of April. Loons and grebes are frequently seen along with considerable numbers of Canada Geese, occasional flocks of Tundra Swans, and a few Snow Geese. Large concentrations of Mallards and American Black Ducks are sometimes present, as well as lesser numbers of Gadwall, Northern Pintail, Green-winged and Blue-winged teals, American Wigeon, Redhead, Ring-necked and Lesser Scaup ducks, Common Goldeneye, Bufflehead, Ruddy Duck, and all three mergansers. During the fall, lowered water levels sometimes create mudflats which attract a variety of shorebirds.

Big Creek Park

On old Ohio 44 in Geauga County three-fourths of a mile north of Chardon. (Map B–6)

Large upland woods, stands of hemlock in shaded valleys, and small lakes create a diversity of habitats attractive to a large variety of birds. The Broad-winged Hawk and Ruffed Grouse nest here along with the Pileated Woodpecker and, possibly, the Long-eared Owl.

Other nesting birds include the Black-capped Chickadee, Veery, Yellow-throated Vireo, Black-and-White Warbler, Cerulean Warbler, Ovenbird, Hooded Warbler, American Redstart, Scarlet Tanager, and Rose-breasted Grosbeak. Blackburnian Warblers are a possibility in the hemlocks, and Chestnut-sided Warblers may be found along some of the woods' brushy edges. Blue-winged Teals, American Wigeons, and Wood Ducks are counted among the waterfowl that occur on the lakes. In winter, look for Common Redpolls, Pine Siskins, Red Crossbills, and White-winged Crossbills—especially in the hemlocks.

Brecksville Reservation   *From Cleveland, take I-77 south to the Brecksville exit and go east on Ohio 82 or turn south on U.S. 21. (Map B–7)*

This 2,768-acre tract of oak-hickory, beech-maple, and hemlock relict forests is another important link in Cleveland's Emerald Necklace system of metropolitan parks. The area is outstanding geologically for its exposed faces of Mississippian age Berea sandstone, Bedford shale, Cleveland shale (containing fragments of giant armored fish), and fossil-rich Chagrin shale. There is a trailside museum, a labeled nature trail, and an asphalt-paved Trail for All People designed for the handicapped.

Migration time, especially in the spring, produces hordes of transient birds. Hawks are apt to be seen soaring overhead (a few species nest), various waterbirds are seen along the Cuyahoga River, and flycatchers, thrushes, vireos, warblers, and finches seem to be everywhere on a good day.

Birds breeding at Brecksville include the Red-tailed Hawk, Kestrel, Eastern Screech, Great Horned and Barred owls, Ruby-throated Hummingbird, Belted Kingfisher, Common Flicker, Red-headed, Hairy, and Downy woodpeckers, Eastern Phoebe, Eastern Wood-Pewee, Northern Rough-winged and Barn swallows, and Purple Martin.

Also the Blue Jay; Common Crow; Black-capped Chickadee; Tufted Titmouse; White-breasted Nuthatch; House Wren; Gray Catbird; Brown Thrasher; American Robin; Wood Thrush; Veery; Eastern Bluebird; Blue-gray Gnatcatcher; Cedar Waxwing; Starling; Yellow-throated, Red-eyed, and Warbling vireos; Black-and-White, Yellow, and Cerulean warblers; Ovenbird; Louisiana Waterthrush; American Redstart; Northern Oriole; Red-winged Blackbird; Common Grackle; Brown-headed Cowbird; Scarlet Tanager; Northern Cardinal; Rose-breasted Grosbeak; Indigo Bunting; American Goldfinch; Rufous-sided Towhee; Chipping, Field, and Song sparrows.

Burke Lakefront Airport   *Leave Ohio 2 at East Ninth Street in*
downtown Cleveland (just east of the
municipal stadium) and follow the
North Marginal Drive. (Map B–8)

An unusual number of rare birds have been attracted to this pocket-sized airport in the heart of downtown Cleveland. Good views of the field can be obtained by following the drive east along the fence. Shorebird rarities frequently put down here during their migrations in the spring, summer, and fall. Species observed have included the Piping Plover, Lesser Golden Plover, Black-bellied Plover, Hudsonian Godwit, Marbled Godwit, Whimbrel, Upland Sandpiper, Willet, Wilson's Phalarope, Red-necked Phalarope, and Buff-breasted Sandpiper.

Even more unexpected have been records such as the Western Meadowlark, Sharp-tailed Sparrow, and Lark Sparrow. The airport is one of the best places in Ohio to find Snowy Owls during the winter months. Look for them on nearby breakwaters and retaining walls along the lake. Snow Buntings are found from late fall to early spring, and Water Pipits are frequently seen from October into December and again in March and April.

Castalia Pond   *Take either U.S. 20 or U.S. 6 to*
Ohio 101, which goes through the
small town of Castalia, southwest of
Sandusky. (Map A–9)

The pond is in the middle of town; it is fed by a steady flow of water from springs associated with the Blue Hole. (The Blue Hole, also in Castalia, is a beautiful, seemingly bottomless 10-acre pool. Every day nearly two million gallons of water well up in it from a vast network of solution channels through the underground limestone of a watershed of higher ground nearly a hundred square miles in area, most of it lying south of Castalia.) Water in this 12-acre pond remains open during the winter and attracts large numbers of waterfowl, which can be observed and photographed at extremely close range.

Some of the birds that can be seen here between December and March include the Pied-billed Grebe, Horned Grebe, Canada Goose, Mallard and American Black ducks, Gadwall, Northern Pintail, Green-winged and Blue-winged teals, American Wigeon, Northern Shoveler, Wood Duck, Redhead, Ring-necked Duck, Canvasback, Lesser Scaup, Common Goldeneye, Bufflehead, Ruddy Duck, and Hooded Merganser. Rarer species have included the Mute Swan and Snow Goose.

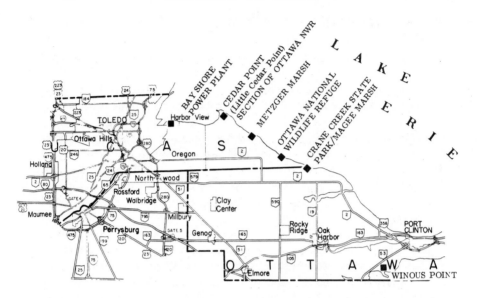

Cedar Point National Wildlife Refuge (Little Cedar Point)

East of Toledo, turn off Ohio 2 onto Decant Road (10.9 miles west of Crane Creek State Park) and proceed north to Cedar Point Road. Look for the sign marking the new entrance to the refuge which is off Corduroy Road and leads onto a scenic drive atop new dikes that encircle the entire marsh. (Map A–10)

Administered by and part of the Ottawa National Wildlife Refuge Complex, this 2,245-acre marsh is one of the best all-round birding areas in the state. Permission to enter the area is difficult to obtain, but a bird census of the area is taken the first Sunday of each month. Organized groups are conducted on tours of the refuge. For further information, write Refuge Manager, Ottawa National Wildlife Refuge Complex, 14000 W. State Route 2, Oak Harbor, Ohio 43449, or phone (419) 897-0211.

One of the ornithological attractions at Cedar Point NWR is the possibility of seeing large numbers of migrating Blue Jays. On favorable days in late April and early May, sometimes several thousand can be seen within a few hours, as flock after flock pass overhead. An even more interesting spectacle is provided by the jays engaged in reverse migration when the flocks stream by in a southeasterly direction.

When walking or driving the dikes, keep a sharp lookout for

migrating hawks. The westward movement of raptors around the end of Lake Erie is an almost daily occurrence from March until the middle of May, and includes birds that have arrived along the lakeshore from as far east as Port Clinton.

During the spring months, the numerous woodlots along Ohio 2 and south of that highway often harbor many hawks seeking food and a place to rest until conditions are favorable for continuing their migration. Species most often seen, when they take to the air, are Sharp-shinned and Broad-winged hawks. Some Cooper's, Red-tailed and Red-shouldered hawks, and Northern Harriers will also be observed during a good flight. Kestrels and Turkey Vultures commonly follow the same flightline. Rough-legged Hawks are decidedly scarce, and Peregrine Falcons and Merlins are rare, although a few are seen each year.

Most birders enter the refuge to see a diversity of waterbirds— herons, egrets, bitterns, geese, ducks, rails, and shorebirds. Landbirds, however, are frequently an equal—if not greater—attraction in late April and May, when prodigious concentrations sometimes occur wherever there are trees or adequate cover.

Open expanses of water and marsh are visible from many vantage points. The deeper pools are a stopping place for most of the duck species and many other waterbirds. In March, Tundra Swans are almost always present, sometimes in the hundreds. Ospreys investigate the marsh during their migrations, but seldom remain for any length of time. One or two Great Horned Owls can usually be flushed out of the trees any time of the year.

Birds that nest or spend the summer at Cedar Point NWR include the Pied-billed Grebe, Great Blue Heron, Green-backed Heron, Cattle Egret, Great Egret, Black-crowned Night Heron, Least and American bitterns, Canada Goose, Mallard, American Black Duck, Gadwall, Northern Pintail, Green-winged and Blue-winged teals, American Wigeon, Northern Shoveler, Wood Duck, Redhead, Ruddy Duck, Hooded Merganser, Turkey Vulture, Red-tailed Hawk, and formerly, the following, all decidedly rare now—the Cooper's, Red-shouldered, and Marsh hawks, Bald Eagle, American Kestrel, Ring-necked Pheasant, King and Virginia rails (both declining in numbers), Sora, Common Gallinule, and American Coot.

Also Killdeer, Spotted Sandpiper, Herring and Ring-billed gulls (occasional breeders, sometimes in goose tubs), Common, Caspian, and Black terns, Mourning Dove, Yellow-billed Cuckoo, Eastern Screech and Great Horned owls, Chimney Swift, Ruby-throated Hummingbird, Belted Kingfisher, Common Flicker, Red-headed (irregular) and Downy woodpeckers, Eastern Kingbird, Great Crested Flycatcher, Eastern Phoebe (now rare or absent), Acadian and Willow flycatchers, Eastern Wood-Pewee, Horned Lark, Tree, Bank, and Northern Rough-winged swallows, Purple Martin, Blue Jay, American Crow, Tufted Titmouse, White-breasted Nuthatch (irregular), House, Marsh, and Sedge wrens (rare and irregular), Gray Catbird, Brown Thrasher, American Robin, Eastern Bluebird (now rare or absent); Cedar Waxwing, European Starling, Red-eyed and Warbling vireos, Yellow Warbler; Common Yellowthroat; House Sparrow, Eastern Meadowlark, Red-winged Blackbird, Northern Oriole, Common Grackle, Brown-headed Blackbird, Northern Cardinal, Indigo Bunting, Dickcissel (irregular), American Goldfinch, and Savannah, Chipping, Field, Swamp (rare), and Song sparrows.

The fall migration of landbirds lacks the dramatic impact of the northward movement in the spring, but there can be moments of excitement. Tree Swallows seem to be everywhere and from midsummer on there are wandering bands of Bobolinks and other early migrants to look for, not to speak of shorebird arrivals and increased numbers of Cattle Egrets and other nomads among the heron tribe. Rarely, the Sharp-tailed Sparrow invades the Lake Erie marshes in late September and October, but by then there are plenty of other things to look for, including the first returning waterbirds.

Chapin Park and State Forest   *Take Ohio 306, in Lake County, to*
U.S. 6. Go west on 6 for about one
mile. (Map B–11)

This heavily wooded 362-acre site is just north of Little Mountain (see p. 34). Beech, maple, and oak trees dominate and are inhabited by an above average population of Ruffed Grouse; other birds characteristic of the deep woods are the Veery and Hooded Warbler. Brushy zones along wooded edges should yield the Chestnut-sided Warbler. Both the Scarlet Tanager and the Rose-breasted Grosbeak nest here.

Charles Mills Lake   *Take Ohio 30 eight miles east of*
Mansfield. (Map A–12)

This large lake (1,350 acres) attracts significant numbers of waterbirds in both spring and fall; in the latter season, many linger until the water freezes. In spring, scan the water for Gadwalls, American Wigeons, and rafts of diving ducks composed of Redheads, Ringnecked Ducks, Canvasbacks, Lesser Scaups, and Buffleheads. In fall, good numbers of Red-breasted Mergansers have been seen here, along with Hooded Mergansers and Common Mergansers.

Surrounding woods, in spring and summer, provide breeding habitats for Red-headed Woodpeckers, Great Crested Flycatchers, Wood Thrushes, Cerulean Warblers, Ovenbirds, Northern Orioles, and Scarlet Tanagers.

Clear Fork Reservoir   *Take I-71 in Richland County to Ohio 97; proceed west one mile past Lexington. (Map A–13)*

Ohio 97 closely follows the south shore of this 1,000-acre reservoir surrounded by beech-maple woods. There are numerous vantage points to look over the water for migrant waterfowl. Ospreys are sometimes seen in April and May and again from late August to mid-October. Common Loons, Horned and Pied-billed grebes, Double-crested Cormorants (becoming more common in Ohio), American Coots, gulls and terns can all be found in season. A few of the summer residents are Cooper's Hawk, Eastern Kingbird, Carolina Chickadee, Wood Thrush, Cedar Waxwing, Yellow-throated Vireo, Cerulean Warbler, Ovenbird, American Redstart, Scarlet Tanager, Summer Tanager (occasionally), and Rose-breasted Grosbeak.

Crane Creek State Park and   *In Ottawa and Lucas counties ten*
Magee Marsh Wildlife Area   *miles north of Oak Harbor. The entrance is on Ohio 2, seventeen miles west of Port Clinton and two miles west of Ohio 19. (Map A–14)*

Crane Creek State Park is an integral part of the Magee Marsh Wildlife Area. The marsh was purchased by the state in 1951, and in 1956 the Crane Creek Wildlife Experiment Station was established. Taken together, the area comprises 2,600 acres of extensive marshes, ponds, woods, Lake Erie beach, and fields. An attractive nature center is located a short drive from the entrance, and a paved road crosses the width of the marsh to the lakeshore, where there are beaches, woods, picnic facilities, and a fine nature trail.

Considerable numbers of Canada Geese have been induced to nest in the area. With the addition of migrants, many thousands of these birds are present in late October and November and again in March. In May and June, proud and protective parent birds shepherd their goslings about the refuge, even up onto the roads, where it is a common sight to see families of geese holding up traffic.

During the greater part of the year, there is good birding from the moment one enters the park. A roadside pond just inside the entrance frequently overflows its banks during wet weather and attracts shorebirds, geese, gulls, egrets, and an occasional rail. In spring and summer, there are Tree Swallows and Purple Martins flying about the visitor center and there is always the possibility of seeing one of the Yellow-headed Blackbirds that have nested nearby in recent years. The shallow ponds behind the center should be searched for shorebirds such as the Dunlin which is a common late spring migrant. Don't get too excited over the assemblage of waterfowl in the ponds immediately behind the center since many of these are pinioned birds and are part of a resident flock. Most noticeable among them are Tundra Swans and Snow Geese.

From the visitor center, turn left and continue down the road to the east, take the bend to the north and slowly follow the road as it intersects the vast width of Magee Marsh. The water levels vary greatly from year to year and season to season affecting the ease with which one can see appreciable numbers of birds. When the water is low, mudflats are exposed and the wading birds tend to concentrate in a few favored places.

From April through October, there should be good numbers of Great Blue Herons, a few Green-backed Herons, plenty of Great Egrets, sometimes very close to the road, and lesser numbers of the more secretive Black-crowned Night Herons. In March and April, ducks are plentiful, along with large flocks of American Coots, and a sprinkling of Pied-billed Grebes. Tundra Swans are a possibility during the first part of the period. Ring-billed and Herring Gulls will be liberally scattered about the marsh, and there's always a good chance of finding a little flock of Water Pipits along the water's edge. Look for migrating hawks in the skies.

Toward the end of April, when many of the waterfowl have departed, there are still some birds that stay behind to nest. And a few other waterbirds arrive daily as the season progresses into May. Coots abound; every once in a while, an American Bittern will flounder into the air on its bi-colored wings and flap across the marsh, and there's always a chance of seeing a King, Virginia, or Sora rail.

Every other willow seems to have its Yellow Warbler, and their *sweet-sweet-sweet* songs fill the air with music. Continuing out the causeway, check the dredged channels on either side of the road for Dunlin, White-rumped Sandpipers, and other small peeps. In recent years, increased numbers of Wilson's Phalaropes have been seen in this area. Be on the lookout for Bonaparte's Gulls and Forster's Terns, each species showing flashes of silvery white in their wings. The Common Tern is often seen over the marsh, along with smaller numbers of the

Black Tern and the large Caspian Tern, with its conspicuous bill of bright coral red.

As the road nears the lake, it turns left through an area that was once used for parking. Pull off here and climb up on the retaining wall along the lake. Scan the slabs of concrete for Sanderlings and Ruddy Turnstones and search the lake for additional gulls and terns. Sometimes Palm Warblers and White-crowned Sparrows will be feeding in the protective shelter provided by the wall. When a good migration is underway, hundreds of swallows can be observed flying westward along the shore and during the early morning hours many other species can be seen in a similar migration.

After returning to the car, carefully look over the old parking lot, which is now mostly grown up in grass, for shorebirds. Then proceed through the new parking lot area, paying particular attention to the elongated pond on the left side of the road. When the water is down, look for shorebirds; when the water is up look for Common Gallinules and Least Bitterns. Portions of the bird trail encircle this pond so you will have a second opportunity to look it over when you are on foot.

The entrance to the bird trail is located near the west end of the parking lots and is marked by a sign. The area traversed by the trail is a fine example of a bird "trap." Surrounded by marsh on three sides and the lake on the fourth, this bit of swamp forest attracts huge numbers of passerine birds during the spring migration and only slightly fewer numbers in the fall. On days after heavy nocturnal migration, many species concentrate here and continue to build up even during the daylight hours. The fact that the lake lies just beyond undoubtedly tempts many spring arrivals to rest and feed here before continuing their journeys. Conversely, in the fall, for many birds this is the first landfall after crossing the lake.

There is a feeding station near the entrance to the trail that attracts an abundance of White-throated Sparrows, White-crowned Sparrows, and a few shy Lincoln's and Swamp sparrows. The large cottonwoods and willows here are frequently swarming with warblers and other migrants. During late April and May, these trees are apt to yield such birds as the Black-and-White Warbler, Golden-winged Warbler, Orange-crowned Warbler (sometimes earlier in April), Northern Parula, Black-throated Blue Warbler, Blackburnian Warbler, American Redstart, Scarlet Tanager, Rose-breasted Grosbeak, Purple Finch, troupes of American Goldfinches, and Chipping Sparrows. Sometimes an Evening Grosbeak is spotted. On a good day, all of these birds—and many more—can be seen all along the bird trail.

In late March and April, grapevine tangles and red cedars are favorite hiding places for Northern Saw-whet Owls. Eastern Screech Owls are permanent residents, but are difficult to find. Great Horned Owls start nesting in February and March, often utilizing goose nesting tubs that have been erected about the swampy woodland. The young owls are usually out of the nest by the first of May and can be seen perched in large cottonwood trees.

The bird trail winds past various inundations, ponds, inlets, and rivulets honeycombing the entire area. From March to April, Rusty Blackbirds frequent these wet places, and there is always a chance of seeing a Brewer's Blackbird. May specialties include several pairs of nesting Prothonotary Warblers, migrant Northern Waterthrushes, Mourning, Hooded, Wilson's, and Canada warblers.

To sum up, Crane Creek State Park is probably the best all-round birding area in Ohio, regardless of season. Over 275 species of birds have been recorded, and every year one or two more are added. Cattle Egrets have increased in numbers, Glossy Ibis show up more frequently, and a few Sandhill Cranes are seen almost every year. The list of western strays grows more impressive with each passing year. Among the shorebirds, there have been dramatic increases in the numbers of Hudsonian and Marbled godwits. American Avocets, Willets, Wilson's and Red-necked phalaropes, and Ruffs show up with increased regularity.

To whet the appetite of a birder wishing to visit the area, these rare birds have been observed: American White Pelican, Little Blue Heron, Louisiana Heron, White-faced Ibis, Mute Swan, Brant, Greater White-fronted Goose, Fulvous Whistling-Duck, Cinnamon Teal, Eurasian Wigeon, Common Eider, Golden Eagle, Gyrfalcon, Peregrine Falcon, Merlin, Piping Plover, Red Phalarope, Buff-breasted Sandpiper, Groove-billed Ani, Snowy Owl, Western Kingbird, Northern Shrike, Townsend's Warbler, Kirtland's Warbler, Western Meadowlark, Brewer's Blackbird, Sharp-tailed Sparrow, and Clay-colored Sparrow.

Deep Lock Quarry Metropolitan Park   *Take I-77 in Summit County to the village of Peninsula; the park is located on Riverview Road south of town. (Map B–15)*

Once a Berea sandstone quarry shipping millstones and grindstones around the world, this 191-acre park was also the site of a lock in the canal between Akron and Cleveland. Now there is a pleasant woodland, with nature trails, plus many mementos of days gone by.

During May migration, flycatchers, thrushes, vireos, tanagers, finches, and swarms of warblers pass among the trees and shrubs. On a red-letter day, you may see as many as thirty warbler species.

In early summer, trails along the old canal and the Cuyahoga River can be especially rewarding. One should see or hear Wood Ducks, both cuckoos, Ruby-throated Hummingbirds, Belted Kingfishers, five woodpecker species, Eastern Kingbirds, Great Crested Flycatchers, Eastern Phoebes, Eastern Wood-Pewees, Northern Rough-winged and Barn swallows, Black-capped Chickadees, Tufted Titmice, White-breasted Nuthatches, House Wrens, Gray Catbirds, Wood Thrushes, Cedar Waxwings, Red-eyed and Warbling Vireos, Yellow Warblers, Cerulean Warblers, Common Yellowthroats, Northern Orioles, grackles and cowbirds, Northern Cardinals, Indigo Buntings, American Goldfinches, Chipping Sparrows, and Song Sparrows.

Dry Creek Access   *On U.S. 24 one mile west of the village of Texas in Henry County. (Map A–16)*

This pocket park along the Maumee River is always worth checking for waterbirds in spring and fall. There are apt to be some surface-feeding ducks along with Common Goldeneyes, Buffleheads, and Common Mergansers. Warbling Vireos and Northern Orioles nest in sycamores along the river, and Ospreys frequently patrol the river during their migrations.

Eagle Creek Nature Preserve   *From the intersection of Ohio 88 and Ohio 82 in Garrettsville, go east on 82 for two blocks to the flashing light. Turn left (north) at the light onto Center Road. Follow Center Road for 2.3 miles to Hopkins Road and turn right (south). Visitors parking lot is on Hopkins Road. (Map B–17)*

These 441 acres are unique in the variety of habitats they offer. A glacial stream cut through Mississippian rock to create a south-facing slope with an inspiring forest featuring huge white oaks, and a north-facing slope of beech-maple forest. There is also a floodplain with attendant buttonbush swamp, a number of small peat bogs, and marshland. Beaver ponds, fox dens, and a fine assortment of breeding birds attest to the wilderness aspects of this spot.

A few of the breeding birds are the Wood Duck, Red-tailed Hawk,

Yellow-billed Cuckoo, Eastern Screech Owl, five species of woodpeckers, five flycatcher species, including the Willow Flycatcher, Black-capped Chickadees, Carolina Wren (cyclic), Wood Thrush, Veery, Yellow-throated and Red-eyed vireos, Blue-winged Warbler, Yellow Warbler, Cerulean Warbler, Ovenbird, Common Yellowthroat, Northern Oriole, Scarlet Tanager, Rufous-sided Towhee, and Chipping, Field, and Song sparrows.

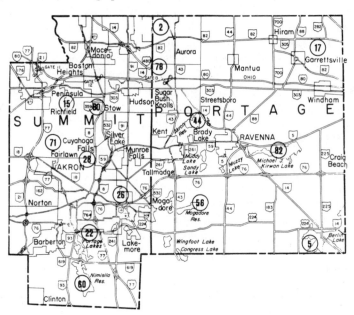

Akron Area

2	Aurora Pond and Bog	56	Mogadore Reservoir
5	Berlin Reservoir	60	Nimisila Reservoir/Portage Lakes
15	Deep Lock Quarry Metropolitan Park	71	Sand Run Metropolitan Park/
17	Eagle Creek Nature Preserve		Seiberling Nature Center
22	Firestone Metropolitan Park	78	Tinkers Creek Nature Preserve
26	Goodyear Heights Metropolitan Park		and State Park
28	Gorge Metropolitan Park	80	Virginia Kendall Metropolitan Park
44	Lake Rockwell	82	West Branch State Park

Edgewater Park and Perkins Beach

Take U.S. 20 to the Edgewater Park exit at West 70th Street in Cleveland. (Map B–18)

An excellent point along Cleveland's lakeshore for observing a fine

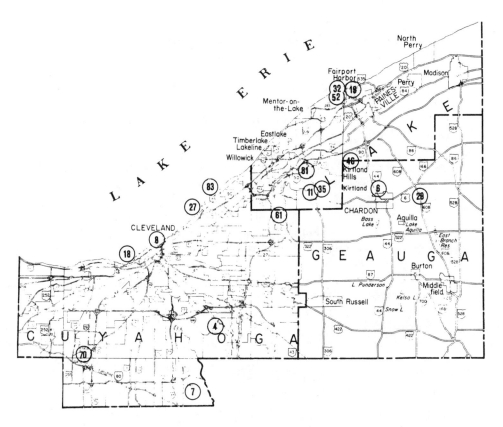

Cleveland Area

variety of loons, grebes, diving ducks, and gulls during the fall, winter, and early spring. This locality includes a wooded drive high atop a bluff that affords an outstanding view of the waters offshore, and a small park at water level combining a small beach and a breakwater. Except in the coldest winters, there is usually some open water. Many rare species have been reported in the vicinity.

Look for Common and Red-throated (rare) loons, Horned and Pied-billed grebes, occasional puddle ducks, Redheads, Ring-necked Ducks, Canvasbacks, Greater and Lesser scaups, Common Goldeneyes, Buffleheads, Red-breasted Mergansers (often the most common duck in early winter), American Coots, Herring, Ring-billed, and Bonaparte's gulls.

Among the decidedly unusual birds that have been observed are the Glossy Ibis, Brant, Common and King eiders, White-winged, Surf, and Black scoters, Sandhill Crane, Red-necked Phalarope, Glaucous, Iceland, Franklin's, and Little gulls, Black-legged Kittiwake, and Snowy Owl. In December 1963, a Rock Wren was identified in the area. Although rare, Purple Sandpipers should be looked for along breakwaters and rocky retaining walls.

During March and April, migrating Blue Jays, Mourning Doves, Common Flickers, and other landbirds sometimes stream by in impressive numbers. At the same time of the year, hawks are frequently seen flying eastward along the lakeshore. During the height of the spring migration, the trees and bushes are often alive with warblers.

Fairport Harbor   *Take I-90 east of Cleveland, exiting*
                                  onto Ohio 44 and proceed north.
                                  (Map B–19)

From October to April, this is an excellent place to find Common Loons, Horned Grebes, a variety of puddle ducks, and most of the diving ducks. Large numbers of gulls gather here in this area of protected water, especially in the late fall and early spring.

Some of the rare species that have been encountered in the harbor and vicinity include the Eared Grebe, White-winged and Black scoters, Whimbrel, Purple Sandpiper, Pomarine and Parasitic jaegers, Northern Gannet, Glaucous, Iceland, and Laughing gulls, Black-legged Kittiwake, and Gull-billed and Roseate terns.

Findlay Reservoirs   *Take Ohio 37 southeast of Findlay*
                                  about three miles to Township Road
                                  234; proceed north to either

*Township Road 205 or 207 and
turn east. Both roads circle the
reservoirs and provide access to two
ramp areas. (Map A-20)*

These sizeable upground reservoirs are excellent for waterfowl after the ice has broken up in the early spring and from October to freeze-up. Geese, ducks, and a few Tundra Swans stop over in the spring, but most of the rarities are seen in the fall. Then be on the lookout for the Red-throated Loon, Red-necked Grebe, Double-crested Cormorants, and rafts of diving ducks that might contain Oldsquaws, White-winged Scoters, Surf Scoters, and Black Scoters. After rainy weather, wet spots in nearby fields lure shorebirds such as the Lesser Golden Plover, Black-bellied Plover, Greater and Lesser yellowlegs, Short-billed Dowitchers, small peeps, and Pectoral Sandpipers. Laughing and Franklin's gulls have been recorded here along with flocks of graceful Bonaparte's Gulls, big Herring Gulls, and Ohio's most common gull, the Ring-billed.

Findley State Park   *On Ohio 58, in Lorain County, four
miles south of Wellington. (Map B–21)*

A 93-acre lake surrounded by beech-maple woods and pine trees attracts a few waterbirds in the spring and from October to freeze-up. In winter, half a dozen bird feeders are in operation and can be observed from the roadways. At these times, Downy Woodpeckers, Hairy Woodpeckers, Blue Jays, Black-capped Chickadees, Tufted Titmice, White-breasted Nuthatches, American Goldfinches, Rufous-sided Towhees, Dark-eyed Juncos, Tree Sparrows, and Song Sparrows can be seen to good advantage. A Varied Thrush visited one of these feeders during the winter of '79-'80.

Evening Grosbeaks, Purple Finches, Common Redpolls, Pine Siskins, Red Crossbills, and White-winged Crossbills are possible in the winter, especially in the area of pine trees. Some of the country roads a few miles north of the park are well worth investigating in winter for the Cooper's Hawk, Horned Larks, Northern Shrike (rare), Lapland Longspurs, and Snow Buntings.

Breeding birds in the park include the Wood Duck, Sharp-shinned Hawk, American Woodcock, Yellow-billed Cuckoo, Barred Owl, Belted Kingfisher, Eastern Wood-Pewee, Veery, Wood Thrush, Yellow Warbler, Cerulean Warbler, Ovenbird, Hooded Warbler, American Redstart, Scarlet Tanager, Rose-breasted Grosbeak, and Rufous-sided Towhee.

Firestone Metropolitan Park   *South of Akron, take I-224 to South*
Main Street, then south to Swartz
Road, east to Harrington Road and
the Tuscarawas parking lot on the
northwest side of Harrington Road.
(Map B–22)

The Tuscarawas River flows through this 250-acre swamp forest of oak, tulip, cherry, ash, elm, and alder trees. The Broad-winged Hawk, as well as the Red-shouldered Hawk probably nest here, in addition to Pileated Woodpecker; Red-headed Woodpecker; Willow Flycatcher (areas of shrub and alder); Black-capped Chickadee; Veery; Cedar Waxwing; Yellow-throated, Red-eyed, and Warbling vireos; Blue-winged Warbler; Cerulean Warbler; Ovenbird; American Redstart; Northern Oriole; Scarlet Tanager; Northern Cardinal; Rufous-sided Towhee; Chipping, Field, and Song sparrows.

Five Mile Creek Access   *On Ohio 111 five miles south of*
Defiance. (Map A–23)

This pocket park on the Auglaize River provides a view of the water above the power dam. Small numbers of waterfowl stop here in spring and late fall including the Canada Goose, Mallard, American Black Duck, Northern Pintail, American Wigeon, Redhead, Ring-necked Duck, Lesser Scaup, Common Goldeneye, Ruddy Duck, and Common Merganser. On cool days in April and May, look for Chimney Swifts and all the swallow species skimming low over the water.

Fowler Woods   *Take Ohio 13, in Richland County,*
six miles northwest of Olivesburg to
Noble Road. Proceed east on Noble
Road to the intersection with the
Olivesburg-Fitchville Road. (Map
A–24)

With trees undisturbed for well over one hundred years, this preserve has eighty acres of forest, about fifty acres in near-virgin condition. Another part of the area is swamp forest, with beech-maple woods on higher ground. Surrounding fields are in various stages of natural succession and should yield Horned Larks, Bobolinks, Savannah Sparrows, Grasshopper Sparrows, Vesper Sparrows, and Field Sparrows.

Barred Owls, Pileated Woodpeckers, Yellow-throated Vireos, Blue-winged Warblers, Eastern Yellow Warblers, Cerulean Warblers, Ovenbirds, Kentucky Warblers, American Redstarts, Northern Orioles, Scarlet Tanagers, and Rose-breasted Grosbeaks are among the nesting birds.

Goll Woods Nature Preserve   *Take Ohio 66 two and a half miles north of Archbold in Fulton County; turn west on Township Road F and proceed 2.9 miles to the third crossroad, then turn south to the parking lot entrance. (Map A–25)*

The 320 acres of this preserve constitute one of the best remnants of the Black Swamp Forest in Ohio. Burr oaks, white oaks, and yellow oaks achieve sizes up to five feet or more in diameter and are estimated to be 400 to 500 years old. Other sections of the woods contain beech-maple, elm, red oak, basswood, and ash trees.

At the parking lot, look and listen for Common Flickers, Eastern Kingbirds, House Wrens, American Robins, Cedar Waxwings, Eastern Meadowlarks, and Field Sparrows.

Nesting birds include the American Woodcock, Red-tailed Hawk, Red-shouldered Hawk, Yellow-billed Cuckoo, Red-headed Woodpecker, Hairy Woodpecker, Great Crested Flycatcher, Acadian Flycatcher, Willow Flycatcher, Black-capped Chickadee, White-breasted Nuthatch, Brown Thrasher, Wood Thrush, Veery, Eastern Bluebird, Yellow-throated Vireo, Red-eyed Vireo, Black-and-White Warbler, Cerulean Warbler, Chestnut-sided Warbler (edges), Ovenbird, American Redstart, Northern Oriole, Scarlet Tanager, Northern Cardinal, and Rose-breasted Grosbeak.

Goodyear Heights Metropolitan Park   *Located on the east side of Akron at Darrow Road and Newton Street, west of Ohio 9, north of I-76. (Map B–26)*

This 372-acre park is an excellent place to see large numbers of spring and fall migrants right in the city of Akron. Grass recreation areas are interspersed with wooded slopes of beech-maple and pine; there is a 15-acre lake, a marshy spot, and numerous thick shrub plantings.

Over-wintering birds include the Common Flicker, Downy and Hairy woodpeckers, Black-capped Chickadee, Tufted Titmouse, White-breasted Nuthatch, Brown Creeper, Golden-crowned Kinglet, Northern Cardinal, Dark-eyed Junco, White-throated Sparrow, and Song Sparrow.

Gordon Park/Illuminating Company

On the near east side of Cleveland, take I-90 to the Liberty Boulevard exit and turn left at the stop sign. (Map B–27)

Located on the lakeshore on Cleveland's near east side, the park benefits in the winter from the warm water outflow of the power plant. In the fall, winter, and early spring, this is a particularly good spot to observe waterbirds that have sought the protection of the breakwaters and they can often be seen at close range.

Among the rare birds that have been seen here are the Red-throated Loon, Double-crested Cormorant, Brant, Harlequin Duck, King Eider, White-winged, Surf, and Black scoters, Glaucous and Little gulls, Black-legged Kittiwake, Northern Gannet, Pomarine and Parasitic jaegers, Snowy Owl, and Loggerhead Shrike.

Other birds found during the cold months include the Common Loon, Horned and Pied-billed grebes, Mallard, American Wigeon, Redhead, Ring-necked Duck, Canvasback, Greater and Lesser scaups, Common Goldeneye, Bufflehead, Oldsquaw (scarce), Common and Red-breasted mergansers, and Herring, Ring-billed, and Bonaparte's gulls. The three latter species sometimes occur in the tens of thousands. Also search the shore and breakwaters for Snow Buntings.

Gorge Metropolitan Park

Located on Front Street between Cuyahoga Falls and Akron, north of the Cuyahoga River, west of North Main Street, and west of Route 8 and the Route 59 expressway. (Map B–28)

Pileated Woodpeckers range through this dramatic 250-acre park where the Cuyahoga River tumbles and splashes over several miles of falls and rapids. There are also nesting Cooper's and Red-shouldered hawks, Great Horned Owls, Barred Owls, Belted Kingfishers, Red-bellied Woodpeckers, Hairy Woodpeckers, Black-capped Chickadees, Black-and-White Warblers, Black-throated Green Warblers, Cerulean Warblers, Chestnut-sided Warblers, Ovenbirds, Common Yellowthroats, Hooded Warblers, American Redstarts, Scarlet Tanagers, Rose-breasted Grosbeaks, House Finches, Rufous-sided Towhees, and Song Sparrows.

Hambden Orchard Wildlife Area

On Ohio 608 three miles south of the village of Hambden in Geauga County. (Map B–29)

Beech-maple and oak-hickory woods dominate this 841-acre tract which also includes two pools, fields, and an old orchard. Mallards, Blue-winged Teals, and Wood Ducks feed and rest on the ponds; Ruffed Grouse, American Woodcocks, Eastern Screech Owls, and Barred Owls inhabit the woods. Also, in spring and summer, look and listen for the Red-headed Woodpecker, Hairy Woodpecker, Great Crested Fly-catcher, Eastern Wood-Pewee, Acadian Flycatcher, Black-capped Chickadee, Tufted Titmouse, White-breasted Nuthatch, House Wren, Brown Thrasher, Wood Thrush, Veery, Yellow-throated and Red-eyed vireos, Cerulean Warbler, Ovenbird, Hooded Warbler, Ameri-can Redstart, Scarlet Tanager, and Rose-breasted Grosbeak.

Tree and Northern Rough-winged swallows and Purple Martins skim over the ponds; flocks of Cedar Waxwings can be found along the forest edges along with Gray Catbirds, Common Yellowthroats, and Chipping, Field, and Song sparrows.

Harrison Lake State Park   *Take U.S. 20 west from Toledo approximately 5.3 miles; turn south on Fulton County Road 26. (Map A–30)*

Beech woods, pine trees, and old fields surround this 105-acre lake in northwestern Ohio. When winter ice breaks up, flocks of Mallards, American Black Ducks, Northern Pintails, American Wigeons, Com-mon Goldeneyes, and Common Mergansers can be seen here to good advantage. Blue-winged Teals and American Coots feed close to the shore and around the marshy end of the lake. Close scrutiny of the neighboring fields should yield Horned Larks and Savannah and Ves-per sparrows.

Hayes State Memorial   *Take U.S. 6 in Fremont to the intersection of Buckland and Hayes avenues. (Map A–31)*

This 25-acre wooded estate was the home of Rutherford B. Hayes, 19th president of the United States. There are walks, driveways, and paths that enable one to explore the gardens, cool wooded slopes, and broad lawns.

In late March and early April, there are Yellow-bellied Sapsuck-ers, Northern Chickadees, Tufted Titmice, White-breasted Nut-hatches, Red-breasted Nuthatches, Brown Creepers, Winter Wrens, Hermit Thrushes, Golden-crowned Kinglets, Ruby-crowned King-lets, Solitary Vireos (late April), Yellow-rumped Warblers, Rusty

Blackbirds, Northern Cardinals, Pine Siskins, Dark-eyed Juncos, and White-throated Sparrows. Later in the spring, large hemlock trees attract migratory Parula, Cape May, Black-throated Green, and Bay-breasted Warblers.

Headlands Beach State Park

Take U.S. 90 east from Cleveland; exit onto Ohio 44 North and follow it to its end. (Map B–32)

This 120-acre parcel of land embraces a beach, a small amount of marsh habitat, picnic facilities, and a bit of swamp forest. The park is near Mentor Marsh and Fairport Harbor.

Loons, grebes, and diving ducks are frequently seen offshore, including rarities such as the Oldsquaw and all three scoters. A surprising number of rare shorebirds turn up here in the spring migration and a few less in the summer and fall. Read the account on Mentor Marsh State Nature Preserve (p. 38) for additional birds found in the vicinity.

Hiestand Woods Park

Off Ohio 127 on Hospital Drive at the edge of Van Wert. (Map A–33)

This pleasant little park has hiking trails through a wooded area and along a small stream. There are some picnic tables set amidst some large oak and honey locust trees that attract numerous warblers and other migrants during the spring migration. Other birds to look for include Red-headed and Pileated woodpeckers, Eastern Kingbirds, Eastern Wood-Pewees, Northern Rough-winged and Barn swallows, Warbling Vireos, Common Yellowthroats, Indigo Buntings, Northern Orioles, and Song Sparrows.

Hinkley Reservation

Take I-71 in Cleveland to Ohio 303; proceed east, then turn south on Bellus Road and drive to a park road on the right that leads to the dam on Hinkley Lake. (Map B–34)

Famous for its roost of Turkey Vultures, the reservation is the southernmost unit of the Cleveland Metropolitan Park District's Emerald Necklace. The region offers hillside woods of beech, oak, maple, and chestnut, and spectacular outcroppings of Pennsylvanian period conglomerate rock.

Among the birds that can be found during the late spring and summer (in addition to permanent residents) are the Great Blue and Green-backed herons; Mallard; Wood Duck; Turkey Vulture; Cooper's, Red-tailed, Red-shouldered, and Broad-winged hawks; American Kestrel; Killdeer; Spotted Sandpiper; Mourning Dove; Black-billed Cuckoo; Eastern Screech, Great Horned, and Barred owls; Ruby-throated Hummingbird; Belted Kingfisher; Common Flicker; Red-headed, Hairy, and Downy woodpeckers; Acadian Flycatcher (infrequent); Eastern Wood-Pewee; Tree, Northern Rough-winged, and Barn swallows; Purple Martin; Blue Jay; Common Crow; and Black-capped Chickadee.

Also the Tufted Titmouse; White-breasted Nuthatch; House Wren; Gray Catbird; Brown Thrasher; American Robin; Wood Thrush; Veery (uncommon); Eastern Bluebird, Blue-gray Gnatcatcher; Cedar Waxwing; Yellow-throated, Red-eyed, and Warbling vireos; Black-and-White, Blue-winged, Yellow, and Cerulean warblers; Ovenbird; Common Yellowthroat; Hooded Warbler; and American Redstart.

Additional summer birds include the Red-winged Blackbird; Northern Oriole; Common Grackle; Brown-headed Cowbird; Scarlet Tanager; Northern Cardinal; Rose-breasted Grosbeak, Indigo Bunting; American Goldfinch; Rufous-sided Towhee; and Chipping, Field, and Song sparrows.

During the summer and early fall, scan the lakeshore for Great Egrets and occasional shorebirds. In spring and fall, the entire area is good for migrating landbirds.

Holden Arboretum   *Located on Sperry Road north of*
                                        U.S. 6 near Mentor. (Map B–35)

A delightful place to visit any time of the year, the arboretum features over five thousand different kinds of cultivated woody plants, flowering trees, and shrubs. Its scenic nature trails meander along the east branch of the Chagrin River past ponds and through wooded ravines. One trail leads to ornithologically interesting Stebbins' Gulch, which is described on p. 59. Other trails wind through a beech-maple climax forest, which also includes oak, sassafras, sour gum, and dogwood trees. Nature courses are offered; there are guided tours and nature walks.

The impressive list of birds seen here includes most of the warblers that occur in Ohio. During the spring and fall migrations, Corning Lake attracts good numbers of waterfowl, including Tundra Swans. Aeration keeps the water open in winter, and Canada Geese and a variety of ducks stay through the winter.

Some of the rare and unusual species that have been observed at the arboretum include the Eared Grebe, Yellow-crowned Night Heron, Least Bittern, Greater White-fronted and Snow geese, Eurasian Wigeon, Barrow's Goldeneye, Peregrine Falcon, Yellow Rail, Northern Saw-whet Owl, Pileated Woodpecker, Western Kingbird, and Black-throated Gray Warbler. One of the first House Finch incursions into Ohio was in this region, and the species is now well established.

Summer birds include the Pied-billed Grebe, Green-backed Heron, Canada Goose, Mallard, Wood Duck, Turkey Vulture, Cooper's, Red-tailed, Red-shouldered, and Broad-winged hawks, American Kestrel, Spotted Sandpiper, Yellow-billed and Black-billed cuckoos, Eastern Screech, Great Horned, and Barred Owls, Ruby-throated Hummingbird, Belted Kingfisher, Common Flicker, Red-bellied, Red-headed, Hairy, and Downy woodpeckers, and Eastern Kingbird.

Also look for the Great Crested Flycatcher, Eastern Phoebe, Willow Flycatcher, Eastern Wood-Pewee, Tree, Northern Rough-winged, Bank, and Barn swallows, Purple Martin, Blue Jay, American Crow, Black-capped Chickadee, Tufted Titmouse, White-breasted and Red-breasted (rare) nuthatches, House Wren, Gray Catbird, Brown Thrasher, American Robin, Wood Thrush, Veery, and Eastern Bluebird.

Other breeding species are the Yellow-throated, Red-eyed, and Warbling vireos, Yellow, Magnolia (rare), and Cerulean warblers, Ovenbird, Common Yellowthroat, American Redstart, Eastern Meadowlark, Red-winged Blackbird, Northern Oriole, Common Grackle, Brown-headed Cowbird, Scarlet Tanager, Northern Cardinal, Rose-breasted Grosbeak, Indigo Bunting, American Goldfinch, Rufous-sided Towhee, and Chipping, Field, and Song sparrows.

Huron Harbor and Breakwater   *Take Ohio 6 into the center of Huron and turn north toward the lake at the intersection with Ohio 13. (Map A–36)*

An impressive number of rare birds have been observed here, especially since silt and sludge has been pumped into an area adjacent to the shore end of the breakwater. To the east of the road to the parking area on the pier, a wide channel is a favorite concentration point for Herring, Ring-billed, and Bonaparte's gulls. Depending on their movement along the lake—east in fall and early winter, west in late winter and spring—sometimes tens of thousands of gulls fill the air with others resting on nearby sand and coal piles. There are usually several dozen Great Black-backed Gulls present in winter with diminished numbers in spring and fall.

To see shorebirds to advantage, walk out on the breakwater for about fifty yards and look for a path through scrub willows and weeds leading off to the left. This will lead to exposed mudflats where sandpipers and their allies are usually present from April to November. A few shorebirds might also be encountered on the wide, flat breakwater. A spotting scope is almost a necessity in locations like this, especially for waterbirds out on the lake. Greater Scaups occur in good numbers each winter from here east along Lake Erie's shore.

Rare birds that have been seen here are the Northern Gannet, Snowy Egret, Oldsquaw, all three scoters, American Avocet, Piping Plover, Hudsonian Godwit, Whimbrel, Spotted Redshank, Red Phalarope, Long-billed Dowitcher, Red Knot, Western Sandpiper, Buff-breasted Sandpiper, Jaeger species, Glaucous Gull, Thayer's Gull; California Gull; Common Black-headed Gull, Laughing Gull, Franklin's Gull, Little Gull, Black-legged Kittiwake, Sabine's Gull, Arctic Tern, Least Tern, Snowy Owl, and Sharp-tailed Sparrow.

Irwin Prairie
From I-475 on the west side of Toledo, take Ohio 120 west to McCord Road; go south to Bancroft Road; turn west and go to Irwin Road; turn north to the entrance.
(Map A–37)

Established in 1974 by the Ohio Department of Natural Resources, this 142-acre remnant of what once were extensive prairies and swamplands is still a splendid place to find unusual birds, especially in late spring and summer. There are parking areas just off the road, and a boardwalk transects part of the marsh.

Between 1951 and 1961, John J. Stophet made a survey of the birdlife now included within the preserve's boundaries. He observed breeding Pied-billed Grebes, Least and American bitterns, Mallards, King and Virginia rails, Soras, Common Moorhens, and Marsh Wrens. Most of these species are still found here, in addition to the following birds reported in more recent years: Broad-winged Hawk, Yellow and Black rails (no positive nesting records), Willow and Alder flycatchers, Sedge Wren, Bell's Vireo, White-eyed Vireo, Golden-winged and Blue-winged warblers, Yellow-breasted Chat, Western Meadowlark, and Le Conte's Sparrow (migrant). For further information on the region, read the account on Oak Openings Metropolitan Park on p. 45.

Kelleys Island

Located about 3.5 miles north of Marblehead Point in Lake Erie, the island can be reached by ferry from Sandusky. (Map A–38)

Kelleys Pond near the village on the south shore of the island, and Carp Pond near the west shore, offer the birder a bit of marsh habitat to explore for puddle ducks, herons, and rails. Otherwise, the bird life is quite similar to that explained in greater detail for South Bass Island (p. 57).

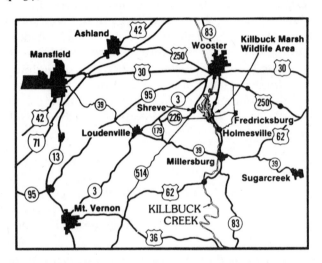

Killbuck Marsh Wildlife Area

From Ohio 83 approximately six miles south of Wooster, turn west onto Clark Road, or proceed farther south and turn west onto Force or Harrison roads. (Map B–39)

The largest remaining inland marsh in Ohio, this state wildlife area extends along Killbuck Creek for some eight miles. The region combines the creek and adjacent large tracts of marsh, ponds, woodland, and fields. There are a number of off-road parking spots that make it easier to explore this fine natural area. The beautiful and rare Prothonotary Warbler can be found along Clark Road and, a bit farther west, along Willow Road. If the warblers cannot be found in these locations, go about a mile south on Route 83 to Force Road and try there, or go another mile south to Harrison Road and check out the areas around the parking spaces and the bridge over the creek.

Bird highlights, in season, include the Great Blue Heron, Green-

backed Heron, Cattle Egret, Great Egret, Least and American bitterns, Canada Goose, Tundra Swan (occasional), Blue-winged Teal,
Wood Duck, a scattering of other surface-feeding ducks, Red-tailed
and Red-shouldered hawks, Northern Harrier, Ring-necked Pheasant, King Rail (rare), Virginia Rail (uncommon), Sora, Common
Moorhen, American Coot, Greater and Lesser yellowlegs, Solitary
and Spotted sandpipers, American Woodcock, and Common Snipe.

In late spring and summer, the Yellowbilled Cuckoo is common,
as is the Red-headed Woodpecker and Eastern Kingbird. Listen for
the distinctive *fitz-bew* song of the Willow Flycatcher. Tree, Northern
Rough-winged, and Barn swallows nest and Marsh Wrens breed in
the dense cattails.

In sycamore and cottonwood trees, look and listen for Warbling
Vireos and Northern Orioles. Yellow Warblers and Common Yellowthroats are common, and in late summer Cedar Waxwings become
abundant. Swamp Sparrows nest in the marsh and a few can probably
be found year-round.

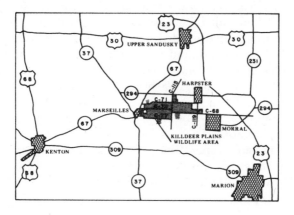

Killdeer Plains Wildlife Area   *From U.S. 23 about fourteen miles*
northwest of Marion, turn east onto
Ohio 294; continue through the
village of Harpster to County Road
115, then drive south for about one
mile. (Map A–40)

Over 8,000 acres of impoundments, cropland, fields in various stages
of succession, and woods are included in this valuable state wildlife
area. Large numbers of Canada Geese and numerous duck species
are present in early spring, late fall, and early winter. Small numbers
of blue-phased Snow Geese are frequently seen from late October

through November. Some Canada Geese and half a dozen kinds of ducks nest in the area. Good observation points are from atop the earthen mound south of the residence on County Road 115, and along the embankment on the north side of County Road 68.

From November to April, Bald Eagles and Snowy Owls are rare visitors, and Short-eared Owls occur regularly, most often in the fields south and west of the headquarters building. Some years a few pairs remain to nest.

Rare birds observed have included the American White Pelican, Snowy Egret, Glossy Ibis, Mute Swan, White-fronted Goose, Fulvous Whistling-Duck, Golden Eagle, Peregrine Falcon, Sandhill Crane, Marbled Godwit, and Sharp-tailed Sparrow.

Representative summer residents are the Pied-billed Grebe; Great Blue Heron; Green-backed Heron; American Bittern; Canada Goose; Mallard; American Black Duck; Blue-winged Teal; Wood Duck; Turkey Vulture; Cooper's, Red-tailed, and Red-shouldered hawks; Northern Harrier (scarce); American Kestrel; Northern Bobwhite; Ring-necked Pheasant; Sora; Killdeer; American Woodcock; Spotted Sandpiper; Yellow-billed Cuckoo; Great Horned Owl, Barred Owl; Belted Kingfisher; Red-headed Woodpecker; Horned Lark; Tree, Northern Rough-winged, and Barn swallows; Purple Martin; Carolina Chickadee; Marsh Wren; Sedge Wren (erratic); Eastern Bluebird; Loggerhead Shrike (rare); Warbling Vireo; Prothonotary Warbler (scarce); Yellow Warbler; Common Yellowthroat; Bobolink; Orchard Oriole (uncommon); Northern Oriole; Scarlet Tanager; Summer Tanager (uncommon); Dickcissel (erratic); Savannah, Grasshopper, Henslow's (erratic), Vesper, Chipping, Field, and Song sparrows.

During winter months, Killdeer Plains is an excellent place to see flocks of Horned Larks and Snow Buntings, and smaller numbers of Lapland Longspurs.

Kingwood Center   *900 West Park Avenue in*
                                       Mansfield. (Map A-41)

This delightful arboretum and garden covers 47 acres and includes a trail that meanders through a woods and meadow. In April and May, many migrant landbirds pass through the trees and shrubs—Hermit Thrushes (early April), Swainson's Thrushes, Veerys, Solitary Vireos, Black-and-White Warblers, Tennessee Warblers, Magnolia Warblers, Cape May Warblers, Chestnut-sided Warblers, Canada Warblers, American Redstarts, Northern Orioles, Scarlet Tanagers, White-throated and White-crowned sparrows. Summering birds include the

Eastern Wood-Pewee, Red-eyed Vireo, Northern Oriole, Indigo Bunting, and Chipping, Field, and Song sparrows.

Kyle Woods   *On Ohio 224, in Mahoning County, about one and a half miles east of Canfield. (Map B–42)*

This 53-acre swamp forest contains sugar maple, black gum, black cherry, oak, and ash trees. Springtime pools of water are alive with salamanders and several species of frogs. A large log house near the preserve was a stopping place on the Underground Railway during the Civil War.

Though modest in size, this preserve offers plenty of food and cover for both migratory and nesting birds. The Winter Wren, Hermit Thrush, Rusty Blackbird, Purple Finch, and Fox Sparrow can be seen here in early spring and again in the fall; Northern Waterthrushes and many of the northern warblers pass through in May.

Breeding birds include the Red-headed Woodpecker, Eastern Wood-Pewee, Black-capped Chickadee, House Wren, Gray Catbird, Cedar Waxwing, Yellow-throated Vireo, Yellow Warbler, Ovenbird, Common Yellowthroat, American Redstart, Scarlet Tanager, Indigo Bunting, Rufous-sided Towhee, Field and Song sparrows.

La Due Reservoir   *On U.S. 422 about ten miles southeast of Chagrin Falls. (Map B–43)*

This reservoir is the stopping place for a wide variety of waterbirds during the spring and fall migrations. Among these transients, look for the Common Loon, Horned and Pied-billed grebes, Herring, Ring-billed, and Bonaparte's gulls, and most of the duck species commonly seen in Ohio. If water levels are down during the late summer and fall, a variety of shorebirds are apt to be found.

Some of the more unusual occurrences have been a Common Loon in July, Greater White-fronted Goose, Oldsquaw, Yellow Rail, Common Moorhen (nested), Willet, and Sandhill Crane.

Lake County Metropolitan Parks: Hidden Valley, Hogback Ridge, Indian Point, and Riverview   *These parks are located along the Grand River and can be reached from Ohio 528. For further information, write: Supervisor, Lake County Metropolitan Parks, 1385 Jackson Street, Painesville, OH 44077.*

Lake Rockwell

*Take County Road 797, in Portage
County, about two miles north of
Kent, or Ohio 14 where it crosses the
upper end of the reservoir.
(Map B–44)*

Originally a swamp forest with glacial bog plants, this 800-acre area
with its large lake provides the city of Akron with water. Surrounding
woods are beech-maple, oak-hickory, and pine. Tundra Swans and
Canada Geese linger here in March along with the modest numbers
of surface-feeding and diving ducks. Herring, Ring-billed, and smaller
numbers of Bonaparte's gulls enliven the sky and water with their
white fluttering. Breeding birds are representative of Portage and
Summit counties.

Leipsic Reservoir

*On Ohio 613 three miles east of Leipsic
in Putnam County. (Map A–45)*

This modest-sized 30-acre reservoir was built on a branch of Beaver
Creek. The groves and thickets around it attract a variety of spring
and fall migrants. Late March and early April arrivals include the
Belted Kingfisher, Common Flicker, Eastern Phoebe, Tree Swallow,
Hermit Thrush, Eastern Bluebird, Yellow-rumped Warbler, and White-
throated and Field sparrows.

A few waterbirds, mostly Mallards and Blue-winged Teals, and
occasional Pied-billed Grebes, pay brief visits to the lake. By the first
of May, Spotted Sandpipers are teetering along the shore, and small
troupes of vireos, warblers, and orioles can be found in the surrounding trees.

Little Mountain

*South of Mentor, take Sperry County
Road north of U.S. 6. (Map B–46)*

Part of Holden Arboretum, this 65-acre site has a stand of white pine
and hemlock at an elevation of 1,200 feet. This delightful spot is
famed as the nesting locale for a number of species that rarely nest
elsewhere in Ohio. These elite birds include the Least Flycatcher;
Red-breasted Nuthatch; Solitary Vireo, and Blackburnian Warbler.
The Pine, Wilson's, and Canada warblers are probable nesters.

The Black-throated Green Warbler is an abundant breeder on
Little Mountain. Each year between 1933 and 1938, B. P. Bole, Jr.,
found ten to nineteen of these warblers nesting in a 75-acre tract. He
also counted fifteen pairs of Ovenbirds in the same area in 1939.
Other breeding warblers include the Black-and-White, Cerulean,

Hooded, and American Redstart. Broad-winged Hawks have been found nesting, and the Ruffed Grouse is an annual breeding bird.

Little Mountain is an exceptionally fine place to find transient landbirds during the spring and fall migrations. On May 4, 1936, a migrating flock of approximately two hundred Black-throated Blue Warblers was encountered by one observer.

Lorain Harbor and Breakwater   *Take U.S. 6 to Oberlin Avenue in downtown Lorain, turn north and go to First Street, which parallels the lake shore. The municipal pier is between the power plant and the coal dock. (Map B–47)*

Thanks to a warm water outflow from the Ohio Edison Power Plant, a sizeable area of the inner harbor never freezes over. Therefore, one can see a multitude of waterbirds in mid-winter without even getting out of the car at dockside.

Search all of the breakwaters and jetties with a spotting scope, especially at the water's edge; sometimes, in mid-winter, a Great Blue Heron or a Black-crowned Night Heron can be found. Other birds to look for are Mallards, American Black Ducks; Redheads, Canvasbacks, Greater and Lesser scaups, Common Goldeneyes, Buffleheads, and an occasional Oldsquaw. A few Common Mergansers are apt to be present along with larger numbers of Red-breasted Mergansers. Among the gulls, there should be thousands of Ring-billed and Bonaparte's, and smaller numbers of Herring gulls. Rarer species of *Laridae* are discussed later in this account.

To get to the breakwater, return to Route 6, proceed east across the bridge on Erie Avenue, turn toward the lake on Arizona Avenue, then drive left one block to Lakeside Avenue. Park along the street and walk down the incline to the breakwater, which is at least half a mile long and angles off into the lake. During the winter months, be sure to bring along plenty of warm clothing, because this can be one of the coldest and windiest places anywhere.

When landbirds are migrating, check out the trees along Lakeside Avenue. Also at the bottom of the incline, there is a thicket that is an excellent trap for warblers, sparrows, and a variety of other birds.

Once out on the breakwater, look for Common Loons and Horned Grebes, all of the ducks mentioned above, plus additional numbers of Greater Scaups, Oldsquaws, occasional scoters, and Common and Red-breasted mergansers. In winter, there is always a chance of seeing a

Purple Sandpiper; during the spring and fall, a few shorebirds frequent the puddles and pools of water that are sometimes present atop the breakwater.

The list of rare birds seen at Lorain, mainly in the two areas described, is impressive. Count among them the Red-throated Loon, Red-necked Grebe; Northern Gannet; Brant, Greater White-fronted Goose, Common and King eiders, Harlequin Duck, all three scoter species, jaegers, and the following gulls: Glaucous, Iceland, Lesser Black-backed, Thayer's, California, Common Black-headed, Laughing, Little; Heermann's, Franklin's, and Blacklegged Kittiwake. Though not rare, the Great Black-backed Gull is seen with regularity during the winter months. A Snowy Owl or two are seen most winters, usually perched on a breakwater.

Lost Creek Reservoir   *Drive one mile east of Lima on High Street Road. (Map A–48)*

This 112-acre reservoir is owned by the city of Lima. The main avian attraction here is the early spring and late fall migration of waterfowl. Species that occur with a fair degree of regularity include Pied-billed and Horned grebes, Canada and Snow (uncommon) geese; Mallards, American Black Ducks, Gadwalls, Northern Pintails, Green-winged and Blue-winged teals, Redheads, Canvasbacks, Lesser Scaups, Common Goldeneyes, Buffleheads, Ruddy Ducks, and Hooded Mergansers.

Magee Marsh State Wildlife Area   *See Crane Creek State Park.*

Malabar Farm   *Take Ohio 95, in Richland County, about five miles northeast of Butler; follow the signs to Bromfield Road. (Map A–49)*

This lovely home surrounded by rolling hills and green fields was the dream and joy of author and environmentalist Louis Bromfield, who converted four worn-out and eroded farms into an agricultural Eden. A tour of the house with its fine furniture, artwork, and memorabilia is highly recommended.

Summer bird residents include the Ruby-throated Hummingbird, Eastern Kingbird, Eastern Phoebe, Northern Rough-winged and Barn swallows, House Wren, Northern Mockingbird, Gray Catbird, Eastern Bluebird, Cedar Waxwing, Yellow Warbler, Northern Yellowthroat, Eastern Meadowlark, Northern Oriole, sometimes the Summer Tanager, Indigo Bunting, American Goldfinch, Chipping Sparrow, Field Sparrow, and Song Sparrow. In the cultivated fields, look for Savannah, Grasshopper, and Vesper sparrows.

Maumee River Rapids   *Follow U.S. 24 southwest from*
                                            Toledo. (Map A–50)

This is a favorite place to find waterfowl during the winter months, and shorebirds in late summer and fall when the water is low. The best birding area is between the community of Maumee and the Providence Dam.

During winter the water remains open, thereby attracting large numbers of ducks, including many Mallards, American Black Ducks, American Wigeons, and Common Goldeneyes. Among these, look for Gadwalls, Northern Pintails, and Green-winged Teals. Diving ducks are sometimes found in the deeper pools of the rapids and, in addition to Common Goldeneyes, include Redheads, Ring-necked Ducks, Canvasbacks, and Common Mergansers. Ring-billed Gulls, along with a few Herring Gulls, are seen almost year-round.

Many species of shorebirds have been found in the rapids, especially during the southward movement extending from July through October. Commonly seen species are the Killdeer, Greater and Lesser yellowlegs, Solitary and Spotted sandpipers, Ruddy Turnstone, Common Snipe, Sanderling, Semi-palmated and Least sandpipers, White-rumped and Pectoral sandpipers, and Dunlin. Other birds to look for include herons and egrets, geese, Ospreys, rails, terns, Belted Kingfishers, swallows, pipits, Rusty Blackbirds, and sparrows.

Maumee State Forest   *Take Fulton County Road B, near*
                                            Swanton, three miles west of
                                            Whitehouse. (Map A–51)

Flat as a tabletop, the 3,071 acres of this forested tract are crisscrossed with thirty-seven miles of trails. At least sixty species of birds nest in this large area and more will probably be discovered with additional fieldwork. Turkey Vultures, Cooper's Hawks, and Red-tailed Hawks nest in the vicinity; Eastern Screech Owls and Barred Owls are resident, and Wood Thrushes, Cerulean Warblers, Scarlet Tanagers, and Rose-breasted Grosbeaks are summer breeders. In surrounding fields, look for Horned Larks, Eastern Meadowlarks (always keep alert for the more melodious song of the Western Meadowlark), Savannah and Vesper sparrows.

Mentor Marsh State
Nature Preserve

Exit I-90 at Ohio 44 and proceed through Painesville, then turn west on Ohio 283. Continue about one-half mile and turn right onto Corduroy Road to the Marsh House. (Map B-52)

Jointly owned by the Ohio Department of Natural Resources and the Cleveland Museum of Natural History, this 619-acre preserve has ponds and adjoining marshy areas bordered by sand dunes and a beech-maple forest.

In the early spring, transient waterfowl throng to the preserve: Mallards, American Black Ducks, Gadwalls, Northern Pintails, Green-winged and Blue-winged teals, American Wigeons, Wood Ducks, Ring-necked Ducks, Lesser Scaups, Ruddy Ducks, and Hooded Mergansers can be found, along with Canada Geese and a few Horned and Pied-billed grebes.

By mid-April, new arrivals include Great Blue Herons, occasional Great Egrets, Black-crowned Night Herons, and Least and American bitterns. Marshy edges yield Virginia Rails, Soras, Common Moor-hens, and American Coots. By the first week in May, all of the swallow species found in Ohio can be found winging over the ponds. As the spring progresses, migrant landbirds are sometimes present in impressive numbers.

On May 1, 1976, a John Carroll University ornithology class, using tape-recorded calls on the Becker Trail, attracted between one and two hundred Soras and Virginia Rails. Prothonotary Warblers nest in the area every year.

A few of the rare birds found in the vicinity, including the municipality of Mentor, are Northern Goshawk, Merlin, Brunnich's Murre, King and Black rails, Short-eared Owl, Violet-green Swallow, Western Tanager, Blue Grosbeak, Red Crossbill, Lark Sparrow, and Clay-colored Sparrow.

Metzger Marsh Wildlife Area

On Ohio 2 about seven miles west of Crane Creek State Park, or one mile east of Bono. (Map A-53)

This state marsh and recreation area can be recognized from the road by the sizeable marina facilities. Follow the access road all the way to the end. From here, there is a good view of a large expanse of water that is a favorite stopping place for Tundra Swans and other water-fowl in March and early April. From the parking lot, look for several sandbars far out in the water. These are loafing places for Herring Gulls, Ring-billed Gulls, and Bonaparte's Gulls and, even into late May, for a few Great Black-backed Gulls. During the warm months, there are usually Common Terns, Caspian Terns, and sometimes a few Forster's Terns and Black Terns flying about or resting on the sandbars.

During spring and fall migrations, there might be transient land-birds in the trees and shrubs near the parking area—Eastern King-birds, Swainson's Thrushes, Yellow-rumped Warblers, Palm Warblers, White-crowned Sparrows, White-throated Sparrows—feeding and resting before continuing their journeys. Before leaving, check out the retaining walls for Spotted Sandpipers, Ruddy Turnstones, and Sanderlings.

Milan Wildlife Area

Take Ohio 113, in Erie County, three miles west of Milan. (Map A–54)

A 200-acre woods of oak, hickory, ash, cottonwood, and maple is transected by the cliff-lined Huron River, providing habitat for a considerable number of nesting birds. Turkey Vultures, Cooper's Hawks, and Red-tailed Hawks nest in or near the area. Other breeding birds include the Yellow-billed Cuckoo, Barred Owl, Pileated Woodpecker, Red-headed Woodpecker, Acadian Flycatcher, Black-capped Chickadee, Brown Thrasher, Wood Thrush, Veery, Yellow-throated Vireo, Black-and-White Warbler, Cerulean Warbler, Ovenbird, Scarlet Tanager, Rose-breasted Grosbeak, Rufous-sided Towhee, and Song Sparrow.

Mill Creek Park

Entrances to this park in Youngstown are at the Mahoning Avenue Bridge at Glenwood and Falls Avenues, and at Canfield Road, which is also U.S. 62. (Map B–55)

The park commences where Mill Creek joins the Mahoning River and then extends southward along a picturesque gorge for seven miles. There are roadways along both sides of the creek. Oak, walnut, sugar maple, and hickory trees cover the hillsides and gorge. Hem-locks grace the slopes of some of the cool, moist spots in the gorge. In addition to the stream, there are three lakes, numerous ponds, and several swamps.

Several productive trails start at the Old Mill on Canfield Road. During the latter part of April and throughout May, large numbers of migrant landbirds can be found in many parts of the park. The vicinity of the lakes, and almost anywhere along the gorge, are especially good areas. Boardman Woods and Flats is relatively undisturbed and can yield hours of enjoyable hiking and birding. It is located at the southern end of the park.

A surprising number of birds nest in the park and include the Green-backed Heron, Red-shouldered Hawk, Kestrel, American Woodcock, Yellow-billed Cuckoo, Eastern Screech and Barred owls, Chimney Swift, Ruby-throated Hummingbird, Belted Kingfisher, Pileated Woodpecker, Red-bellied, Red-headed, Hairy, and Downy woodpeckers, Eastern Kingbird, Eastern Phoebe, Acadian and Willow Flycatchers, and Northern Rough-winged and Barn swallows.

Also the Black-capped Chickadee, House Wren, Gray Catbird, Brown Thrasher, Wood Thrush, Veery, Yellow-throated, Red-eyed, and Warbling vireos, Black-and-White Warbler, Blue-winged and Yellow warblers, Cerulean Warbler, Ovenbird, Louisiana Waterthrush, Common Yellowthroat, Yellow-breasted Chat, American Redstart, Orchard and Northern orioles, Scarlet Tanager, Northern Cardinal, Rose-breasted Grosbeak, Indigo Bunting, Purple Finch, House Finch, Rufous-sided Towhee, and Henslow's, Chipping, Field, and Song sparrows.

Mogadore Reservoir

Take Ohio 43 about three miles south of I-76 just east of Akron. (Map B–56)

This 1,015-acre site contains a large reservoir partly surrounded with pine plantations, beech-maple and oak-hickory woods. Mallards, Wood Ducks and, probably, Blue-winged Teals nest; from mid-March to early April, Tundra Swans are frequently present, along with large flocks of ducks, chiefly Mallards, American Black Ducks, Green-winged and Blue-winged teals, American Wigeons, Redheads, Ring-necked Ducks, Canvasbacks, Lesser Scaups, Common Goldeneyes, Ruddy Ducks, and Red-breasted and Hooded mergansers. In the fall, before the water freezes, Horned Grebes are sometimes plentiful and there is a chance to see rarities such as the Oldsquaw, and all three scoters.

Mohican State Park and State Forest

Take I-71 to the Ohio 97 exit and proceed east to Loudonville, then go two miles south on Ohio 3. (Map A–56)

Together, Mohican State Park and the forest which surrounds it make up a scenic and wooded recreation area of over five thousand acres.

The park features a lodge, dining facilities, meeting rooms, gift shop, indoor and outdoor pools, tennis courts, a beach, boating, fishing, hiking trails—and birding.

The Lyons Falls hiking trail affords spectacular views of a Black Hand sandstone (see p. 75) overhang, great stands of oak-hickory and beech-maple forest, and an abundance of wildflowers. There are also extensive pine plantations, as well as native pines, and giant hemlocks along many of the rugged slopes.

Pleasant Hill Lake is reached by taking Ohio 95 northeast from Butler. Extending two or more miles from Pleasant Hill Dam to the Mohican River is beautiful Clear Fork Gorge, which may be explored by a nature trail on the north side. Along its banks can be found red maple, Canadian yew, and a stand of virgin white pine and hemlock. The sunny northern slope provides suitable habitat for red and white oaks, tulip trees, beech, and magnificent sycamores.

Birds that are permanent residents include Cooper's and Red-tailed hawks, Kestrel, Ruffed Grouse, Ring-necked Pheasant, Mourning Dove, Eastern Screech, Great Horned, and Barred owls, Belted Kingfisher, Pileated, Red-bellied, Red-headed, Hairy, and Downy woodpeckers, Blue Jay, American Crow, Black-capped Chickadee, Tufted Titmouse, White-breasted Nuthatch, Carolina Wren (now rare), Eastern Bluebird, European Starling, House Sparrow, Northern Cardinal, American Goldfinch, Rufous-sided Towhee, and Song Sparrow.

Summer residents and nesting birds include a wide variety of attractive species, many of which can be seen and heard by canoeing through the region. Wood Ducks inhabit the Mohican River; Bank, Northern Rough-winged, and Barn swallows skim over the fields, and Northern Orioles and attendant Warbling Vireos are abundant in the streamside sycamores. In 1974 I counted 36 pairs of Warbling Vireos and 30 pairs of Northern Orioles along a six-mile stretch of the river.

In the more open, brushy areas, a few Golden-winged Warblers cohabit with numerous Blue-winged Warblers, and Yellow Warblers and Common Yellowthroats are common. Once in a while, a Yellow-breasted Chat squawks and chatters; Summer Tanagers are possible, and Indigo Buntings and Chipping, Field, and Song sparrows are almost always within earshot. Blue-gray Gnatcatchers and Cedar Waxwings ply the areas between open spaces and wooded edges.

Where there are deeper woods, and gorges, look and listen for the many Wood Thrushes present, plus Black-and-White and Cerulean warblers, Parulas in the hemlocks, Ovenbirds, American Redstarts, and Scarlet Tanagers. A Solitary Vireo was once observed along the river in late May, and a Lawrence's Warbler, the rare recessive hybrid of the Golden-winged and Blue-winged warblers, was observed in June. Further investigation of the region should reveal additional breeding birds.

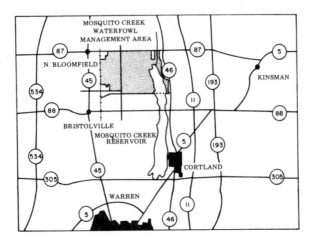

Mosquito Creek Reservoir   *Take the Ohio 5 Outerbelt northeast*
                                          of Warren and exit at Ohio 46 or 305.
                                                       (Map B–58)

The 11,857-acre state park and wildlife area that surrounds the reservoir is a first-rate spot for observing waterfowl and shorebirds in season. The reservoir covers 7,850 acres and attracts numerous ducks and geese in the spring and fall. Most of the puddle ducks are common, and rafts of diving ducks are often seen on the wider expanses of water. Non-resident Canada Geese are regular visitors as are flocks of Tundra Swans in March and November. On the south side of the reservoir is the park, which combines a beech-maple forest, a swamp, and old fields. Canada Geese now nest here as a result of a program started in 1957.

Shorebirding is good in the summer and fall if the water level drops enough to create mudflats. Among the species seen at such times are the Killdeer, Semi-palmated Plover, Lesser Golden and Black-bellied plovers, Greater and Lesser yellowlegs, Solitary and Common Spotted sandpipers, Ruddy Turnstone, Red-necked Phalarope, Common Snipe, Short-billed Dowitcher, Western Sandpiper, Least and White-rumped sandpipers, Baird's and Pectoral sandpipers, and Stilt Sandpiper.

Bald Eagles and Ospreys are seen occasionally. Common Loons,

Horned Grebes, and Double-crested Cormorants occur in migration. Cattle Egrets are now seen with some frequency, and the Glossy Ibis, Snow Goose, Oldsquaw, Merlin, Whimbrel, Long-billed Dowitcher, and Buff-breasted Sandpiper are among the rare birds that have been recorded.

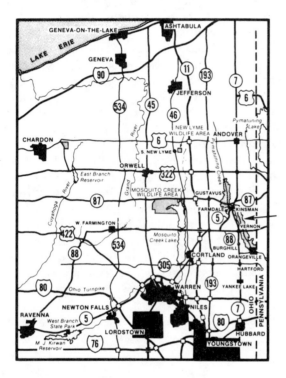

New Lyme Wildlife Area   *On Ohio 46 one mile east of South New Lyme, in Ashtabula County.*
(Map B–59)

This 529-acre swamp forest is composed of pin oak, swamp oak, ash, and elm on ground that stays wet until mid-summer. There are fine opportunities here for finding nesting birds rare in other parts of Ohio.

During the spring, Ruffed Grouse can often be heard drumming, and American Woodcocks can be observed performing their nuptial sky dances. In June, this is a breeding place for the Least Flycatcher, Black-capped Chickadee, Veery, Solitary Vireo (rare), Nashville Warbler (rare), Purple Finch, Rufous-sided Towhee, and Rose-breasted Grosbeak.

Nimisila Reservoir/
Portage Lakes

Take Ohio 619 south from
Barberton, or Ohio 93 south from
Akron. There are numerous parking
spots and access roads. (Map B–60)

About seven miles long, these irregularly shaped reservoirs are over 3,000 acres in area and are an excellent region to study waterfowl, shorebirds, and many landbirds.

Loons and grebes occur in spring and fall, along with Tundra Swans, Canada Geese, and good numbers of ducks. From April to October, Great Blue Herons, Green-backed Herons, Cattle Egrets, Great Egrets, and occasional Black-crowned Night Herons can be found with a fair degree of certainty. Green-backed Herons are the first to depart, while a few Great Blue Herons linger into December. North of East Nimisila Road and east of Christman Road there is an open bog meadow where bitterns have been found, and Virginia Rails and Soras can be flushed out of the wet spots. In summer and early fall, this entire region should be checked for Marsh Wrens, the much rarer Sedge Wren, Bobolinks, Savannah Sparrows, and Henslow's Sparrows. Some of the plants found here include sphagnum, fringed gentian, shrubby cinquefoil, blazing star, and small orchids.

Ospreys are seen regularly each spring and fall; shorebirds in good numbers can be discovered where there are mudflats or shallow water from mid-July to mid-October.

North Chagrin Reservation

Take I-90 east of Cleveland and go
south on Ohio 91, or from the I-271
exit at Mayfield Heights, drive east a
short distance to Route 91 (SOM
Center Road) and drive north
several miles. Park entrances will be
on the right. (Map B–61)

This large tract of wooded hills along the Chagrin River constitutes the northeast link of Cleveland's Emerald Necklace. The 1,719-acre park contains wildflower and nature trails that meander through the beech-maple climax forest and hemlocks along the deeper ravines. Sunset Pond has an aerating system that keeps some of the water open for ducks and geese all winter.

Canada Geese, Mallards, American Black Ducks, and a few American Wigeons frequently overwinter. Some of the resident birds are the Red-tailed and Red-shouldered hawks, Ruffed Grouse, Barred

Owl, Pileated, Red-bellied, Hairy, and Downy woodpeckers, Blue Jay, American Crow, Black-capped Chickadee, Tufted Titmouse, White-breasted Nuthatch, Northern Cardinal, and Song Sparrow.

Summer visitors and nesting birds are Great Egret, Black-crowned Night Heron, Least Bittern (has nested), Canada Goose, Mallard, Sharp-shinned Hawk (has nested), Red-tailed Hawk, American Kestrel, Virginia Rail (nesting record at the Forest Lane Pond), American Woodcock, Yellow-billed and Black-billed cuckoos, Chimney Swift, Ruby-throated Hummingbird, Belted Kingfisher, Common Flicker; Eastern Kingbird, Great Crested Flycatcher, Eastern Phoebe, Acadian Flycatcher, Eastern Wood-Pewee, Tree, Northern Rough-winged, and Barn swallows, and Purple Martin.

Also the House Wren, Sedge Wren, Carolina Wren (now scarce), Gray Catbird, Brown Thrasher, American Robin, Wood Thrush, Veery, Eastern Bluebird (cyclic), Cedar Waxwing, Yellow-throated, Red-eyed, and Warbling vireos, Yellow, Black-throated Green, Cerulean, and probably the Chestnut-sided warblers, Ovenbird, Louisiana Waterthrush, Common Yellowthroat, Hooded Warbler, American Redstart, House Sparrow, Red-winged Blackbird, Northern Oriole, Common Grackle, Brown-headed Cowbird, Scarlet Tanager, Northern Cardinal, Rose-breasted Grosbeak, Indigo Bunting, American Goldfinch, Rufous-sided Towhee, and Chipping, Field, and Song sparrows.

During the spring migration, migrants pour through the reservation and a large list of species can be compiled in a single morning. Usually fewer birds are seen in the fall.

Oak Openings Metropolitan Park   *Take Ohio 2 west from downtown Toledo. Proceed for 18 miles, going under the Ohio Turnpike and 3 miles west of the Toledo Express Airport, then turn left on Wilkins Road and continue to the main entrance on the right. (Map A–62)*

Broad sand dunes, dry soil plants and bog flora, open oak woods, swamp forest, alder bogs, wet prairies, and dry prairies all contribute to making this a unique 3,400-acre naturalists' paradise. During the first part of the century, much of the region was drained, cut, and burned. Although much reduced in area and integrity, small pockets of valuable habitat have been saved, and other areas are returning to their original state. Ohio's only moving or "living" sand dunes are preserved within this park. Nature hikes are a regular part of the park program during the warmer months. Except in the winter, be sure to take along a good insect repellent.

The open oak woods on the dunes consist of black and white oaks with a forest floor of bracken fern, huckleberry and blueberry bushes, wintergreen, wild indigo, lupine, goldenrods, and asters. Within the swamp forests, situated among the dunes, are pin oaks, elms, soft maples, wild cherries, tupelos, aspens, and poplars. Beneath these trees are buttonbush; blackberry tangles; spicebush; wild spirea; spikenard; bedstraw; and royal, cinnamon, and sensitive ferns. Some of the wildflowers still found are the blazing star, wild phlox, lance-leafed and bird's-foot violets, and wild lily-of-the-valley.

The bogs provide the proper habitat for willows, alders, elder-berry, and wild spirea. Large trees are few in number, but the under-growth is almost impenetrable, consisting of wild raspberry, skunk cabbage, marsh marigold, jewelweed, boneset, prairie nettle, golden-rods, and a variety of other plants. When rainfall is normal, the scat-tered remnants of wet prairie retain water until mid-summer. According to Lou Campbell in his *Birds of the Toledo Area*, the dominant plants are blue joint-grass, slough-grass, clumps of willows, cornel, button-bush, nine-bark, and aspens.

Special birds to look for in sloughs and wet spots from early May through the nesting season are the Least and American bitterns, both of which are difficult to find, and the equally elusive King and Vir-ginia rails, plus the more plentiful Sora, occasional Pied-billed Grebes, Green-backed Herons, Common Gallinules, and American Coots.

Both cuckoos nest here; the Black-billed is slightly more com-mon. A few pairs of Whip-poor-wills are present most years. The flycatchers are represented by the Eastern Kingbird, Great Crested, Eastern Phoebe, Acadian, Willow, Least (rare), and Eastern Wood-Pewee. The *fee-bee-o* of the Alder Flycatcher should be listened for since it has been reported in the area several times.

The scarce Bewick's Wren has been known to nest, as well as the Sedge and Marsh wrens and, of course, the House Wren. Black-capped Chickadees nest regularly as do the Tufted Titmouse, White-breasted Nuthatch, Gray Catbird, Brown Thrasher, American Robin, Wood Thrush, Veery, Eastern Bluebird, Blue-gray Gnatcatcher, Cedar Waxwing, and the White-eyed, Bell's (rare), Yellow-throated, Red-eyed, and Warbling vireos.

A late spring or early summer visit to the Oak Openings should yield a good list of warblers. Look for the Black-and-White (rare), Golden-winged and Blue-winged, the hybrid Brewster's and Lawrence's (rare) warblers, Yellow Warbler, Cerulean and Chestnut-sided warblers, Ovenbird, Kentucky (rare), Mourning (rare), Common Yellowthroat, Yellow-breasted Chat, Hooded, Canada (rare), and American Redstart.

Those three spectacular birds the Northern Oriole, the Scarlet Tanager, and the Rose-breasted Grosbeak nest in the Oak Openings, but in fewer numbers than in preceding years. A few Orchard Orioles have also been known to nest in the area and the erratic Dickcissel is always a possibility in the patches of wet prairie.

Rufous-sided Towhees are numerous and sometimes can be heard singing and calling from a number of locations at the same time. Nine species of sparrows have been known to nest in the park: Savannah, Grasshopper, Henslow's, Vesper, Lark, Chipping, Field, Swamp, and Song sparrows.

Oregon Power Plant/Bay Shore Power Plant

Take Ohio 2 to Wynn Road east of Toledo along the shore of Maumee Bay; proceed north to Bay Shore Road, turn west and enter the trucking road just east of the power plant. (Map A–63)

Birders should ask permission to be on the premises (usually freely given) at the guardhouse, which is a short distance from the gate. The area is only open Monday through Friday from 7:30 a.m. to 3:30 p.m.

Search the nearby shoreline; in late summer and fall, this is a good place to find flocks of Black-bellied plover, a few Sanderlings, various peeps, and Ruddy Turnstones.

Farther on there are several large, shallow impoundments—and a good view of Maumee Bay. The impoundments attract shorebirds in season, including Hudsonian and Marbled godwits, Willets, and American Avocets. Up to four White Pelicans were present during most of July 1982.

The waters of the bay are visited by impressive numbers of diving ducks—Ring-necked Duck, Canvasback, Lesser Scaup, Ruddy Duck, and others—from October until ice forces them on their way, usually in late December. The entire area has a diversity of habitats, both natural and man-made, and lies at a strategic conflux of migration routes.

In recent years considerable numbers of Ring-billed and some Herring gulls have nested in the area of the impoundments. Common Terns sometimes attempt nesting, but their efforts are usually frustrated by the gulls.

Ottawa National Wildlife
Refuge

Located on Ohio 2 approximately midway between Toledo and Port Clinton and about half a mile west of Crane Creek State Park. (Map A–64)

The Ottawa National Wildlife Refuge Complex encompasses over 8,000 acres in an island and a series of marshes that hopscotch along the shores of Lake Erie from west of Port Clinton nearly to Toledo. West Sister Island, nine miles offshore, supports an important heron and egret rookery.

The largest marsh, described here, abuts the Crane Creek State Park-Magee Marsh Wildlife Area and is headquarters for the entire Ottawa Complex. Little Cedar Point, the westernmost link in the system, is discussed on p. 10. Since the above locations are reviewed in this book and are representative of the region, a detailed account of the Navarre and Darby marshes is omitted. The Navarre Marsh is jointly owned by the Toledo Edison and Cleveland Electric Illuminating companies and is the site of the Davis-Besse Nuclear Power Station. Darby Marsh, at this writing, is still being developed as a wildlife refuge.

The "backside" of the Ottawa Refuge, a productive birding area, is accessible from Veler Road, which is about five miles west of the headquarters building on Ohio 2 (directions on p. 51).

When birding any of the Lake Erie marshes, a can of insect repellent should be standard equipment during the warm months. Another word of precaution: always bring extra clothing, especially jackets and sweaters—even if the weather is warm when you start out. Sudden changes in the weather and precipitous drops in temperature are commonplace along the lake.

An overflow channel parallels the right side of the entrance road to the headquarters building and parking lot of the main refuge. Behind the channel is a wetland of grasses and sedges which is a favorite feeding ground of geese and puddle ducks. Shorebirds also inhabit this fine environment, and it is a good place to find Semi-palmated Plovers, Black-bellied Plovers, Greater and Lesser yellow-legs, Solitary Sandpipers, Wilson's and Red-necked phalaropes, Common Snipe, and a variety of peeps. In late summer and fall, look for the scarce Long-billed Dowitcher.

A few puddle ducks and occasional shorebirds can be found in the pond behind the headquarters building. Except in mid-winter, Canada Geese will be everywhere and their clamorous honking will fill the air.

Most of the six miles of walking trails are atop the dikes surrounding the large impoundments. Before investigating them, check the brushy area and woods immediately west of the parking lot for small landbirds.

March, April, and early May are the best months to see migrating hawks. Scan the sky every few minutes; use binoculars to look at, around, and under clouds where hawks might be riding the updrafts high overhead. This vicinity is one of the best in the state to find appreciable numbers of Cooper's, Sharp-shinned, and Red-shouldered hawks. In late April, May, and again in September, it is a common sight to see spiraling kettles of Broad-winged Hawks. Other raptors to look for are the Red-tailed Hawk and Northern Harrier, Peregrine Falcon (rare), Merlin (rare), and American Kestrel. Bald Eagles nest on the refuge and one or two can usually be found year-round. Small numbers of Ospreys are usually present during each migration, but seldom are more than one or two seen in a day. Rough-legged Hawks are uncommon winter residents and decidedly scarce in migration.

The water level of the several impoundments varies from season to season. Water is regulated to achieve the growth of specific plant associations and to maintain proper soil-water combinations. By following the trail from the parking lot around the first impoundment, a loop of about two miles, most of the birds present can be observed. Heavy though they are to carry, a spotting scope on a tripod is almost a necessity.

Tundra Swans appear soon after the ice melts each spring. Through March several thousand will probably be present throughout the region, although less than a hundred are apt to be on the impoundments. Also look for Mallards, American Black Ducks, Gadwalls, Northern Pintails, Green-winged and Blue-winged teals, American Wigeons, Northern Shovelers, and Wood Ducks. Along with the surface-feeding ducks there should be a few diving ducks such as the Ring-necked Duck, Canvasback, Lesser Scaup, Bufflehead, and Ruddy Duck. The majority of diving ducks fly over the Lake Erie marshes; however, larger numbers can be found on Maumee Bay to the west, Sandusky Bay to the east, on borrow pits, and sometimes there are scattered rafts offshore along the lake.

In spring and fall, when a big migration is under way, small landbirds seek cover in marginal willows and shrubs and along the edges of the marsh. Such birds include Brown Thrashers, Hermit Thrushes, Ruby-crowned Kinglets, Yellow-rumped Warblers, Palm

Warblers, and Swamp Sparrows in early spring and again in October. The small birds that pop up out of the grass and fly twenty or thirty yards only to disappear again are probably Savannah Sparrows.

At the extreme north end of the dikes is a patch of flooded trees and tree-lined banks along a channel. These spots can be excellent for everything from Prothonotary Warblers and other songbirds to herons, Blue-winged Teal, Wood Ducks, Common Moorhens, American Coots, and Belted Kingfishers.

For shorebirds, the best time for a visit is May and again from mid-July to October. When water levels are ideal, impressive numbers of birds are often present. Species such as the Short-billed Dowitcher are common, and Dunlin (May and late September-October) at such times throng the mudflats. Other shorebirds regular in migration are the Semi-palmated Plover, Greater and Lesser yellowlegs, Solitary Sandpiper, Spotted Sandpiper, Semi-palmated Sandpiper, Least Sandpiper, and Pectoral Sandpiper. Rarer species to look for include the Lesser Golden Plover, Black-bellied Plover, Ruddy Turnstone, Red Knot, Sanderling, Western Sandpiper, White-rumped Sandpiper, Baird's Sandpiper, and Stilt Sandpiper.

Ring-billed Gulls are almost always present, and in August and September there are noticeable increases in Green-backed Herons, Cattle Egrets, Great Egrets, Common Terns, Caspian Terns, and Black Terns. By the end of the period, Forster's Terns are mixed in with the Common Terns in appreciable numbers.

To get to the Veler Road section of the Ottawa Complex, take Ohio 2 five miles west, turn to the right, and proceed to the gate. The large tract combines large expanses of marsh, mudflats, meadows, and croplands. During the first half of the seventies, this part of the refuge was extremely good for shorebirds and it is still an excellent place to visit for a variety of interesting species.

Beyond the gate, the road extends back into the marsh, in the process passing the site of an old farmhouse, orchard, and large fields. The first two locations are good for small flocks of migratory songbirds in the spring and fall. Eastern Kingbirds, Willow Flycatchers, vireos, warblers, Orchard Orioles, Indigo Buntings, and Pine Siskins have been noted here. In March and April, it is a good place to find Rusty Blackbirds and an occasional Brewer's Blackbird.

The fields and fallow meadows along the road sometimes become slightly flooded; when this happens, look for Lesser Golden Plovers, Black-bellied Plovers, Upland Sandpipers, Greater and Lesser yellowlegs, Solitary Sandpipers, Pectoral Sandpipers, and Dunlins. This is also a good habitat for Water Pipits, Bobolinks, Eastern Meadowlarks, Dickcissels, Savannah Sparrows, and Grasshopper Sparrows.

Look for Northern Harriers over the fields and marshes; Bald Eagles frequently fly over, and Peregrine Falcons are seen in spring and fall with some regularity.

Farther down the road is an area of dense cattail growth on the left and, just beyond, a section that sometimes develops into mudflats. The rare little Piping Plover has been seen here, along with flocks of Lesser Golden Plovers, Black-bellied Plovers, Ruddy Turnstones, White-rumped Sandpipers; Baird's, Stilt, and Buff-breasted Sandpipers. If this area is not productive or is overgrown with vegetation, walk another half a mile and there might be flooded fields and flats on the right side of the road.

In addition to shorebirds, in season the Veler Road location is a veritable spa for herons, egrets, geese, surface-feeding ducks, and large numbers of Common Terns. Among the latter, look for Forster's, Caspian, and Black terns. Before leaving, scan the skyline to the east—chances are good that you will see a Bald Eagle perched in one of the distant trees.

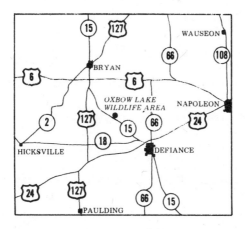

Oxbow Lake Wildlife Area   *On Ohio 15 eight miles northeast of Defiance. (Map A–65)*

A sizeable lake, two ponds, a bit of marsh, woods, fields, and farmland grace this attractive state wildlife area. Look for Pied-billed Grebes in the spring and fall; an occasional Great Blue or Green-backed heron, Blue-winged Teals, Wood Ducks, Ring-necked Pheasants, American

Coots, American Woodcocks and, sometimes, a Sora Rail in the marshy places.

Other species to look for include Red-headed Woodpeckers; Willow Flycatchers; Tree, Northern Rough-winged, and Barn swallows; Mockingbirds; Gray Catbirds; Brown Thrashers; Eastern Bluebirds; Blue-winged Warblers; Yellow Warblers; Cerulean Warblers; Common Yellowthroats; Northern Orioles; Savannah, Vesper, and Song sparrows.

Paulding Ponds   *On Paulding County Road 107 on the southern edge of Paulding near the fairgrounds. (Map A–66)*

In early spring, after the water is free of ice, these three ponds attract Mallards, American Black Ducks, Gadwalls, Blue-winged Teals (April–May), American Wigeons, Northern Shovelers, and a few diving ducks—Redheads, Ring-necked Ducks, Buffleheads, and Hooded Mergansers. Shorebirds such as Greater and Lesser yellowlegs and Solitary and Spotted sandpipers sometimes find spots to feed along the pond's edges. All the swallow species can be seen during the spring migration.

Pearson Metropolitan Park   *On Ohio 2 two miles east of the Toledo-Detroit Expressway in Toledo. (Map A–67)*

Three miles of hiking trails wander through woods and past several ponds. In addition, there are all kinds of recreational activities such as picnicking, horseback riding, and pedal boating.

This is a fairly good place to look for migrating landbirds in late April and throughout the month of May. On mornings after a really heavy migration, the trees will be full of flycatchers, thrushes, vireos, warblers, orioles, tanagers, and grosbeaks. A few Broad-winged Hawks can be flushed out of the trees from April 20 to May 10. Wood Ducks are sometimes found on the ponds, and a pair of Belted Kingfishers is frequently present.

Nesting birds include the Common Flicker, Red-headed Woodpecker, Eastern Wood-Pewee, Barn Swallow, Black-capped Chickadee, White-breasted Nuthatch, House Wren, Gray Catbird, Brown Thrasher, Wood Thrush, Red-eyed Vireo, Cerulean Warbler, Common Yellowthroat, Northern Oriole, Scarlet Tanager, Indigo Bunting, and Rose-breasted Grosbeak.

Pymatuning State Park

Take either U.S. 6 or Ohio 7 to this large park, which is east of Andover. Many good observation points are located in Pennsylvania and can be reached by continuing north and then east on U.S. 6 to Linesville. (Map B–68)

This state park is a tract of 8,919 acres along the shores of the 17,000-acre reservoir. The surrounding land is quite flat, with swamp forests in the low areas, and beech-maple woods on higher ground. The reservoir is shallow and has twenty-one low islands, in addition to several extensive mudflats. The islands are covered with trees, underbrush, and marshy spots; many inlets and bays occur along the shore.

Waterfowl that breed around the reservoir include Canada Goose, Mallard, American Black Duck, Gadwall, Blue-winged Teal, Northern Shoveler, Wood Duck, and Hooded Merganser. Spring migration for waterbirds peaks between mid-March and mid-April; the major fall migration is between mid-October and the first of December. Substantial numbers of all the surface-feeding and diving ducks occur, including rarities such as the Eurasian Wigeon, Greater Scaup, Oldsquaw, and all three scoters.

The list of birds that nest or summer in the region is impressive and includes the Pied-billed Grebe; Great Blue Heron; Green-backed Heron; Cattle Egret; Great Egret; Least and American bitterns; the waterfowl mentioned above; Red-tailed Hawk; Northern Harrier; Bald Eagle; American Kestrel; Ring-necked Pheasant; King Rail; Virginia Rail; Sora; Common Moorhen; American Coot; Killdeer; Upland Sandpiper; Spotted Sandpiper; Herring and Ring-billed gulls; Common, Caspian, and Black terns; Mourning Dove; Yellow-billed and Black-billed cuckoos; Eastern Screech, Great Horned, and Barred owls; Common Nighthawk; Chimney Swift; Ruby-throated Hummingbird; and Belted Kingfisher.

Other summering birds are the Common Flicker; Pileated, Downy, and Hairy woodpeckers; Eastern Kingbird; Great Crested, Acadian, and Willow flycatchers; Eastern Wood-Pewee; Horned Lark; Tree, Northern Rough-winged, Barn, and Cliff swallows; Purple Martin; Black-capped Chickadee; Tufted Titmouse; White-breasted Nuthatch; House, Marsh, and Sedge wrens; Gray Catbird; Brown Thrasher; Eastern Bluebird; Cedar Waxwing; Yellow-throated, Red-eyed, and Warbling vireos; Blue-winged, Yellow, and Cerulean warblers; Common Yellowthroat; American Redstart; Northern Oriole; Scarlet Tanager; Northern Cardinal; Indigo Bunting; Rufous-sided

Towhee; Savannah, Grasshopper, Henslow's, Vesper, Chipping, Field, and Song sparrows.

Birds frequently seen during the winter months are the Canada Goose; Mallard; American Black Duck; Common Goldeneye; Red-tailed and Rough-legged hawks; Northern Harrier; Bald Eagle; most of the woodpeckers; Horned Lark; Black-capped Chickadee; Tufted Titmouse; White-breasted and Red-breasted nuthatches; Brown Creeper; Eastern Bluebird; Golden-crowned Kinglet; Cedar Waxwing; Evening Grosbeak; Common Redpoll (erratic); Red Crossbill; White-winged Crossbill; Dark-eyed Junco; American Tree, White-throated, Swamp, and Song sparrows.

River Park   *On Hiram-Rapids Road three miles*
                                  south of Burton in Geauga County.
                                  (Map B–69)

Located along the upper reaches of the Cuyahoga River, this 50-acre spot includes an interesting marsh with deeper pools that attract migratory waterfowl in spring and fall. Congregations of swifts and swallows skim the water on cool days in the spring and Hermit Thrushes and Rusty Blackbirds are present until early May. Least and American bitterns occur rarely; Wood Ducks, Soras, and American Coots more commonly. In areas of deadwood, Tree Swallows and Prothonotary Warblers nest; Marsh Wrens are sometimes found in the cattails, and Willow Flycatchers in the willow and alder scrub.

Rocky River Reservation   *Take U.S. 20 in Cleveland to Ohio*
                                  252, go south on 252 to Cedar Point
                                  Road, then east for a quarter-mile to
                                  the parking lot. (Map B–70)

This 5,614-acre tract, which runs north and south along the Rocky River on the western limits of Cleveland and Lakewood, is an excellent place to find a variety of birds at all seasons of the year. Within the park are remnant Indian fortifications, small ponds, a lagoon, wooded hills and valleys, a picturesque river, and a mill with a millrace. Nature trails, special wildflower trails, the services of a resident naturalist, and a pleasant picnic area are all available.

Nesting and summering birds found here are quite similar to those listed for the North Chagrin Reservation on p. 44 and Hinkley Reservation on p. 26.

Some of the more unusual birds that have been found here are the Brewster's and Lawrence's warbler (hybrids), Yellow-throated

Warbler, Bohemian Waxwing; Brewer's Blackbird, Blue Grosbeak, Red Crossbill, and Le Conte's Sparrow. In late April and early May, Broad-winged Hawks are frequently seen overhead, plus smaller numbers of other raptors including Sharp-shinned, Cooper's, Red-tailed, Red-shouldered, and Rough-legged (uncommon) hawks and the Northern Harrier. An occasional Osprey can be seen soaring over on a good migration day.

Sand Run Metropolitan Park/   *In northwest Akron. Take I-77 to*
Seiberling Nature Center   *Route 18, then go east for 2.3 miles*
to Smith Road. Proceed east on
Smith Road for 1.5 miles to the
entrance. (Map B–71)

This 987-acre park is steeped in Indian history; the fortifications and villages of many tribes and nations once dotted the promontories and terraces along the Cuyahoga River valley. The Seiberling Nature Center is located within the park, and there are picturesque trails through the woods and up to high bluffs.

Today, Turkey Vultures soar overhead; Sharp-shinned Hawks sit quietly on the inside branches of large trees, and the reverberating yelps of Pileated Woodpeckers ring through the less frequented areas of forest. Wood Thrushes and Veeries sing duets of silvery music. Very little has changed from earlier years.

Yellow-billed and Black-billed cuckoos are both known to nest here. All of Ohio's breeding woodpeckers are represented, and the roster of breeding flycatchers includes the Eastern Kingbird, Great Crested Flycatcher, Eastern Phoebe, Acadian Flycatcher, Willow Flycatcher (in the bottomlands), Least Flycatcher (rare), and Eastern Phoebe.

Nesting warblers include the Black-and-White, Blue-winged, Yellow, Cerulean, Chestnut-sided, Ovenbird, Louisiana Waterthrush, Common Yellowthroat, Yellow-breasted Chat, Hooded, and American Redstart.

Secor Metropolitan Park and   *Eight miles west of downtown Toledo*
Arboretum   *on Central Avenue. (Map A–72)*

Low sand dunes are a feature of the southern section of this park, which is adjacent to the Oak Openings. The dunes are separated by swamp-forest remnants of ash, cottonwood, and maple with oak trees on the more stabilized dunes. In the lower half of the park the Dogwood Trail circles through a woodland of oak, tulip, basswood, red maple, and black gum. The northern part of the tract is an arboretum. There is also a nature interpretive center, a number of trails, and a year-round park naturalist.

Summer birds found in the vicinity include the Great Crested Flycatcher, Acadian Flycatcher, Willow Flycatcher, Eastern Wood-Pewee, Black-capped Chickadee, Blue-gray Gnatcatcher (scarce), Wood Thrush, Veery (scarce), Warbling Vireo, Golden-winged Warbler, Blue-winged Warbler, Yellow-breasted Chat (scarce), Scarlet Tanager, Rose-breasted Grosbeak, Rufous-sided Towhee, and Savannah, Henslow's, Vesper, Lark (rare), Chipping, Field, and Song sparrows.

For additional information on this region, read the Oak Openings Metropolitan Park description on p. 45.

Secrest Arboretum   *Take Ohio 83 about a mile south of*
the Wooster city limits. (Map B–73)

Part of the nearly two thousand-acre Ohio Agricultural Research and Development Center, the arboretum has over eighteen hundred species and cultivated varieties of trees and shrubs in a natural setting. Walnut Hollow features over one hundred and fifty kinds of azaleas and rhododendron plantings. Trails through the mixed hardwood forest allow visitors to enjoy a host of wildflowers, ferns, mosses, and birds. Other highlights include twisted silver fir trees, young bristle-cone pines, dawn redwoods, and well over a hundred varieties of flowering crab apple trees. Hundreds of different kinds of roses are displayed in an old-fashioned garden, and nearby is a collection of more than one hundred kinds of holly.

Spring and summer birds that can be seen in this pleasant environment are the Eastern Kingbird, Barn Swallow, Carolina Chickadee, House Wren, Gray Catbird, and Cedar Waxwing. Listen for the songs of Red-eyed Vireos, Yellow Warblers, Common Yellowthroats, and Northern Orioles. Northern Cardinals, Indigo Buntings, American Goldfinches, Chipping, and Song sparrows are common summer residents. During the spring migration, other birds are to be seen, including a good showing of flycatchers, vireos, warblers, and sparrows.

Seiberling Nature Center   *See Sand Run Metropolitan Park.*

Sheldon's Folly Nature Preserve   *Take U.S. 6 to the first entrance west*
of the Sawmill Creek State Lodge, in
Erie County. (Map A–75)

This pleasant tract on Lake Erie combines a managed woodland, a sandy beach, marshland, a pond, cultivated fields, a tree farm, a multiflora rose hedge, and tangles of brush. The area is extremely attractive to migrating birds in late April and May.

On a good day, twenty-five or more species of warblers can be tallied, along with remarkable numbers of orioles, tanagers, grosbeaks, and all the other birds that go to make up a big wave. Black-bellied Plovers, Ruddy Turnstones, Sanderlings, and Dunlins are frequently seen on the beach. Offshore, there are apt to be Herring Gulls, Ring-billed Gulls, Bonaparte's Gulls, Common Terns, Caspian Terns and, around the pond and marsh, Black Terns.

South Bass Island

Take the ferry boat from Port Clinton, Lakeside, or Sandusky.
(Map A–74)

Located several miles north of Catawba, this island is 3.5 miles long and 1.5 miles wide with a low, slightly rolling terrain, which consists of cultivated vineyards, old fields, and numerous patches of woods and brushy tangles. The village of Put-in-Bay is on the island, as is the Franz Theodore Stone Laboratory, a biological research station operated by The Ohio State University. The most prominent landmark, visible for miles around, is Perry's Victory and International Peace Monument. Over the years, many migrating birds have been killed on windy nights as a result of eddies of air slamming them into this edifice.

The best birding is around the middle of May, especially during inclement weather. At such times, large numbers of transient landbirds seek refuge on the island. One of the best places to find these concentrations is the wooded area along the western shoreline, between the southern tip of the island and Peach Point, which juts northward toward Middle Bass Island.

The first spring migrants reach the island during the first part of March, and include Killdeers, Mourning Doves, Eastern Meadowlarks, Purple Finches, and some of the early sparrows. Between the middle of March and the first of April, Common Loons can often be seen offshore, along with Horned Grebes, Double-crested Cormorants, and Red-breasted Mergansers. A variety of other ducks frequent the harbor, along with Herring, Ring-billed, and newly arrived Bonaparte's gulls. By April first, Belted Kingfishers, Eastern Phoebes, Cedar Waxwings, and Rufous-sided Towhees are in evidence.

Warblers reach the island about May 3, but the really big waves occur between May 10 and May 20. The raptor migration extends through April into the first part of May, when Sharp-shinned, Cooper's, Red-tailed, Red-shouldered, and Broad-winged hawks fly over, sometimes in large numbers. The fall migration of hawks is never as good, although a flight of Rough-legged Hawks sometimes passes high over the island about mid-October.

Migrating shorebirds appear on the reefs and mudflats around the island in July. The species seen most often are the Semi-palmated Plover, Greater and Lesser yellowlegs, Solitary and Spotted sandpipers, Ruddy Turnstone, Sanderling, Semi-palmated Sandpiper, and Least Sandpiper. A few Short-billed Dowitchers can be found during the season and, occasionally, a Red Knot.

Summer residents and visitors include the Great Blue Heron, Green-backed Heron, Great Egret, Black-crowned Night Heron, Mallard, American Black Duck, Wood Duck, Killdeer, Spotted Sandpiper, American Woodcock, Herring Gull, Common Tern, Black Tern, Mourning Dove, Yellow-billed Cuckoo, Black-billed Cuckoo, Chimney Swift, Ruby-throated Hummingbird, Belted Kingfisher, Common Flicker, Downy Woodpecker, Eastern Kingbird, Great Crested Flycatcher, Willow Flycatcher (uncommon), Eastern Pewee, Tree Swallow, Northern Rough-winged Swallow, Barn Swallow, Purple Martin, American Crow, House Wren, Bewick's Wren (rare), Carolina Wren (present status unknown), Gray Catbird, Brown Thrasher, American Robin, Cedar Waxwing, European Starling, Red-eyed Vireo, Yellow Warbler, Common Yellowthroat, Yellow-breasted Chat, American Redstart (uncommon), House Sparrow, Eastern Meadowlark, Red-winged Blackbird, Orchard Oriole, Northern Oriole, Common Grackle, Northern Cardinal, Indigo Bunting, American Goldfinch, Rufous-sided Towhee, Savannah Sparrow, Grasshopper Sparrow, Chipping Sparrow, Field Sparrow, and Song Sparrow.

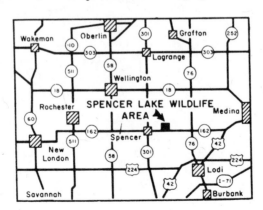

Spencer Lake Wildlife Area

Take Ohio 162 in Medina County;
about two miles east of Spencer, turn
north on the access road. (Map B–76)

A 70-acre lake is situated in this 595-acre wooded park, which includes stands of beech-maple and oak-hickory forest. There are grassy fields where one should look for Horned Larks and Savannah Sparrows, and pockets of marsh vegetation around the lake where a few Mallards and Blue-winged Teals nest.

In spring and fall Water Pipits can sometimes be found in the fields and near the water's edge, Ospreys investigate the lake, and small numbers of grebes and ducks stop over.

Springville Marsh

Take U.S. 23 north of Carey to
Township Road 24; turn west and
cross the railroad tracks. (Map A–77)

This 200-acre marsh is adjacent to and just west of a fertilizer plant. It is one of the largest remnants of wetland in the interior of northwestern Ohio. Birds to look for during the warm months are the Green-backed Heron, Mallard, Wood Duck, Cooper's Hawk, Ring-necked Pheasant, Sora, Killdeer, Yellow-billed Cuckoo, Belted Kingfisher, Eastern Kingbird, Willow Flycatcher, Marsh Wren, Warbling Vireo, Yellow Warbler, Common Yellowthroat, and Northern Oriole.

Small numbers of surface-feeding ducks stop here in migration (nine Fulvous Tree Ducks were spotted in April of 1975). A pond with mudflats is close to the road, and in the spring, summer, and fall it frequently attracts Semi-palmated Plovers, Short-billed Dowitchers, Greater and Lesser yellowlegs, Solitary and Spotted sandpipers, Common Snipes, Semi-palmated and Least sandpipers, Pectoral Sandpipers, and Dunlins.

Stebbins' Gulch

Take Ohio 6 to Chardon; the gorge is
just off Mitchell Mills and Wisner
roads north of Route 6. (Map B–35)

This rugged little gorge formed by erosion many eons ago was named after Hosea Stebbins who purchased the property in 1860. The gulch and adjoining land was given to the Holden Arboretum in 1958. In places the steep walls rise several hundred feet above the stream bed. Along one section, the stream drops almost three hundred feet in a mile and is festooned with numerous falls and cascades along its course. In the deeper parts of the gulch, the temperature seldom rises above seventy-five degrees on the hottest summer days; thus trees and plants of more northern climes thrive here. The gulch contains a mixed hardwood forest of mature hemlocks and white pines on the north-facing slopes.

Among the bird specialties that are found nesting here, or are present during the breeding season, are Acadian and Least flycatchers, Black-capped Chickadee, Brown Creeper, Winter Wren, Solitary Vireo, Brewster's Warbler (hybrid), Nashville Warbler, Magnolia Warbler, Black-throated Green Warbler, Blackburnian-Warbler, Louisiana Waterthrush, Mourning Warbler, Canada Warbler, and Dark-eyed Junco.

Tinkers Creek Nature Preserve and State Park   *Take I-480 to the Twinsburg-Aurora exit. The park and preserve are four miles southwest of Aurora, one and a half miles west of Hudson-Aurora Road on Davis Road. (Map B–78)*

The 1,086-acre state park combines upland woods, fields, and marsh. About 500 acres of marsh and a number of spring-fed ponds constitute the nature preserve. All of this provides a nice habitat-mix and a morning's birding can yield everything from Veeries, Cerulean and Hooded warblers, and Louisiana Waterthrushes to Great Egrets, American Bitterns, rails, and good numbers of waterfowl.

Van Buren State Park   *Take I-75 in Hancock County about seven miles north of Findlay and drive east on Ohio 613 for one mile. (Map A–79)*

Grassland and patches of beech-maple woods create a pretty setting for the 70-acre lake located here. Small numbers of ducks, geese, and gulls can be seen in early April and late fall. A few of the summer birds are the Red-headed Woodpecker, Great Crested Flycatcher, Horned Lark, Barn Swallow, Tufted Titmouse, Eastern Bluebird, Cedar Waxwing, Red-eyed Vireo, Northern Oriole and, some years, Summer Tanager.

Virginia Kendall Metropolitan Park   *Take Ohio 8 north from Akron, or south from I-80 (Ohio Turnpike Gate 12); turn west on Ohio 359. (Map B–80)*

This large park (2,039 acres) brings together beech-maple and oak-hickory woods, hemlock-lined rugged ravines, a twelve-acre lake, fields, meadows, and marsh. Over twelve miles of delightful trails wind through all the various habitats.

Lookout points on some of the higher cliffs are frequently manned by birders in spring and fall scanning the skies for birds of prey. Turkey Vultures follow the flight line, as do modest numbers of Sharp-shinned and Cooper's hawks, Red-tailed Hawks, a few Red-shouldered Hawks, kettles of Broad-winged Hawks, an occasional Rough-legged Hawk, Northern Harriers, Ospreys, a Peregrine Falcon on a red-letter day, and American Kestrels. Sometimes even a Northern Goshawk is seen in late fall or winter.

On May mornings, the areas around the lake, wooded edges, and groves of trees are sometimes alive with transient warblers and other landbirds. After mid-May, this is a good place for Yellow-bellied Flycatchers, Olive-sided flycatchers (perched on dead branches atop tall trees), Gray-cheeked Thrushes, Philadelphia Vireos, Bay-breasted Warblers, Blackpoll Warblers, Wilson's Warblers, and Canada Warblers.

Rare winter birds—Evening Grosbeaks, Common Redpolls, Pine Siskins, Red Crossbills, and White-winged Crossbills— have been seen, although some winters there are none.

Waite Hill   *Take I-90 east of Cleveland to Ohio
                                  306; drive south about a mile and a
                                  half, then turn right into any one of
                                  several streets and proceed through
                                  the scenic neighborhood. (Map B–81)*

Waite Hill is a wooded, park-like residential area where Annette Flanigan made a bit of ornithological history before retiring and moving to Florida. On some days during the spring and fall migrations, she would mist-net and band as many as fifteen warbler species in a single day. Some of her outstanding banding records and observations follow.

On 8 August 1974, a Yellow-bellied Flycatcher was banded, and two days later it was seen with another bird of the same species; undoubtedly early migrants. A Black-backed Woodpecker was seen on 7 January 1959. Thirty Bohemian Waxwings were observed in nearby Kirtland Hills on 2 January 1963, and one was seen at Waite Hill on 27 March 1966. A Boreal Chickadee was netted, banded, and photographed on 23 December 1972. Northern Shrikes have been seen several times. A very late Hermit Thrush was banded on 3 June 1974, and a Swainson's Thrush on 10 August 1974. An extremely young Swainson's Thrush was banded on 2 August 1976.

A late Red-eyed Vireo was banded on 2 November 1975, a late Warbling Vireo on 15 October 1973. Early Tennessee Warblers were banded 12 August 1975; a Cape May Warbler on 18 August 1970, and a Yellow-rumped Warbler on 13 August 1975. A very late Lincoln's Sparrow was banded on 5 June 1975.

Some other good records for the region include sightings of Tundra Swans and Sandhill Cranes flying over, Cattle Egret, Northern Saw-whet Owl, White-winged Crossbill, Sharp-tailed Sparrow, and the Gambel's race of the White-crowned Sparrow. House Finches have been common for quite a few years.

West Branch State Park

On Ohio 5 in Portage County about six miles east of Ravenna. (Map B–82)

Michael J. Kirwin Lake, a 2,650-acre reservoir, was formed by building a long earthen dam across a tributary of the Mahoning River. The rolling terrain combines old fields and beech-maple woods.

The lake is visited by transient waterbirds in migration and into the winter—as long as it is ice-free. Common Loons, Horned and Pied-billed grebes, Double-crested Cormorants, Tundra Swans, Canada Geese, and most duck species can be found from March through April, and again from October into December. Marshy edges here and there invite American Coots and a few rails and gallinules. In summer, listen for the rattling songs of Marsh Wrens. Late summer Bobolinks sometimes gather in fallow fields and, through September, stands of giant ragweed should be searched for migrant *parulidae* such as the Nashville, Yellow, Magnolia, Blackpoll, Bay-breasted, Palm, and sometimes, Connecticut warblers. During the cold months, Bald Eagles have been spotted, and Rough-legged Hawks, Northern Harriers, and Short-eared Owls are possible.

White City Park

Take I-90 east from downtown Cleveland; exit north onto 136th Street, turn east on Ohio 283 (Lake Shore Boulevard), then turn left on the road just before the intersection with East 140th Street. This will be a short distance east of the Easterly Sewage Treatment Plant. (Map B–83)

This park is an excellent spot to find rare shorebirds during the summer and fall months; offshore waterbirds during the fall, winter, and spring, and multitudes of gulls from late fall to early spring. During the cold months, look out on the lake for Common Loons, Horned Grebes, Redheads, Canvasbacks, Greater and Lesser scaups,

Common Goldeneyes, Buffleheads, and Ruddy Ducks. Sometimes in November and December, thousands of Red-breasted Mergansers can be seen rafted up or flying offshore.

During the winter, this is a good place to try for a few Oldsquaws, and there is always a chance of seeing Common and King eiders, all three scoter species, and an occasional Harlequin Duck. Along the retaining walls and jetties, look for the rare Purple Sandpiper. Searching for rare gulls among the thousands of gulls sometimes assembled can be tedious, but it is immensely rewarding to discover a rarity. The White City roster of gulls includes the Glaucous, Iceland, Great Black-backed, Herring, Ring-billed, Common Black-headed, Laughing, Franklin's, Bonaparte's, Little, Black-legged Kittiwake, and Sabine's. Pomarine and Parasitic jaegers have been seen several times, usually in September and October.

Considering the rather limited area, a surprisingly large number of shorebirds stop off here during their leisurely southward migration. Be sure to check out every nook and cranny, including the breakwaters, jetties, and any landfill that might be present. Among the rarities that have been found are the American Avocet, Piping Plover, Hudsonian Godwit, Whimbrel, Willet, Wilson's Phalarope, Red-necked Phalarope, Red Phalarope, Long-billed Dowitcher, Red Knot, Stilt Sandpiper, and Buff-breasted Sandpiper.

Winous Point Shooting Club

Take Ohio 53 south from Port Clinton about two miles past the Ohio 2 overpass. The area is on the east side of the road and is marked by a WPSC sign on a utility pole. (Map A–84)

Permission must be obtained in advance to enter this fine marsh on Sandusky Bay. In May, look for Cattle Egrets, Bobolinks, and Dickcissels in the field just beyond the farmhouse. Search the shrubs along the gravel road leading into the marsh; they are often full of Yellow Warblers, Yellow-rumped Warblers, Palm Warblers, Common Yellowthroats, and White-crowned, White-throated, and Swamp sparrows. Swarms of Tree Swallows fill the air over their nesting cavities in the many dead trees.

Stop the car frequently and check the channels paralleling the road for Least Bitterns, Wood Ducks, Ring-necked Ducks, Soras, American Coots, Solitary and Spotted sandpipers, and Dunlins. The first pull-off to the left is always worth investigating. Yellow Warblers and Common Yellowthroats are abundant in this pleasant nook and,

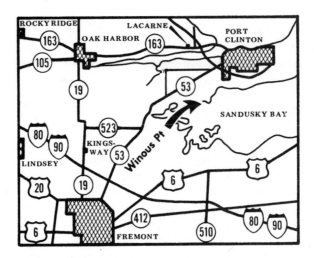

in late May, Connecticut and Mourning warblers might be present. Beyond the small pond, there is a wet meadow that attracts Greater and Lesser yellowlegs, Solitary Sandpipers, and Common Snipes. Sedge Wrens have been known to nest in the tall grasses and reeds. A rookery of Great Blue Heron nests can be seen from here.

Another good observation point is at the first pull-off on the right where there is a pump. Set up a spotting scope to best see the waterfowl in the impoundments and bays on both sides of the road. In addition to all the surface-feeding ducks, look for Tundra Swans (March), Redheads, Ring-necked Ducks, Canvasbacks, Lesser Scaups, Common Goldeneyes (March and early April), Buffleheads, Ruddy Ducks, Hooded Mergansers, Red-breasted Mergansers, and Common Mergansers. Almost a dozen duck species nest in the marsh.

Gulls and terns are constantly flying overhead; Ospreys are present during migration; Cooper's Hawks, Red-tailed Hawks, and two pairs of Bald Eagles nest in the vicinity.

The flooded woods between the pump and the headquarters complex attracts many passerine birds in migration including Hermit Thrushes (April), Swainson's Thrushes, Veeries, Warbling Vireos, and at least thirty species of warblers, plus Orchard Orioles, Northern Orioles, Scarlet Tanagers, and Rose-breasted Grosbeaks. This is also a good place to find the elusive Prothonotary Warbler.

PART II

The West-Central Counties

Once FOREST LAND broken only by occasional swaths of prairie, marsh, and a few large swamps—and traversed by clear rivers and streams—the counties of central and western Ohio are now predominantly farmland dotted with small towns and the urban-industrial sprawl of larger cities. Yet, in this drastically altered environment, there still exist a significant number of natural areas—forests and ungrazed woodlots, remnant bogs, lakes, and tree-lined rivers—many of them wisely set aside as parks and nature preserves. In this century, numerous reservoirs and thousands of farm ponds—not to speak of such specialized environments as sewerage treatment ponds, golf courses, airports, quarries, and landfills—have further changed the landscape. In spite of all these changes, each spring and fall millions of bird migrants of several hundred species pass through our state to and from their breeding grounds. About one-third of these nest in the west-central region.

Part II describes sites in 22 counties. The westernmost counties of the region and birding sites therein, shown on Map C, are Auglaize, Champaign, Clark, Darke, Greene, Hardin, Mercer, Miami, Logan, Montgomery, Preble, and Shelby. The central counties, shown on Map D, are Delaware, Fayette, Franklin, Knox, Licking, Madison, Marion, Morrow, Pickaway, and Union. Descriptions of, and directions to, the sites are presented in alphabetical order.

Alum Creek Reservoir

Take Ohio 23 north from Columbus to Lewis Center Road and follow it east to the dam. To reach the upper part of the reservoir, take Ohio 42 east from Delaware. (Map D–1)

This sizeable reservoir was first fully filled in 1975. The surrounding land is maintained for recreational purposes by the Ohio Department of Natural Resources. Less than a mile from the dam on the west side of the reservoir is a woods that extends along both sides of Lewis Center Road. Along the wooded edges, look for migrant songbirds in the spring and fall. In late spring and summer, the sloping field that leads to the water's edge is excellent for such erratics as the Dickcissel and Henslow's Sparrow and, more commonly, Horned Larks, Bobolinks, Eastern Meadowlarks, Savannah Sparrows, and Grasshopper Sparrows.

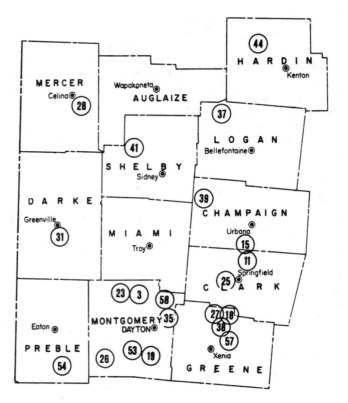

MAP C

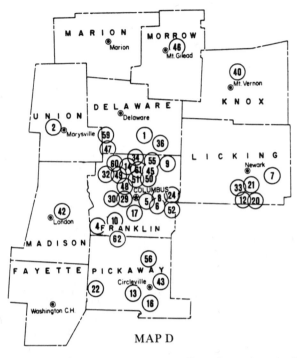

MAP D

A long man-made beach, accessible from Lewis Center Road, stretches northward along the shore and is a good place to look for Water Pipits, Ruddy Turnstones, Sanderlings, and a scattering of other shorebirds, in the spring and during the early morning in the late summer. Scan the water for loons, grebes, gulls, terns, and ducks in spring and fall.

Africa Road parallels the east side of the reservoir—the boat ramp areas are the best places for observing the water. Bird records for the reservoir are relatively few because it is new and has fall waterfowl hunting. Indications are that the majority of waterfowl, including large numbers of American Coots, concentrate around inlets on the western shore. During the summer, fallow fields along Africa Road sometimes attract Sedge Wrens, Bobolinks, and Dickcissels.

A circuit of the upper end of the reservoir is possible by taking Old State Road north from Ohio 42, turning east on Ohio 521 for a short distance, then returning south along Hogback Road, which offers some scenic views of the upper reservoir in addition to good birding in surrounding woods and fields. The rare Bachman's Sparrow has been recorded in the area of Pugh Road about a half mile west of Hogback Road.

American Aggregates Quarry
See City of Columbus Sewerage Treatment Plant/American Aggregates Quarry

American Legion Memorial Park
Located off U.S. 33 on the northwest edge of Marysville. (Map D–2)

This is a pleasant spot to visit in April and May to look for warblers and other arboreal migrants. Trails wander through groves of large deciduous trees with an understory sprinkled with wildflowers and along a tree-lined stream.

Aullwood Audubon Center
From I-70, exit at Ohio 48, proceed north to Englewood Dam and turn east to Center. From I-75, exit at U.S. 40, drive through Vandalia and turn south at Frederick Road. (Map C–3)

The 70-acre center was once a farm. In 1957 Mrs. John W. Aull gave it to the National Audubon Society to be used as an outdoor education

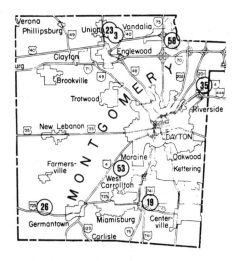

Dayton Area

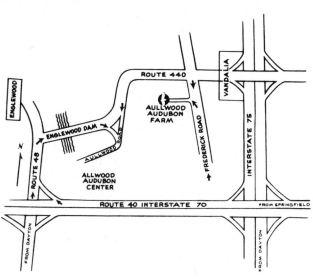

center. Almost two hundred bird species have been recorded since the center was established. Of these, eighty-one have nested or were observed during the nesting season. The area is also a haven for foxes, raccoons, skunks, opossums, and many smaller mammals. Fish, frogs, and turtles inhabit the freshwater ponds and streams. There is a splendid variety of native trees and wildflowers, as well as big blue-stem and Indian grasses towering ten feet high.

The ponds and bordering marshes have attracted Great Blue, Green-backed, Little Blue, and Black-crowned Night herons; Least and American bitterns; Great Egrets; Canada and Snow geese; Mallards; Black Ducks; Green-winged and Blue-winged teals; American Wigeons; Wood Ducks; Redheads; Ring-necked Ducks; Canvasbacks; Lesser Scaups; Common Goldeneyes; Buffleheads; Common Mergansers; Ospreys; Sandhill Cranes; Virginia Rails; Soras; American Coots; Killdeer; Upland Sandpipers; Solitary and Spotted sandpipers; Common Snipes; Semi-palmated, Least, Pectoral, and Stilt sandpipers; and Herring, Ring-billed, and Bonaparte's gulls.

During the warm months, one may find American Woodcocks; Yellow-billed and Black-billed cuckoos; Ruby-throated Hummingbirds; Eastern Kingbirds; Great Crested Flycatchers; Eastern Phoebes; Acadian and Willow flycatchers; Eastern Wood-Pewees; Northern Rough-winged and Barn swallows; Purple Martins; Gray Catbirds; Brown Thrashers; Wood Thrushes; Eastern Bluebirds; Blue-gray Gnatcatchers; Cedar Waxwings; White-eyed, Yellow-throated, Red-eyed, and Warbling vireos; Blue-winged, Yellow, Cerulean, and Kentucky warblers; Common Yellowthroats; Yellow-breasted Chats; Eastern Meadowlarks; Orchard and Northern orioles; Northern Cardinals; Indigo Buntings; American Goldfinches; Rufous-sided Towhees; and Chipping, Field, and Song sparrows.

Battelle-Darby Creek   *Drive west of Columbus on U.S. 40*
Metropolitan Park   *to Darby Creek Drive (5.3 miles west*
                                  of I-270); turn south and proceed
                                  for three miles. (Map D–4)

This attractive natural area has benefited from a Battelle Memorial Institute Foundation grant which has enabled an ongoing expansion program. The park area now includes 1,521 acres of oak-hickory woodlands and habitat-rich bottomlands bordering two creeks. The bluffs overlooking Darby Creek are known for their prairie wildflowers.

Beginning at the parking lot, several trails lead into the woods, follow the ravines, and emerge at the creek. The trails to the north eventually come out onto the higher bluffs; there is also one trail that follows the creek. In the spring and fall, most landbird species can be found here, and because of the diversity of habitat, a surprising number of waterfowl, shorebirds, and marsh inhabitants have been recorded.

Great Blue Herons and Green-backed Herons are often seen along the creek, and Great Egrets, Black-crowned and Yellow-crowned Night herons, and American Bitterns have been seen on occasion. Waterfowl that have been observed include the Canada Goose, Mallard, Northern Pintail, Blue-winged Teal, American Wigeon, Wood Duck, Redhead, Canvasback, and Hooded Merganser.

Turkey Vultures are frequently seen soaring over the scenic valley, and there is even one record of a stray Black Vulture. Small numbers of hawks and Ospreys follow the creek valley in their migrations.

In March and April the American Woodcock can be watched putting on its fascinating aerial nuptial dance after the sun goes down. Eastern Screech, Great Horned, and Barred owls have all been observed and presumably nest.

Other birds seen regularly during the breeding season are Yellow-billed Cuckoos, Ruby-throated Hummingbirds, Belted Kingfishers, all of the Ohio-nesting woodpeckers, Eastern Phoebe, Acadian and Willow flycatchers, and Eastern Wood-Pewee.

Barn and Northern Rough-winged swallows skim over the fields and along the creek; Carolina Chickadees, Tufted Titmice, and White-breasted Nuthatches are commonly found in the woods, and House Wrens, Northern Mockingbirds, Gray Catbirds, Brown Thrashers, and Blue-gray Gnatcatchers can be found along the edges. Wood Thrushes, Yellow-throated Vireos, Cerulean Warblers, Ovenbirds, and Scarlet Tanagers can be found, or at least heard, in the deep woods. One or two pairs of Louisiana Waterthrushes nest along the deep ravines.

To get to the recently acquired Little Darby Creek section of the park, continue south on Darby Creek Drive to Alkire Road, proceed west (right) a short distance to Gardner Road and turn north (right) to the parking area.

There are two trails. One leads along the creek and another ascends an incline, cuts through an old orchard, and winds through a large area of mature woodland, brushy tangles, grassland, old fields and pastures, and large plots of planned ecological succession.

A pair of Red-tailed Hawks, and Great Horned and Barred owls are permanent resident nesting birds. Among other breeding species are the American Kestrel; Ring-necked Pheasant; American Wood-cock; Yellow-billed Cuckoo; Red-bellied, Red-headed, Hairy, and Downy woodpeckers; Eastern Kingbird; Great Crested Flycatcher; Eastern Wood-Pewee; Northern Mockingbird; Gray Catbird; Brown Thrasher; Eastern Bluebird; Blue-gray Gnatcatcher; Cedar Waxwing; White-eyed, Yellow-throated, Red-eyed, and Warbling vireos, and the following warblers—Blue-winged, Yellow, Cerulean, Yellow-throated, Louisiana Waterthrush, Common Yellowthroat, and Yellow-breasted Chat.

Eastern Meadowlarks nest in the fields; several pairs of Northern Orioles can be found along the creek, and Northern Cardinals, Indigo Buntings, and American Goldfinches are common throughout the park along with Chipping, Field, and Song sparrows.

Bexley City Park

Take Nelson Road in Columbus north from East Broad Street and turn right at Clifton Avenue. If the park entrance is closed, continue to Parkview Avenue, turn left and enter the driveway just north of the large mansion that is located on the grounds. There is a parking lot at the end of the driveway. (Map D–5)

Located on the banks of Alum Creek, this is a pleasant place to hike any time of the year. Trails lead along the creek and through the woods. Resident birds include the Mourning Dove, Barred Owl (in the pine grove), Downy Woodpecker, Blue Jay, Common Crow, Carolina Chickadee, Tufted Titmouse, White-breasted Nuthatch, Carolina Wren, Robin (a few even in winter), Northern Cardinal, Rufous-sided Towhee, and Song Sparrow.

A colorful array of summering birds can be found—from Great Crested Flycatchers and Wood Thrushes to Northern Orioles and Indigo Buntings. The trail along the creek and the trees and shrubs around the parking lot can be excellent for migrating warblers and other landbirds.

Big Walnut Park

Take I-70 in Columbus and exit at Hamilton Road, North; continue on Hamilton Road to Livingston. Drive east on Livingston about 1.5 miles. (Map D–6)

This Columbus park features a mature river bottom forest of sycamores, cottonwoods, and sugar maples which run in a narrow strip
along the creek between Livingston Avenue and East Main Street.
There is also a small pond, parkland, brush, and weed fields.

In late April and most of May, this is a fine place to find migratory landbirds in good numbers. Green-backed Herons, Wood Ducks,
Greater and Lesser yellowlegs, Solitary Sandpipers, and Spotted
Sandpipers occur along the creek. In late April and mid-September,
look for kettles of Broad-winged Hawks. Resident birds are similar to
those described for Blacklick Woods Metropolitan Park. Stephen W.
Kress compiled a list of one hundred and twenty species of birds in
this park, including thirty-two species of warblers.

Black Hand Gorge State Nature Preserve

From Newark take Ohio 16 east to Ohio 146, then south to County Road 273. Continue south a short distance to the entrance near the village of Toboso. (Map D–7)

About 300 million years ago Ohio was covered by an inland sea. Sand
and rock eroding from the mountains of Pennsylvania formed a vast
delta that eventually became what is known as Black Hand sandstone,
after the large black hand drawn by Indians on the walls of this deep
gorge cut by the Licking River. It is thought the hand pointed the way
to the flint deposits of nearby Flint Ridge. Picturesque trails developed by the Ohio Department of Natural Resources lead to the gorge.
Oak, hickory, Virginia pine, and mountain laurel abound on the hillsides, where birds like the Pileated and Red-bellied woodpeckers,
Acadian Flycatcher, Ovenbird, and Kentucky and Hooded warblers
nest. In the floodplain, sycamores, cottonwoods, and box elders provide
habitat for Eastern Kingbirds, Cedar Waxwings, Warbling Vireos,
Northern Orioles, and Indigo Buntings. In spring, troupes of warblers, vireos, tanagers, and grosbeaks sometimes fill the treetops with
color and song. At such times, fifty species can be seen in an hour or
two on the trails.

Blacklick Woods Metropolitan Park

Take I-70 in Columbus to the north exit at Brice Road. Proceed north on Brice Road to Livingston Avenue and turn east. The park is about one mile distant. (Map D–8)

The forest areas of this large park are laced with paths that wind through lowlands of swamp forest with white oak, pin oak, bur oak, and silver maple trees. Typical trees of the higher ground include beech, sugar maple, white ash, black cherry, hickory, white oak, and red elm.

Between the several parking lots, there are groves of trees, playgrounds, and expanses of grassy parkland. Vantage points for birding are the clearing around the Beech-Maple Lodge, the nearby parking spaces and small pond, clearings within the woods, and an old roadway between the woods and the golf course. In spring and summer, scan the golf course for Killdeers, Upland Sandpipers, Barn Swallows, and Purple Martins. Overhead, look for Kestrels and Red-tailed and Red-shouldered hawks. Ring-necked Pheasants and Common Bobwhites occur in weedy fields and along woody edges.

Frequently seen April and early May migrants include the Yellow-bellied Sapsucker; Eastern Phoebe; Red-breasted Nuthatch; Winter Wren; Brown Thrasher; Hermit Thrush; Eastern Bluebird; Blue-gray Gnatcatcher; Golden-crowned and Ruby-crowned Kinglets; Solitary Vireo; Black-and-White, Blue-winged, Orange-crowned, Yellow-rumped, Pine, and Palm warblers; Louisiana Waterthrush; Rusty Blackbird; Purple Finch; Rufous-sided Towhee; Chipping, Field, White-crowned, White-throated, Fox, Swamp, and Song sparrows.

Some representative nesting birds to look for are the Wood Duck; Red-tailed and Red-shouldered hawks; Kestrel; Yellow-billed and, more rarely, Black-billed cuckoos; Pileated, Red-bellied, and Red-headed woodpeckers; Eastern Kingbird; Great Crested and Acadian flycatchers; Eastern Phoebe; Eastern Wood-Pewee; Northern Mockingbird; Brown Thrasher; Wood Thrush; Eastern Bluebird; Blue-gray Gnatcatcher; Cedar Waxwing; Red-eyed Vireo; Yellow Warbler; Common Yellowthroat; Yellow-breasted Chat; American Redstart (uncommon); Northern Oriole; and Scarlet Tanager.

Eastern Screech, Great Horned, and Barred owls are year-round residents in the deeper woods; American Woodcock perform their courtship flights each spring over the fields east of the Interpretive Center.

The Interpretive Center is located within the Walter A. Tucker Nature Preserve at the end of the main driveway. The Center has one-way windows for viewing bird feeders and a sizeable pond. In late afternoon, white-tailed deer frequently feed close to the windows.

Blendon Woods Metropolitan Park

From I-270 in Columbus, exit east onto Ohio 161 and proceed for one mile. An alternate route is to take Sunbury Road north from Columbus and turn right at Ohio 161. (Map D–9)

In addition to extensive wooded ravines and uplands, this splendid park embraces the 118-acre Walden Wildlife Refuge with its 11-acre Thoreau Pond and elevated observation shelters equipped with spotting scopes for viewing the waterfowl. The pond is kept free of ice during the coldest winters by an underwater aerating system; ducks and geese are attracted by the grain put out for them. The refuge is open from October through April.

The Nature Interpretive Center, near the entrance to the refuge, has two large picture windows overlooking feeders that attract a steady stream of birds. Bird walks and other nature activities are scheduled on a regular basis throughout the park; there are miles of hiking trails.

Waterbirds frequently seen at Thoreau Pond in season include: Horned and Pied-billed grebes, Great Blue Heron, Canada Goose (nests), Mallard, American Black Duck, Gadwall, Northern Pintail, Green-winged and Blue-winged teals, American Wigeon, Northern Shoveler, Wood Duck, Redhead, Ring-necked Duck, Canvasback, Lesser Scaup, Common Goldeneye, Bufflehead, Ruddy Duck, and Hooded Merganser. Less common species have included the Double-crested Cormorant, Great Egret, American Bittern, Tundra Swan, Snow Goose, Greater Scaup, and Common Merganser. Occasionally gulls and terns investigate the pond, and Ospreys are sometimes sighted.

Migrants at Blendon Woods are essentially the same as those described for Greenlawn Cemetery. An impressive list of nesting birds includes the Green-backed Heron; Red-tailed, Red-shouldered, and Broad-winged hawks; American Woodcock; Spotted Sandpiper; Eastern Screech, Great Horned, and Barred owls; Ruby-throated Hummingbird; all of the summering woodpeckers; Eastern Kingbird; Great Crested, Acadian, and Willow flycatchers; Eastern Phoebe and Eastern Wood-Pewee; House and Carolina wrens; Wood Thrush; Eastern Bluebird; Blue-gray Gnatcatcher; Cedar Waxwing; White-eyed, Yellow-throated, and Red-eyed vireos; Blue-winged, Yellow, and Cerulean warblers; Ovenbird; Louisiana Waterthrush; Kentucky Warbler; Common Yellowthroat; Yellow-breasted Chat; Northern Oriole; Scarlet and Summer tanagers; Rose-breasted Grosbeak; and Rufous-sided Towhee.

Bolton Field Airport

Drive west on West Broad Street in Columbus to Norton Road, which is on the eastern edge of New Rome. Proceed south on Norton Road for three miles, or exit I-270 at Georgesville Road and proceed south to Norton Road. (Map D–10)

Lots of grassland and a number of low wet spots attract migrating shorebirds, especially if there has been ample rain. The best area is along the entrance driveway leading to the administration building. Migrants in the spring include Killdeer, Common Snipe, Solitary and Upland sandpipers, Greater and Lesser yellowlegs, and various peeps, including occasional large flocks of Pectoral Sandpipers. Some years flocks of Lesser Golden Plovers stop over for short visits.

Several pairs of Upland Sandpipers usually stay to nest, along with Horned Larks, Eastern Meadowlarks, and Savannah and Grasshopper sparrows. Johnson Road, bordering the south edge of the airport, is worth checking for all the above species, plus Snow Buntings and Lapland Longspurs in winter.

Buck Creek State Park and Clarence J. Brown Reservoir

Exit from I-70 north of Springfield onto Ohio 40, proceed west 2.4 miles, then turn right onto Bird Road and continue 1.7 miles to the park entrance. (Map C–11)

This attractive park offers birders a variety of habitats to investigate: a deep-water lake, shallow inlets, seasonal mudflats, patches of woods, extensive grasslands, fishing ponds, a picturesque wooded creek, numerous brushy areas, and fallow fields in the surrounding countryside.

The boat ramp, parking areas, and Robert Eastman Road near the entrance are good observation spots for waterbirds. While cruising the roads that circle the reservoir, look for Great Blue and Green-backed herons, Belted Kingfishers, hawks of half a dozen species, and a wide variety of other birds.

Waterfowl are prevalent in March and early April and again from late October until freeze-up. Horned and Pied-billed grebes and Common Loons are frequent fall and early winter visitors. Shorebirds are present in late July, August, and September, when water levels are down. Little Blue Herons, Snowy Egrets, and other scarce wading birds are occasional visitors at such times. Horned Larks are year-round residents in the grassy areas of the park.

Buckeye Lake   *Take I-70 about 20 miles east of*
Columbus and go south for one mile
on Ohio 79. (Map D-12)

This 3,300-acre impoundment is surrounded by remnant woods, fallow and cultivated fields, resort and year-round housing, and several small towns and villages. Waterfowl that visit the lake are substantially less numerous than they were before 1960; however, nearly all species of ducks that occur in Ohio may be found on the lake in spring and fall. The largest concentrations are usually found in March when there is a minimum of boating and no hunting. Fairly large assemblages of dabbling ducks—Mallards, American Black Ducks, Gadwalls, Northern Pintails, Green-winged Teals, American Wigeons, Northern Shovelers and, toward the end of the month, newly arrived Blue-winged Teals and Wood Ducks—associate with rafts of bay ducks such as Redheads, Ring-necked Ducks, Canvasbacks, Lesser Scaups, Common Goldeneyes, Buffleheads, Ruddy Ducks, and all three merganser species. Common Loons, Horned and Pied-billed grebes, and a few Double-crested Cormorants are usually present by late March—along with considerable numbers of Herring and Ring-billed gulls, and occasional flocks of dainty Bonaparte's Gulls.

Most waterbirds prefer the deeper middle and western parts of the lake. Highways circle the lake from which access roads lead to numerous lookout points, woods, and remnants of marsh. Boats may be put in the water or rented at numerous docks and marinas. Seller's Point, west of Buckeye Lake State Park (an amusement area) on the north side of the lake, can be reached off Ohio 79 on Ohio 360.

Bounds Woods, about a mile east of Buckeye Lake State Park, is a rewarding place to observe transient landbirds—including Connecticut and Mourning warblers—plus such breeders as the Great Blue Heron, Barred Owl, Red-bellied Woodpecker, Great Crested Flycatcher, Brown Thrasher, Wood Thrush, Blue-gray Gnatcatcher, Yellow-throated Vireo, Red-eyed Vireo, Ovenbird, American Redstart, Scarlet Tanager (scarce), and Rufous-sided Towhee. Around the brushy edges and in clearings, nesting species include the American Woodcock, Willow Flycatcher, Gray Catbird, Yellow Warbler, Common Yellowthroat, Yellow-breasted Chat, Northern Cardinal, Indigo Bunting, and Song Sparrow.

Big Woods, another fine swamp forest, can be viewed from the southernmost dikes of the Hebron Fish Hatchery (see p. 99.) Its large trees, woodland pools, and dense thickets and tangles are sometimes alive with small landbird migrants in late April and May.

Aquatic vegetation and cattail swamps around the lake that once contained good populations of nesting marsh birds are now greatly reduced in extent, but remnants of this habitat, mostly at the east end of the lake, still attract a few rails, gallinules, bitterns, and Marsh Wrens.

For a complete ornithological history of the entire area, refer to *The Birds of Buckeye Lake*, by Milton B. Trautman, University of Michigan Press, Ann Arbor, Michigan, 1940.

Calamus Marsh   *On Ohio 104 about 0.7 mile south of*
                                     Ohio 22 west of Circleville. (Map
                                     D–13)

This moderately sized marsh lies along an abandoned railroad spur and is densely vegetated with calamus, cattails, and sedges with relatively few patches of water. According to Edward S. Thomas, Calamus Marsh has been well known to local ornithologists for at least a hundred years.

During the spring and fall, small flocks of puddle ducks can be found feeding and resting in the marsh. These include Mallards, American Black Ducks, Northern Pintails, American Wigeon, Northern Shovelers, and Blue-winged and Green-winged teals. Wood Ducks nest in the vicinity. Sometimes a few bay—or diving—ducks can be found, such as Redheads, Ring-necked Ducks, and Hooded Mergansers.

Pied-billed Grebes are regular visitors, and probably a few pairs nest here. The same is true of the American Bittern, Sora and Virginia rails, American Coots, and Common Moorhens. Early in the spring, look for Rusty Blackbirds, Rufous-sided Towhees, Fox and Swamp sparrows. Later, during the spring migration, hike back along the railroad tracks to turn up migrant landbirds and—possibly—a pair of nesting Prothonotary Warblers.

Summer birds include the Great Blue and Green-backed herons, Turkey Vulture, Kestrel, Northern Bobwhite, Ring-necked Pheasant, Killdeer, Mourning Dove; Chimney Swift, Belted Kingfisher, Common Flicker, Red-headed and Downy woodpeckers, Eastern Kingbird, Eastern Wood-Pewee, Barn Swallow, Blue Jay, Common Crow, House and Marsh wrens, Gray Catbird, American Robin, Cedar Waxwing, Starling, Red-eyed and Warbling vireos, Yellow Warbler, Common Yellowthroat, Yellow-breasted Chat, Eastern Meadowlark,

Red-winged Blackbird, Northern Oriole, Summer Tanager, Northern Cardinal, Indigo Bunting, American Goldfinch, Field and Song
sparrows.

Camps Johnson and Mary   *Take I-270 north of Columbus and*
Orton   *turn north onto Ohio 23 and proceed*
                                    for about one mile. (Map D–14)

Camp Johnson features a deep-wooded ravine that cuts through the
Ohio shale, exposing interesting jointing patterns and concretions.
Camp Mary Orton has a number of buildings, wide fields, and the
same wooded ravine habitat described above. There is also wooded
acreage along the Olentangy River at both camps. Woods are predominantly beech-maple-ash with plantings of pine trees and stands of
large hemlocks.

   A hike along the roadways and trails of either of these wooded
tracts is always enjoyable. Eastern Screech, Great Horned, and Barred
owls haunt the woods and can be attracted by playing their tape-
recorded calls. A few of the breeding birds include the Wood Duck,
Yellow-billed Cuckoo, Red-headed Woodpecker, Acadian Flycatcher,
Wood Thrush, Blue-gray Gnatcatcher, Yellow-throated and Red-eyed
vireos, Blue-winged, Yellow, and Cerulean warblers, Ovenbird, Louisiana Waterthrush, Common Yellowthroat, Scarlet Tanager, Northern Oriole, Indigo Bunting, and Rufous-sided Towhee. Bachman's
Sparrow has been known to nest among sparsely planted trees in a
fallow field, and there is at least one recent record of the Yellow-
throated Warbler nesting along this stretch of the Olentangy River.

Cedar Bog State Memorial   *Drive 9.5 miles north of Springfield*
                                    on Ohio 68 to Woodburn Road and
                                    turn left. Or, from Urbana drive 3.5
                                    miles south on Ohio 68 to Woodburn
                                    Road. (Map C–15)

Cedar Bog, a 50-acre remnant of what once was a marl swamp of
over seven thousand acres, was created by limestone glacial deposits,
surface water, and groundwater saturation. About one hundred and
fifty acres have been added to the preserve in order to provide a
protective buffer zone.

   This remnant of the last ice age is the only place in Ohio where
arborvitae trees occur in a bog, and it also boasts a white cedar forest
of excellent quality. Cool alkaline spring water oozes to the surface
enabling many plants which bordered the glaciers as recently as ten
thousand years ago to survive in this remaining northern micro-climate.

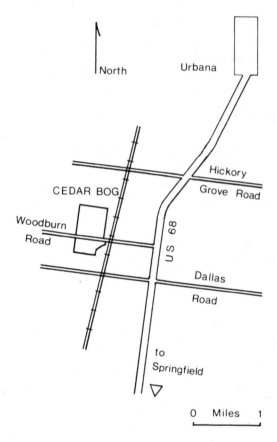

North

Urbana

Hickory

CEDAR BOG

Grove Road

Woodburn
Road

US 68

Dallas

Road

to
Springfield

0   Miles   1

Among the plants found at Cedar Bog are the dwarf birch, lady's-slipper orchid, marsh marigold, large-flowered trillium, fringed gentian, grass-pink orchid, sundew, grass-of-Parnassus, Jack-in-the-pulpit, large-flowered bellwort, drooping trillium, bishop's cap, two-leaf Solomon's plume, yellow lady's-slipper, shrubby cinquefoil, and poison sumac.

Cedar Run, a constantly flowing stream with practically no seasonal fluctuation in temperature or volume, provides cool waters that contain brook trout and the spotted turtle with its bright yellow polkadots. The Massasauga, or swamp rattlesnake, is another reptile that distinguishes the bog. Several rare butterflies dependent on this unique habitat are the Milbert's tortoise shell, the silvery checkerspot, and the swamp metalmark.

Mallards and Wood Ducks seen through the spring and summer probably nest nearby. Turkey Vultures, Red-tailed Hawks, and Kestrels are commonly seen. Northern Bobwhites and Ring-necked Pheasants are both resident; Killdeers nest, as do occasional American Woodcocks. American Bitterns, Sora and Virginia rails are sometimes seen during migrations.

Other birds that summer or nest in the area include the Mourning Dove, Yellow-billed Cuckoo, Barred Owl, Chimney Swift, Ruby-throated Hummingbird, Belted Kingfisher, Common Flicker, Red-bellied, Red-headed, Hairy, and Downy woodpeckers, Eastern Kingbird, Eastern Phoebe, Great Crested and Acadian flycatchers, Eastern Wood-Pewee, Horned Lark, Barn Swallow, Blue Jay, Common Crow, Carolina Chickadee, Tufted Titmouse, White-breasted Nuthatch, House and Carolina wrens, Gray Catbird, American Robin, Wood Thrush, Blue-gray Gnatcatcher, Cedar Waxwing, Starling, White-eyed and Red-eyed vireos, Blue-winged and Yellow warblers, Common Yellowthroat, Yellow-breasted Chat, Eastern Meadowlark, Red-winged Blackbird, Common Grackle, Brown-headed Cowbird, Northern Oriole, Northern Cardinal, Indigo Bunting, American Goldfinch, and Song and Field sparrows.

The bog is open from April through October Wednesday through Sunday. Tours are conducted on Saturday and Sunday at 9 and 11 A.M. and 1 and 3 P.M. During the winter months the bog is open by reservation only. Cedar Bog is administered jointly by the Ohio Historical Society and the Ohio Department of Natural Resources.

Charlie's Pond   *Take Ohio 23 south from Circleville*
for 4.3 miles and turn west at
Radcliff Road. Proceed another mile
to the slough. (Map D–16)

Sometimes called Upper Davenport, the area is located in the Scioto bottomlands and has attracted a surprising number of birds considering its small size. Although there is more water on the north side of the road, don't ignore the opposite side which is boggy and contains tangles of underbrush. An occasional heron or egret is found at the pond, in addition to migrating bitterns, puddle ducks, rails, and shorebirds. A few Common Snipes can usually be flushed up from wet spots along the edges in the spring and during the fall migration. Bands of swallows frequently feed over the pond, Swamp Sparrows can be found in the brush in April and May and again from September until early winter, and Water Pipits sometimes linger in the vicinity.

After checking out the pond, continue west on Radcliff Road and turn north on River Road and drive a mile or so to its end. Watch for Red-tailed Hawks and Kestrels anytime, and Rough-legged Hawks and Northern Harriers from November to April. A Golden Eagle and a Merlin have been reported here in the past. The wide, gently rolling fields also attract shorebirds, especially during the spring months when the ground has been plowed and sky ponds appear after heavy rains. At such times, the chances of seeing flocks of Lesser Golden Plover and Pectoral Sandpipers are particularly good.

Horned Larks are common and from the end of January through June this is a fine place to see the males perform their courtship (or territorial) flight songs. Snow Buntings and, more rarely, Lapland Longspurs can be found in flocks of Horned Larks during winter months. In the past quarter-century, the Smith's Longspur has been showing up in central and southwestern Ohio, mostly in March and April. They have been recorded near Charlie's Pond several times.

Spring and summer birds around the pond include the Upland Sandpiper, Eastern Kingbird, Barn Swallow, Eastern Bluebird, Loggerhead Shrike (rare), Eastern Meadowlark, Red-winged Blackbird, Dickcissel (erratic), American Goldfinch, and Grasshopper, Vesper, Field, and Song sparrows.

City of Columbus Sewerage Treatment Plant/American Aggregates Quarry

Take I-71 south of Columbus to the Frank Road exit; turn right, and right again, onto Ohio 104. Proceed about 0.5 mile to the entrance on the left side of the road. Check at the administration building for permission to be on the grounds. Then follow the road to the left of the plant; where it dead-ends, turn right and proceed to the area of ponds and settling basins. (Map D–17)

If your olfactory senses are easily offended, discretion might be the better part of valor: don't bird here. Besides the spectrum of odors emanating from the disposal plant itself, there is a malodorous rendering plant right next door. On the other hand, if you have a hardy stomach and believe almost any risk is worth seeing a new bird, then you are in the right place.

The first two or three small ponds on the right side of the road might produce a Great Blue Heron or a Belted Kingfisher, but are most noteworthy for songbirds attracted to the surrounding brushy tangles and patches of weeds. Continue down the gravel road past the foundations of several razed buildings and up a slight incline. On the right will be a sludge pond that attracts shorebirds from April through October. Some of the rarities that have been seen here include the Piping, Lesser Golden, and Black-bellied plovers; Whimbrel; Willet; Ruddy Turnstone; Wilson's and Red-necked phalaropes; Long-billed Dowitcher; Red Knot; Western, White-rumped, Baird's, Stilt, and Buff-breasted sandpipers. During the late summer movement of shorebirds, the most commonly seen species are Greater and Lesser yellowlegs, Solitary Sandpipers, and Pectoral Sandpipers.

The pond a bit farther on the left is attractive to Blue-winged Teals, Wood Ducks, and American Coots—plus a scattering of other waterbirds. American Bitterns and Glossy Ibis have been found here and, when the water is low, shorebirds feed along the muddy edges. From early May to September, it is a sure place to find Bank Swallows.

A large American Aggregates Company quarry can be viewed by following the dirt and gravel road, turning left at the first fork, and continuing for about a hundred yards. A few waterbirds can be found here year-round, but the best times are in March and November. With the advent of warmer weather in late February or early March, hundreds of ducks gather here, along with occasional loons, grebes, geese, and large numbers of American Coots, to feed and rest. At the peak of migration, there is a good chance of seeing hundreds of Redheads, Ring-necked Ducks, Lesser Scaups, and Common Goldeneyes, along with other diving ducks and substantial numbers of puddle ducks. The fall migration is usually less pronounced than in spring. In all but the most severe winters, flocks of ducks—mostly Mallards, American Black Ducks, and Common Goldeneyes—manage to keep at least one hole open in the ice. The best time to see waterfowl at the quarry is about an hour before sunset.

Among the rare birds that have been recorded in the area are the Red-throated Loon, Red-necked and Eared grebes, American White Pelican, Double-crested Cormorant, Mute and Tundra swans, Snow Goose, Oldsquaw, White-winged Scoter, Bald Eagle, Osprey, Peregrine Falcon, and Laughing Gull.

When birding in the area of the quarry, care must be taken to remain on the high ground atop an old landfill since visitors are not allowed on American Aggregate property.

Clarence J. Brown Reservoir *See Buck Creek State Park.*

Clifton Gorge (John L. Rich State Nature Preserve) *Follow Ohio 343 east of Yellow Springs, turn south on Ohio 370 and proceed a short distance past John Bryan State Park. (Map C–18)*

Hemlocks, yews, and mountain maples inhabit the steep slopes of this gorge through which the Little Miami River flows. Hiking trails skirt the north side of the gorge and pass through fine habitat for the Barred Owl, Acadian Flycatcher, Eastern Wood-Pewee, Wood Thrush, Yellow-throated Vireo, Black-and-White Warbler (rare), Louisiana Waterthrush, Scarlet Tanager, and Rufous-sided Towhee. For other birds of the area, see the account for Glen Helen.

Cox Arboretum

On Ohio 741 one mile north of Ohio 725 in south Dayton. (Map C–19)

Shade trees, rock, herb, and shrub gardens, a conifer hillside, greenhouses, and natural areas—a pond, a seral (succession) meadow, a stream, and woods—make up this outstanding area managed by the Dayton-Montgomery County Park District. In late April and May, warblers and other migrants are seen and heard in many parts of the arboretum—over 70 species have been seen in the woods alone. The entire area provides excellent opportunities to learn some of the basic songs of breeding birds in May and June. Listen for the songs of House Wrens, Gray Catbirds, Wood Thrushes, Red-eyed Vireos, Yellow Warblers, Common Yellowthroats, Northern Orioles, Indigo Buntings, and Chipping, Field, and Song sparrows.

Cranberry Bog Nature Preserve

Take I-70 east from Columbus to State Route 79; proceed south about half a mile, turn left and follow the road to Hunt's Landing. (Map D–20)

This nine-acre floating island composed entirely of sphagnum moss and other compacted vegetation is just off the north shore of Buckeye Lake. Wave action from storms, wind, and power boats has drastically reduced the size of the bog. Plants found here in addition to cranberry include poison sumac, pitcher plant, swamp pink orchid, and rose pogonia.

Under the hot sun of late summer, chunks and matted pieces of partly submerged bog float to the surface of the water, especially near the east end of the island. This provides favorable habitat for migrating shorebirds which can be observed close at hand from a boat. Among them look for Semi-palmated, Lesser Golden, and Black-bellied plovers; Greater and Lesser yellowlegs, Solitary and Spotted sandpipers; Wilson's and Red-necked phalaropes; Short-billed Dowitcher; Semi-palmated, Western, White-rumped, Baird's, and Pectoral sandpipers; Dunlin later in the season; Stilt and Buff-breasted sandpipers.

During the late spring and summer, there is a good chance of seeing wading birds such as the Great Blue and Green-backed herons and American Bittern. Wood Ducks can usually be seen around the island along with Belted Kingfishers; Bank, Northern Rough-winged, and Barn swallows; and Purple Martins. On the island itself, look for Carolina Chickadees, House Wrens, Cedar Waxwings, Prothonotary and Yellow warblers, Common Yellowthroats, Red-winged Black-birds, Common Grackles, Brown-headed Cowbirds, and Song Sparrows.

Because the ecology of the island is very fragile, access is limited. Written permission for visitations may be obtained from the Division of Natural Areas and Preserves, Ohio Department of Natural Resources, Fountain Square, Columbus, Ohio 43224. For most birding activities, a trip around the island by boat is entirely adequate.

Darby Creek Metropolitan Park *See Battelle-Darby Creek Metropolitan Park.*

The Dawes Arboretum *Take I-70 east from Columbus to Ohio 13 and drive north a short distance past U.S. 40. (Map D–21)*

Over 2500 different woody plants grow in this botanist's and naturalist's wonderland. Winding drives and trails traverse an area that contains a 5-acre lake, a cypress swamp, pine plantings, native and exotic trees, including the rare Franklinia discovered in the 1700s by William Bartram in Georgia, streams that meander through woods and meadows, a Japanese garden, administrative buildings, a greenhouse—and a good sample of seasonal birds.

Late April and May are especially recommended since this is a fine place to witness the parade of warblers and other songbirds that pass through the state at that time. Nesting birds are typical of central Ohio. Descriptive literature can be obtained by writing: The Dawes Arboretum, Rte. 5, Newark, Ohio 43055.

Deer Creek State Park *Take I-71 southeast from Columbus about 16 miles to the Mt. Sterling exit; follow Ohio 56 into Mt. Sterling to the junction with Ohio 207, turn east on 207 and proceed five miles to the lake. (Map D–22)*

This 1,277-acre lake is located amidst parkland totaling over 7,000

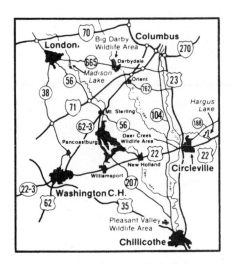

acres. Most parts of the lake are easily reached by a network of all-weather access roads.

Shorebirds can be found in spring in wet meadows, on the sand beach near the dam, and on muddy points of land. In late summer, mudflats appear first in inlets and at the upper end, which can be reached from Ohio 207. Trails through a marsh and a meadow are located near the park office near Dawson Yankeetown Road.

Common Loons, Horned Grebes, Canada Geese, and rafts of ducks are common sights in March and November; Tundra Swans and Double-crested Cormorants are seen less frequently. Great Blue Herons are present most of the year; Green-backed Herons can be found during the warm months and, rarely, an American Bittern is discovered hiding in grassy margins and marshy areas.

Notable landbirds that have been seen in the vicinity include the Rough-legged Hawk, Bald Eagle, Great Horned and Barred owls, Whip-poor-will, Pileated Woodpecker, Willow Flycatcher, Cliff Swallow, Loggerhead Shrike, Mourning Warbler, Summer Tanager, and Henslow's Sparrow.

Edward S. Thomas Nature Preserve   *See Sharon Woods Metropolitan Park.*

Englewood Reserve   *From I-70, north of Dayton, exit at Ohio 48 and go north to U.S. 40; exit and drive east across the dam and turn north into the reserve entrance. (Map C–23)*

A lake with a waterfowl sanctuary, hiking and bridle trails, picnicking sites, Aullwood Garden, canoeing, ice skating, fishing, and *birding* are some of the year-round attractions. There are also fields and meadows, woods, the Stillwater River, plantings of pines and shrubs, and increasing areas of marsh—all of which attract a wide variety of birds.

Breeding species range from the Cooper's Hawk, Great Horned, Eastern Screech, and Barred owls to Red-bellied and Red-headed woodpeckers, Acadian and Willow flycatchers, White-eyed Vireos, Blue-winged and Kentucky warblers, Orchard and Northern orioles, and Rufous-sided Towhees. American Woodcocks put on their dramatic aerial shows on March and April evenings, Pileated Woodpeckers are sometimes sighted, and Warbling Vireos can be counted on in the cottonwoods along the river.

The Englewood Reserve is one of eight "Green Mansions" operated by the Dayton-Montgomery County Park District and is across the highway from the Aullwood Audubon Center.

Gahanna Woods Park and State Nature Preserve

Take Ohio 16 east from Columbus and turn left on Ohio 317; proceed to Taylor Station Road and turn right. (Map D–24)

Besides 50 acres of woods and swamp forest, there are adjoining acres of fields, hedgerows, thickets, and groves of trees. The woods are composed of mature beech, maple, cherry, and ash, while other portions contain predominantly swamp forest species such as pin oak and silver maple.

During the spring migration, this is an excellent area in which to find a host of landbirds, including the Mourning and Connecticut warblers during the last two-thirds of May.

George Rogers Clark State Park

Exit from I-70 three miles west of Springfield, or take U.S. 40 to Ohio 369 and drive south to the park entrance. (Map C–25)

A seven-acre lake, groves of trees, an oak-maple forest, and open grasslands attract numerous migrants in the spring and fall. In late April and May, the park is a good place to find many species of warblers, vireos, and other passerine birds. Small numbers of waterbirds stop briefly on the lake.

Germantown Reservoir   *In Dayton, take Ohio 4 southwest*
about ten miles; go west on Ohio 725
for several miles to the entrance.
(Map C–26)

An old earthen flood-control dam is at the east end of this 1,000-acre site, which includes a large tract of giant beech and maple trees, a bass stream, and land in various stages of plant progression. Over seven miles of trails provide access to most sections of the park and its rich birdlife.

Breeding species include the Wood Duck, Red-tailed and Sharp-shinned hawks, American Woodcock, Great Horned, Eastern Screech, and Barred owls, Whip-poor-will, Pileated Woodpecker, Yellow-throated Vireo, Worm-eating Warbler, Blue-winged and Yellow warblers, and Summer Tanager. The Chuck-wills-widow has been seen here.

Glen Helen Nature Preserve   *Take U.S. 42 to Yellow Springs and*
then Ohio 343 east to the entrance.
(Map C–27)

Scenic and geologically valuable, this 960-acre tract embraces a steep-sided valley, good hiking trails, and a lovely cascade. The preserve is part of Antioch College and includes a 100-acre study forest managed by Yellow Springs High School. Much of the wooded area is resplend-ent with wildflowers in the spring. Hardwood trees include chin-quapin, white and bur oaks, sugar maple, basswood, and black walnut. The understory is composed largely of redbud and spicebush.

Nesting in the woods are such birds as the Cooper's, Red-tailed, and Red-shouldered hawks; Eastern Screech, Great Horned, and Barred owls; Pileated Woodpecker; Great Crested and Acadian fly-catchers; Eastern Wood-Pewee; Wood Thrush; Blue-gray Gnat-catcher; Red-eyed Vireo; Cerulean Warbler; Ovenbird; Louisiana Waterthrush; Scarlet Tanager; and Rufous-sided Towhee.

Other birds nesting in clearings and along wooded edges are the American Woodcock; Yellow-billed Cuckoo; Eastern Kingbird; House and Carolina wrens; Northern Mockingbird; Gray Catbird; Brown Thrasher; Eastern Bluebird; Warbling Vireo; Blue-winged, Yellow, and Cerulean warblers; Common Yellowthroat; Yellow-breasted Chat; Northern Oriole; Summer Tanager; Northern Cardinal; Indigo Bunting; American Goldfinch; Chipping, Field, and Song sparrows.

Great Blue and Green-backed herons nest sparingly, as well as Black-crowned and Yellow-crowned Night herons, Mallards, and Wood Ducks.

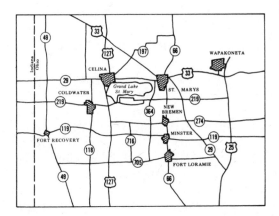

Grand Lake St. Mary

*Take I-75 to Wapakoneta and exit
west onto Ohio 29. To reach the State
Fish Farm, turn south on Ohio 364.
To get to the Mercer County
Waterfowl Refuge, continue south on
Ohio 364, then turn west onto Ohio
703 and follow it to the southwest
shore beyond the village of
Montezuma. (Map C–28)*

Sometimes known as Lake St. Marys, this is the largest body of water
wholly within the state of Ohio. The lake covers approximately 12,500
acres and was created over a century ago by the construction of two
earthen dams. Hundreds of Double-crested Cormorants nested at
that time in tree snags along the south shore and flocks of American
White Pelicans were sometimes present in late summer. Shortly before the turn of the century, the lake was lowered by a severe drought;
surrounding land was cleared, intensive agriculture begun, and most
of the timber was cleared from the exposed lake bed.

The Mercer County Waterfowl Refuge is an excellent area to
observe geese and ducks each spring and fall; the State Fish Farm
attracts shorebirds and waterfowl, plus having the added advantage
of ice-free circulating water in some of the ponds in winter, and the
discharge of warm water at the power plant in Celina provides wintering fish-eating waterbirds with an abundance of small shad. Winter
winds and wave action usually create ribbons of open water on the
lake in all but the coldest weather. Among species seen with regularity
from October through April are the Common Loon, Horned and
Pied-billed grebes, Double-crested Cormorant, Mallard, American

Black Duck, American Wigeon, Green-winged and Blue-winged teals, Redhead, Ring-necked Duck, Canvasback, Lesser Scaup, Common Goldeneye, Bufflehead, and Hooded, Common, and Red-breasted mergansers.

Some of the scarcer waterbirds recorded are the Red-throated Loon, Red-necked Grebe, American White Pelican, Mute Swan, Brant, Greater White-fronted Goose, Cinnamon Teal, Eurasian Wigeon, Greater Scaup, Oldsquaw, and White-winged, Surf, and Black scoters.

A decline in aquatic vegetation has reduced the numbers of marsh-inhabiting birds in recent years and almost eliminated bitterns and rails as breeding species. Great Blue Herons are common and nest in a rookery about four miles to the south, and a scattering of Green-backed Herons nest in wooded spots around the margins of the lake. Infrequent waders and marsh-loving visitors include the Little Blue Heron, Cattle Egret, Great Egret, Snowy Egret, Black-crowned Night Heron, Least and American bitterns, Glossy Ibis, Sandhill Crane, King, Virginia, Sora, Yellow, and Black rails, Common Moorhen, and Marsh Wren. American Coots are common migrants, but rare nesting birds.

The State Fish Farm on Ohio 364 south of Villanova is the choice location to find migrant shorebirds from April to June and July to November. Other shorebirds can be found on emerging mudflats, especially along the south shore, depending on water levels. Some of the good records have included the Whimbrel, Willet, Red Knot, Buff-breasted Sandpiper, Marbled and Hudsonian godwits, American Avocet, Black-necked Stilt, and Red Phalarope.

Gulls that have been recorded at the lake are the Glaucous, Iceland, Great Black-backed, Herring, Ring-billed, Franklin's, Bonaparte's, and Sabine's. Tern species found here are the Forster's, Common, Caspian, and Black, in addition to sightings of such rarities as the Gull-billed and Roseate.

A diversity of habitat exists around the shores of the lake—cultivated and fallow fields, wet meadows, drainage ditches, tree and brush-lined creeks, hedgerows, patches of woods, forests, orchards, dooryards, cemeteries, and small towns. Kessler's Woods is located northeast of the lake; Elm Grove Cemetery is off Greenville Road at the east end of the lake; Liette-Wealock Woods is to the east of Route 364 at the southeast corner of the lake; the State Park headquarters is on Route 29 just west of Villanova; and many good observation points for viewing the lake—and varied land habitats—can be reached along the south side of the lake from Route 703. Some of these latter locations, such as Karafit and Cottonwood roads, Club Island Road, and Behm Road—where they pass close to inlets with dead trees—are excellent places to find nesting Prothonotary Warblers.

Some other breeding birds of interest are the Upland Sandpiper, American Woodcock, Red-headed Woodpecker, Willow Flycatcher, all of the swallows with the possible exception of the Cliff, Yellow-throated Vireo, Yellow Warbler, Cerulean Warbler, Ovenbird, Yellow-breasted Chat, Orchard and Northern orioles, and Scarlet Tanager. In open fields, especially those planted in alfalfa and clover, look for Bobolinks, Dickcissels, and Grasshopper and Savannah sparrows.

Greenlawn Avenue Dam, Reservoir and Bike Path

Take I-71 south of downtown Columbus to the Greenlawn Avenue exit and drive east about one mile. Just before reaching the bridge, turn north into the dead end street paralleling the Scioto River. Or from South High Street, drive west on Whittier Street to the small park and boat ramp at the river. (Map D–29)

On the west side of the river, the bike path passes under the bridge and continues south of Greenlawn Avenue to Frank Road. From mid-April through May, many migrant birds that follow the river can be seen to advantage. Common Flickers, Yellow-bellied Sapsuckers, Winter Wrens, Brown Thrashers, flocks of American Robins, Hermit Thrushes, Ruby-crowned Kinglets, Yellow-rumped Warblers, Purple Finches, Rufous-sided Towhees, Dark-eyed Juncos, and bands of sparrows give way to flycatchers, vireos, warblers of many species, tanagers, and grosbeaks as the spring progresses.

By the end of April, House Wrens appear and seem to be everywhere along the path. This is also one of the best places around Columbus to look for the first returning Yellow Warblers. Listen for the *skeow* call of recently arrived Green-backed Herons along the river bank, and overhead watch for diurnal migrants such as Chimney Swifts, Barn Swallows, and mixed flocks of blackbirds. There is also aways a chance of seeing a few Black-crowned Night Herons or an Osprey along this stretch of the river.

By the first of May, there will be an abundance of Common Yellowthroats, Indigo Buntings, and many other migrating songbirds. The bike path is especially good for Yellow-billed Cuckoos, Wood and Swainson's thrushes, Veeries, Ovenbirds, Scarlet Tanagers, Rose-breasted Grosbeaks, and large numbers of transient Indigo

Buntings. Warbling Vireos and Northern Orioles show up early in May and stay to nest in the cottonwoods above the dam. The rapids below the dam should be scanned for Green-backed Herons, a few shorebirds—most likely Lesser or Greater yellowlegs—and a pair of Belted Kingfishers.

The reservoir behind the dam attracts waterbirds in the fall, during open winters, and in early spring. Mallards, American Black Ducks, Blue-winged Teals, and American Wigeons appear by mid-September. Later in the season, and again in early spring, look for Horned and Pied-billed grebes, Redheads, Ring-necked Ducks, Canvasbacks, Lesser Scaups, Buffleheads, Common Goldeneyes, and any of the three merganser species. Flocks of Ring-billed Gulls and occasional Bonaparte's Gulls are seen in spring and fall, and a few Herring Gulls join wintering Ring-bills during the colder months.

Some of the more unusual birds that have been seen here include the Double-crested Cormorant, Little Blue Heron, Cattle Egret, Tundra Swan, Eurasian Wigeon, Greater Scaup, Oldsquaw, White-winged Scoter, Merlin, Hudsonian and Marbled godwits, Franklin's Gull, Snowy Owl, and Lark Bunting.

Greenlawn Cemetery   *Take I-71 south of downtown*
Columbus to the Greenlawn Avenue
exit and drive west on Greenlawn
Avenue for 0.7 mile to the entrance.
(Map D–30)

On a good day in late April or early May, an experienced observer may record sixty to eighty species of birds in two or three hours in this wooded, park-like cemetery. On arriving, park outside the gate and investigate the nearby bushes, trees, and the wooded ravine behind the administration building. In March and April, the ravine is an excellent place to find the American Woodcock (a pair or two sometimes nest), Louisiana Waterthrush, Rusty Blackbird, Rufous-sided Towhee, and Fox Sparrow.

Go around the south gatepost and shrubbery to the small woods nearby and walk along its western edge. Look for Killdeers, large flocks of American Robins, and Common Flickers during March and April in the adjoining field.

Follow the woods around its perimeter, paying special attention to the surrounding brushy slopes and scrub trees. These are good places to find Connecticut and Mourning warblers, Yellow-breasted Chats, Wilson's and Canada warblers, and Lincoln's Sparrows in May.

Columbus Area

Among the nesting birds are the American Kestrel, Ring-necked Pheasant, Yellow-billed Cuckoo, Willow Flycatcher, Eastern Wood-Pewee, Carolina Chickadee, House and Carolina wrens, Gray Catbird, Brown Thrasher, Cedar Waxwing, Red-eyed Vireo, Yellow Warbler, Common Yellowthroat, Yellow-breasted Chat, Northern Oriole, Indigo Bunting, American Goldfinch, and Chipping, Field, and Song sparrows.

The most popular birding spot at Greenlawn is the site of what was once a small quarry now called the "pit." Surrounded by trees and bushes, this pleasant pond is near the center of the cemetery. To get there, drive past the gate following the red center stripe, then turn right between cemetery sections 77 and 47 and take the first turn to the right. The pit is on the left behind the Hayden mausoleum. In addition to being a fine place to observe birds at close hand, it is also *the* meeting place for Columbus area birders to exchange information and get together with kindred spirits.

When not depleted by Great Horned Owls and a resident pair of red foxes, a noisy flock of domestic fowl including Mallards reside at the pit. However, wild waterbirds—Pied-billed Grebes, Mallards, Blue-winged Teals, Wood Ducks, Black-crowned and Yellow-crowned night herons, American Coots, Solitary and Spotted sandpipers, and Belted Kingfishers—are also sometimes seen.

All of the warblers and vireos that regularly migrate through Ohio can be found sooner or later in the trees and dense shrubbery around the pit. The tangles at the east end are attractive to Hooded Warblers in late April and early May and, more rarely, Connecticut and Mourning warblers a bit later. The grove of trees just east of the tangle also deserves close scrutiny. Flocks of Pine Siskins and Purple Finches are frequently found in the treetops associating with American Goldfinches. Rose-breasted Grosbeaks—as many as several dozen in a single tree–are quite common by the fifth of May. These are also good warbler trees and sometimes an Evening Grosbeak puts in an appearance.

During March and April, look for such birds as the Yellow-bellied Sapsucker, Eastern Phoebe, Red-breasted Nuthatch, Winter Wren, Brown Thrasher, Hermit Thrush, Blue-gray Gnatcatcher, Golden-crowned and Ruby-crowned kinglets, Cedar Waxwing, Solitary Vireo, Black-and-White, Orange-crowned, Black-throated Green, and Yellow-rumped warblers, Louisiana Waterthrush, Rusty Blackbird, and Chipping, White-throated, Fox, Swamp, and Song sparrows. Search the upper limbs of large pine trees for the creeping movements of the Pine Warbler. In large evergreen trees also look for the Long-eared Owl, and in smaller plantings, the Northern Saw-whet Owl. Great Horned Owls are year-round residents.

Scan the skies for migrating Broad-winged Hawks during late April and early May. On good flight days, modest numbers of them can be seen spiraling in kettles as they pass over the cemetery. A few individuals can invariably be flushed out of trees anywhere on the grounds. Other raptors—Sharp-shinned, Cooper's, Red-shouldered, and Red-tailed hawks, Northern Harriers, Ospreys, and American Kestrels—also fly over, usually singly.

Birds of prey are usually noticed flying over between 9 A.M. and 2 P.M. Other in-passage species are seen most often during early morning hours. A partial list includes the Common Loon, Double-crested Cormorant, Great Blue and Little Blue herons, American Bittern, Tundra Swan, Canada Goose, Herring, Ring-billed, and Franklin's gulls, Common Tern, Common Nighthawk, Chimney Swift, all of the swallows, flocks of Blue Jays, and Bobolink.

Another good spot at Greenlawn is an old iron bridge spanning a shallow ravine. To get there from the west end of the pit, drive or walk south to the first roadway to the right and proceed west for about a hundred yards. Near the bridge look for Yellow-bellied Sapsuckers, Winter Wrens, Hermit Thrushes, Rufous-sided Towhees, and Fox Sparrows in early spring. Later in the season, along the gentle slopes of the ravine, there are apt to be Wood, Swainson's, and Gray-cheeked thrushes, Veeries, Ovenbirds, Kentucky, Hooded, and Canada warblers, and American Redstarts. Before leaving the ravine, check the large pines just beyond the Smith monument. Barn, Barred, Long-eared, and Great Horned owls have been found in the higher branches. The grove of maple and sweetgum trees up over the south slope frequently yields an abundance of thrushes, Pine Siskins, Purple Finches, and assorted warblers.

A long, low wooded ridge extends much of the length of Greenlawn from near the bridge all the way to the north boundary of the cemetery. It can be easily reached from the pit by walking a short distance westward. Large oaks are interspersed among many other kinds of trees, all of which attract good numbers of flycatchers, vireos, warblers, orioles, tanagers, and grosbeaks on red-letter days. The oaks have the added advantage of being late leafers, thus offering easy viewing until the middle of May.

The spring migration usually peaks in central Ohio between May 5 and 10, although there is some yearly variation. Additional large numbers of birds continue to migrate through the area as late as May 25, trickling on until June 10.

The fall migration at Greenlawn is unpredictable and seldom impressive. Southbound migrants, including warblers, are not only quiet, but are difficult to see because of the foliage. The woods, brushy areas, and weedy edges on the east side of the cemetery are usually the most productive—although the pit is always worth checking out.

During winter, occasional hawks and owls can be found, along with Common Flickers, Hairy and Downy woodpeckers, Black-capped and Carolina chickadees, Tufted Titmice, White-breasted and Red-breasted nuthatches, Golden-crowned Kinglets, Pine Siskins, American Goldfinches, Dark-eyed Juncos, and White-throated Sparrows. Infrequently, Common Redpolls and both kinds of crossbills appear in small numbers.

Greenville City Park   *Located in the city of Greenville,*
Darke County, along Harmon and
Park Drives. (Map C–31)

The Altar of Peace, commemorating treaties between Anthony Wayne and a consortium of Indian tribes, is located here along with a replica of a stockade, a stream, a woodland, a cemetery, lakes, and ponds. From mid-March through May, this is a good place to witness the progress of landbird migration and to observe occasional migrant waterfowl.

Griggs Dam   *Follow Ohio 33 northwest from*
downtown Columbus and turn left
into the park entrance. Take the road
to the left, then the unimproved road
to the right. (Map D–32)

Scan the rapids below the dam for Yellow-crowned Night Herons from April to mid-September. Three or four pairs of these prehistoric-looking waders nest in trees along the shore or in nearby ravines. The river below the dam remains free of ice except in the coldest weather. A few waterfowl take advantage of the open water and they can be observed from the road that goes through the campground. Most numerous are Mallards, some of them members of the semi-domesticated resident flock, but they are sometimes joined by Pied-billed Grebes, American Black Ducks, Green-winged Teals, American Wigeons, Common Goldeneyes, and Hooded Mergansers.

After returning to near the entrance, take the drive to the right, which follows the Scioto River for several miles above the dam. In the spring, modest numbers of ducks can be found strung out along the river including Redheads, Ring-necked Ducks, Canvasbacks, and Lesser Scaups.

About two miles north of Ohio 161, at the Franklin-Delaware county line, there is a pull-off on the left side of the road. This is a pleasant spot from which to bird right out of the car window. During the cold months, it is possible to see Common Goldeneyes shooting the rapid currents of the river. In summer, a sizeable roost of Turkey Vultures may be observed in nearby trees.

Hebron National Fish Hatchery

Take I-70 about thirty miles east of Columbus. Exit at Ohio 37 and turn south, continuing for approximately one mile. Go left on Ohio 79 for 1.3 miles, then turn left again and drive along the old canal for another mile to the entrance and parking lot. (Map D–33)

Constructed in 1938 with Works Progress Administration funds, the Hebron Hatchery produced its first crop of fish in 1941. Largemouth bass, redear, bluegill sunfish, and channel catfish are propagated for stocking in lakes and reservoirs all over Ohio. In recent years, walleyes, northern pike, and muskellunge were added to the fish raised here. Due to federal budget cutting in 1981, the future of the hatchery remains in some doubt.

The grounds include about seventy-five acres of woods, fields, and marsh habitat in addition to forty ponds which cover about fifty-seven acres. Nature trails connect the ponds and woods; other miles can be logged by walking the pond dikes looking for shorebirds. Wooded stream banks, remnant swamp forest, and wet meadows provide an abundance of plant life. Elm, ash, and soft maples in wet places give way to beech, sugar maple, white oak, pin oak, and honey locust on high ground.

The first ponds to look over are immediately south of the parking lot, with another a short distance to the northeast. After checking these for shorebirds, walk east behind the nearby houses. Over thirty ponds are in this area: at any given time some are full, some are half-empty, and some are drained. After working these, turn your attention to the half-dozen large ponds located south of the wooded stream. Take the footbridge or hike around the west end where conduits carry the water underground. The area of the large ponds has a more natural setting: open water, mudflats, grassy bottoms, and a good amount of cattail and other marsh vegetation.

Shorebirds are the pieces de resistance at the hatchery and, like all good things, they can't always be counted on unless conditions are exactly right. The perfect habitat for sandpipers and plovers is a recently drained pond with a few pools of shallow water or seepage to keep the bottom damp. May is the big shorebird month in spring. Southbound migrants appear early in July and the fall movement continues through most of October, peaking in late August and the first part of September. Rare species that have been recorded are American Avocet, Piping Plover, Hudsonian and Marbled godwits, Willet, all three phalaropes, Long-billed Dowitcher, Red Knot, Western, White-rumped, and Baird's sandpipers, Stilt and Buff-breasted sandpipers, and Ruff.

In late summer, fresh arrivals also include non-resident Green-backed Herons, Blue-winged Teals, a few Green-winged Teals, and Black Terns. Swallows increase in numbers, thousands of Red-winged Blackbirds roost in the cattails; Wood Ducks become numerous and their shrill, screaming notes are frequently heard. Yellow-billed Cuckoos are still quite vociferous, and Willow Flycatchers and Yellow Warblers are conspicuous until their departure in late August.

Mid-April is a good time to visit the hatchery for scatterings of puddle and diving ducks on the ponds, a chance to find Virginia and Sora rails in marshy areas, and an occasional Osprey. Later in the month, increased numbers of shorebirds appear—Semi-palmated Plovers, Greater and Lesser yellowlegs, Solitary and Spotted sandpipers, Semi-palmated, Least, and Pectoral sandpipers—and can be studied at close hand. Flocks of brightly colored Dunlins make their debut in May.

With the influx of birds that arrive in April and May, keep an eye out for Horned Grebes in brilliant breeding plumage, an occasional Great Egret headed for Lake Erie marshes, American Bitterns, and elusive Common Moorhens. Listen for the rattle-like songs of Marsh Wrens coming from the cattails—where they sometimes nest.

Since 1958, 246 species of birds have been observed at the hatchery. Some other good records are Western Grebe, Little Blue Heron, Cattle Egret, Yellow-crowned Night Heron, Glossy Ibis, Mute Swan, Tundra Swan, Snow Goose, Oldsquaw, King Eider, White-winged, Surf, and Black scoters, King Rail, Yellow Rail, Purple Gallinule, Little Tern, Forster's Tern, five species of owls including the Snowy and Short-eared, Bewick's Wren, Sedge Wren, Loggerhead Shrike, Prothonotary Warbler, Evening Grosbeak, Common Redpoll, Lapland Longspur, and Snow Bunting.

A word of warning: between April and November, take a can of insect repellent along, especially when investigating the larger ponds, or hiking in the woods. Massasaugas, or swamp rattlesnakes, are present at the hatchery and in nearby swamp forests. A bit of caution is advised.

Highbanks Metropolitan Park   *Take U.S. 23 north of Columbus to the park entrance which is 2.7 miles north of I-270. (Map D–34)*

This 1,055-acre park is remarkable for its scenery, archaeological features (prehistoric Indian earthworks), and birds. Trails lead through a medley of habitats, including rugged wooded ravines, open fields, brush, forest edges, parkland, and wooded riverbanks.

Counted among the breeding birds are Green-backed Herons, Mallards, Wood Ducks, Spotted Sandpipers, Belted Kingfishers, Northern Rough-winged Swallows, Cedar Waxwings, Warbling Vireos, and Northern Orioles nesting along the river. Fallow fields, strips of weeds, and grassland are preferred by Ring-necked Pheasants, Killdeers, Eastern Meadowlarks, and Field Sparrows. Wooded edges and thickets attract American Woodcocks, Yellow-billed Cuckoos and, occasionally, Black-billed Cuckoos, Ruby-throated Hummingbirds, Eastern Kingbirds, House Wrens, Gray Catbirds, Brown Thrashers; Blue-gray Gnatcatchers, Blue-winged Warblers, Yellow Warblers, Common Yellowthroats, Yellow-breasted Chats, Northern Cardinals, Indigo Buntings, and Chipping Sparrows.

Nesting in deep woods are such birds as Eastern Screech, Great Horned, and Barred owls, Pileated Woodpeckers, Hairy and Downy woodpeckers, Red-bellied and Red-headed woodpeckers, Acadian Flycatchers, Eastern Wood-Pewees, Wood Thrushes, Yellow-throated and Red-eyed vireos, Black-and-White and Cerulean warblers, Ovenbirds, Louisiana Waterthrushes, American Redstarts, Scarlet Tanagers, and Rufous-sided Towhees.

Hoover Reservoir
Take Ohio 161 or I-270 north of Columbus to Sunbury Road, then proceed north through the village of Central College to the dam.
(Map D–36)

The flooding of the Hoover Reservoir basin in 1956 attracted large numbers of waterbirds to central Ohio for the first time in memory. The first two years an estimated 30,000 ducks were present at one time at the peaks of spring migration. Even though silting and deoxidation of the water has drastically reduced the number of birds from those highs, the reservoir still can be exceptionally good at times.

The park area below the dam, including the overflow basin, rapids, willow thickets, and a tree-lined drainage ditch, is always productive and should be checked out before proceeding north on Sunbury Road. Along the way there are several pull-offs and boat-ramp areas from which to scan the water for Common Loons, Horned and Pied-billed grebes, and small rafts of ducks from late October to mid-April. In the spring and fall, American Coots feed along the shore and on the grassy banks.

Continue north along Sunbury Road and turn off onto the second gravel road just above the Smothers Road bridge. In late summer and fall, when the water is low, this is a good place to find small numbers of shorebirds, including the possibility of Buff-breasted Sandpipers. Ring-billed Gulls seen during the summer are non-breeding birds; occasional Common and Black terns are early southbound migrants.

Cross the second bridge and continue on to County Road 31; turn left and proceed for 0.9 mile and turn left into a cul-de-sac. Park at the barricade and hike down the abandoned road, which passes numerous thickets and groves of cottonwoods and willows. A good observation point for seeing waterbirds can be reached by taking the first dirt road to the left (opposite the red brick house) and following it to a knoll that overlooks the reservoir. When water levels are low during late summer and fall, inlets along this part of the shore are among the first to produce mudflats that are attractive to shorebirds. In late October and November, flocks of Canada Geese and, more rarely, blue-phased Snow Geese feed on the upper flats that are covered with burr marigolds.

A canoe or small boat is extremely useful for exploring all the inlets, in addition to the entire upper part of the reservoir. The widely fluctuating water levels of the reservoir have made it difficult for aquatic plants to maintain much continuity of growth. Some years, however, there is enough cattail marsh habitat to attract a few pairs of nesting Marsh Wrens.

To continue a circuit of the reservoir, proceed north on County Road 31 (Sunbury Road) to Galena. For good shorebirding in late summer and fall, circle south around the back side of the town square and park near the slope that leads along a creek channel to the extensive mudflats. For best results, take a spotting scope mounted on a tripod.

On the flats, look for the Semi-palmated Plover, Lesser Golden and Black-bellied plovers, Greater and Lesser yellowlegs, Spotted and Solitary sandpipers, Common Snipe, Short-billed Dowitchers, and a potpourri of peeps. Shorebird rarities have included the American Avocet, Piping Plover, Hudsonian Godwit, Whimbrel, Willet, Ruddy Turnstone, all three phalaropes, Long-billed Dowitcher, Red Knot, and White-rumped, Western, Baird's, Stilt, and Buff-breasted sandpipers. Scan the many snags protruding from the water for Double-crested Cormorants, gulls, and terns. In late fall, flocks of Snow Buntings can sometimes be found feeding around old tree trunks and driftwood.

From Galena, drive west from the town square, cross the bridge and notice the pond at the bottom of an embankment on the right side of the road. A quick look should ascertain whether any birds are present. Turn left at the Wiese Precision Laboratory onto Wiese Road and look for birds as you drive slowly to the next road right. In fall and early winter, keep an eye out for Black-capped Chickadees, Ruby-crowned Kinglets, Yellow-rumped Warblers, flocks of Tree Sparrows, and smaller numbers of Field, White-crowned, White-throated, Swamp, and Song sparrows. During shorebird season, cross the ditch and follow one of several paths to mudflats along the shore.

Take Plumb Road right to get to the Old 3 C Road; turn left and drive 1.6 miles to Tussic Street, then turn left to Oxbow Road, turn left and follow it just past a gate and turn left into a parking area. A good view of the reservoir can be obtained here, and the surrounding shrubbery is a haven for landbirds any time of the year. In spring and fall, look over the wide expanse of water for transients that have stopped over, especially before and at the time of passing storm fronts. At such times, be on the lookout for the Common Loons, scatterings of Horned and Pied-billed grebes, Tundra Swans, and rafts of dabbling and diving ducks. Among the latter, Redheads, Ring-necked Ducks, Canvasbacks, Lesser Scaups, Common Goldeneyes, Buffleheads, Ruddy Ducks, and the three merganser species are often present. Eurasian Wigeons, Greater Scaups, Oldsquaws, White-winged, Surf, and Black scoters are sometimes recorded on red-letter days.

Other rare birds have included the Red-throated Loon, American White Pelican, Little Blue Heron, Bald Eagle, Peregrine Falcon, Franklin's, Laughing, and Sabine's gulls, Black-legged Kittiwake, Roseate Tern, and Western Kingbird.

Huffman Reserve

Located astride Ohio 4 a short distance northwest of Dayton. Enter on the east side of the highway. (Map C–35)

A thirty-acre lake, woods, parkland, bits of pasture, and the Mad River provide the setting for this Dayton-Montgomery County Park District reserve. Situated near Wright-Patterson Air Force Base and the Wright Memorial, the lake attracts good numbers of transient waterbirds—Great Blue and Green-backed herons, Canada Geese, Gadwalls, Northern Pintails, Blue-winged Teals, Common Shovelers, Redheads and Lesser Scaups, Buffleheads and Ruddy Ducks, Semipalmated Plovers, Greater and Lesser yellowlegs, Common Snipe and Pectoral Sandpipers—during their migrations.

Resident nesting birds include the Red-tailed Hawk, Great Horned Owl, Yellow-billed Cuckoo, Great Crested Flycatcher, Eastern Bluebird, Warbling Vireo, Yellow Warbler, Common Yellowthroat, Northern Oriole, Indigo Bunting, and Chipping Sparrow.

Rarities seen on the lake have included the Western Grebe and the White-winged Scoter.

Indian Lake

Located adjacent to U.S. 33 in Logan County. The State Park is off Ohio 273. (Map C–37)

Patches of woods on the northwest shore, a few marshy inlets, fallow and cultivated fields, and widespread development surround this 6,448-acre man-made lake. Although less productive for waterfowl than in the first half of the century, considerable numbers of ducks and geese still stop briefly in spring and again in fall until freeze-up. Ohio 368 at the east end of the lake connects several offshore islands and provides a number of good observation points.

Spring shorebirds occur in wet fields, sky ponds, and along muddy edges; in fall they are dispersed around the lake, mainly in bays and inlets with mudflats. In late spring and early summer, birds of the open fields include the American Kestrel, Ring-necked Pheasant, Killdeer, Barn Swallow, Eastern Kingbird, Horned Lark, Bobolink, Eastern Meadowlark, Red-winged Blackbird, Savannah (scarce), Grasshopper, and Field sparrows.

John Bryan State Park   *Take Ohio 343 about two miles east of Yellow Springs; turn south on Ohio 370 and proceed to the park entrance. (Map C–38)*

This forested valley and ravine is situated between Glen Helen Nature Reserve and Clifton Gorge. Grist mills and an old homestead are added historical attractions. See the Glen Helen account for birds typical of the region.

John L. Rich State Nature Preserve.   *See Clifton Gorge.*

Johnson, Camp   *See Camps Johnson and Mary Orton.*

Kiser Lake State Park   *Take U.S. 36 west from Urbana to the intersection of Ohio 235; turn north and drive about five miles to the entrance. (Map C–39)*

The park encompasses 864 acres of forest and parkland, a shallow lake, and bordering marshland. North of the campground, an amphitheater and nature center are the focal points for park activities, which include a summer nature program.

This is a pleasant and relaxing spot for birding and hiking any time of the year. During the spring months, a host of warblers and other arboreal species can be found in the woods and fields around the lake. Nesting birds include the Yellow-billed Cuckoo, Red-headed Woodpecker, Eastern Wood-Pewee, Barn Swallow, Carolina Chickadee, Gray Catbird, Red-eyed Vireo, Common Yellowthroat, Northern Oriole, Indigo Bunting, Field Sparrow, and Song Sparrow.

The lake attracts modest numbers of waterfowl, including Red-heads, Ring-necked Ducks, and Lesser Scaups during the spring, and waterbirds such as Green-backed Herons, Wood Ducks, and Belted Kingfishers in the summer.

Knox Woods Nature Preserve   *Located in Knox County three miles northeast of Mt. Vernon on the south side of U.S. 36, east of the former Knox County Children's Home. (Map D–40)*

This 30-acre tract of near-virgin mixed deciduous trees contains fine examples of black, red, white, and scarlet oak, sugar maple, shagbark hickory, black walnut, and American beech. Wildflowers include Jack-in-the-pulpit, hepatica, bloodroot, and large-flowered trillium. A trail circles through the woods providing access to spring nesting territories of such birds as the Barred Owl, Red-headed Woodpecker, Great Crested Flycatcher, Carolina Chickadee, Wood Thrush, Yellow-throated Vireo, Cerulean Warbler, Rose-breasted Grosbeak, and Scarlet Tanager.

Lake Loramie State Park   *In Shelby County, located on Ohio 362 between Fort Laramie and Minster. (Map C–41)*

Surrounded by farm fields, woods, and parkland, the 825-acre lake attracts grebes, ducks, and occasional flocks of Ring-billed Gulls during spring and fall. Paths wind through wildflower-dotted woods on the south shore.

Lake St. Marys   *See Grand Lake St. Mary.*

Madison Lake State Park   *In Madison County, on Ohio 665 about five miles east of London. (Map D–42)*

Small numbers of waterfowl—American Wigeons, Redheads, Ring-necked Ducks, and Lesser Scaups—stop in spring and fall at this 100-acre impoundment. Horned Larks and Vesper Sparrows nest in surrounding fields and, in mid-century, the introduced Gray Partridge flourished in the region.

A. W. Marion State Park   *In Pickaway County, take either U.S. 22 or Ohio 188 about five miles east of Circleville and turn off onto the marked roads. (Map D–43)*

Rolling parkland, beech-maple forests, and a 145-acre lake are here;

the lake is visited briefly in March and April and again in late October and November by migrant flocks of American Wigeons, Redheads, Ring-necked Ducks, Lesser Scaups and their allies. A trail starting at the campground circles through fields and woods from which seasonal birdlife can be observed.

Mary Orton, Camp   *See Camps Johnson and Mary Orton.*

Matson Nature Study and   *In Hardin County, on County Road*
Recreation Area   *60 one mile north of Ohio 701.*
                                        (Map C–44)

Trails wind through mixed deciduous woods, plantings of pines and shrubs, expanses of grassland, past a small pond, and bits of marsh habitat. These year-round hiking facilities provide opportunities to check out the seasonal movements of a representative variety of birds.

Minerva Park   *In northeast Columbus, take*
                                        Cleveland Avenue north to Minerva
                                        Lake Road which is about one mile
                                        north of Morse Road. Park at the
                                        community building or the firehouse.
                                        (Map D–45)

This attractive residential area includes a lagoon and a wooded park, both attractive to birdlife. During winter months, the extensive plantings of European Alders around the lagoon are a magnet to flocks of Pine Siskins, occasional Common Redpolls and, rarely, Red Crossbills, and White-winged Crossbills. The siskins, sometimes numbering several hundred, are encountered from November through April.

A footpath crosses a spillway and winds part way around the lagoon providing an opportunity to see May warblers close-at-hand. The patch of woods adjoining the golf course can also yield a sizeable list of migrants, including shy forest-loving species such as Least Flycatchers, Ovenbirds, Kentucky Warblers, Connecticut Warblers, and Mourning Warblers.

A surprising number of birds winter in the area, including all of the Ohio woodpeckers; gleaners like Black-capped and Carolina chickadees, White-breasted and Red-breasted nuthatches, and Brown Creepers; Yellow-rumped Warblers; Purple Finches; House Finches; American Goldfinches; and White-throated Sparrows. Ernie Limes, a longtime resident of Minerva Park, has compiled a list of 140 species seen in or from his backyard.

Mt. Gilead State Park

*In Morrow County, on Ohio 95
about three miles east of Mt. Gilead.
(Map D–46)*

A 30-acre lake with a twin dam on Whetstone Creek and the surrounding wooded slopes provide a nice setting for this 172-acre park. Plantings of pine and spruce, an old orchard, fields, and bits of swamp add to the diversity of habitats, which attract breeding birds like the Barred Owl, Eastern Kingbird, Great Crested Flycatcher, Rough-winged Swallow, Cedar Waxwing, Yellow-throated Vireo, Cerulean Warbler, Eastern Meadowlark, Orchard and Northern orioles, and Rufous-sided Towhee.

Northmoor Park

See Whetstone Park.

O'Shaughnessy Reservoir

*Drive north of Columbus on Ohio
257 for approximately 12 miles.
(Map D–47)*

Before the Hoover, Delaware, and Alum Creek dams were built, O'Shaughnessy Reservoir and Buckeye Lake were the principal places to look for waterfowl in central Ohio. With the advent of the newer and larger reservoirs, O'Shaughnessy doesn't receive the attention it once did, but it is still worth visiting.

Late summer mudflats are good for Great Blue Herons, increased numbers of Green-backed Herons, and a scattering of shorebirds. Yellow-crowned Night Herons nest along the tree-lined shores of the river below the dam.

Just north of the Columbus Zoo, there is a lagoon that is difficult to observe from the road, but can be seen from inside the zoo. From October to April, wild Canada Geese join the zoo flock. An occasional Snow Goose (usually the blue phase) or Richardson's Goose (the small race of the Canada) can also be discovered. Route 257 closely follows the Scioto River from the zoo to Bellpoint, a distance of six miles, along which there are numerous pull-offs for observing any waterbirds that might be present. Many ducks hug the far shore, so use of a spotting scope is advised.

OSU South Woodlot and Pond

*Take I-71 to Ohio 315 in Columbus
to Kinnear Road; go west for about
a mile to The Ohio State University
Electro Science Building and follow
the road to the west side of the woods.
(Map D–48)*

Follow the bike path along the north side of the woods to a small clearing and the pond just beyond. The entire area acts as a bird "trap" during the spring and fall migrations. Listen and look for flycatchers, thrushes, vireos, a variety of warblers, and numerous sparrows. The brushy thickets around the pond are especially productive. Mallards, American Black Ducks, Blue-winged Teals, and Wood Ducks have been noted on the pond.

Summer residents include the American Kestrel, Ring-necked Pheasant, Common Flicker, Downy Woodpecker, Willow Flycatcher, Barn Swallow, Blue Jay, Common Crow, Carolina and House wrens, Northern Mockingbird, Gray Catbird, Brown Thrasher, American Robin, Cedar Waxwing, Red-eyed Vireo, Yellow Warbler, Common Yellowthroat, Red-winged Blackbird, Northern Cardinal, Indigo Bunting, American Goldfinch, Field Sparrow, and Song Sparrow.

OSU Woodlot
Turn west from the Olentangy River Road or Ohio 315 onto Lane Avenue; go west for about half a mile, then turn north onto Carmack Road and follow it through the farm to the woods. (Map D–49)

The entrance road wends its way through fields and orchards before arriving at the woodlot; on the way look for such birds as the American Kestrel, Ring-necked Pheasant, large flocks of Rock Doves, Eastern Kingbird, Horned Lark, Barn Swallow, American Crow, Eastern Meadowlark, and American Goldfinch.

Several trails lead through the woods, but some of the best birding can be done along the south and east edges. During the spring migration, at least 27 species of warblers, in addition to many other songbirds, have been seen here. A pair of Red-tailed Hawks and Great Horned Owls are residents. Occasional Lapland Longspurs and Snow Buntings join Horned Larks in winter in the surrounding fields. Rarely, a Snowy or Short-eared Owl is discovered.

Overbrook Drive East
In the northern part of Columbus, Overbrook Drive intersects with Indianola Avenue and dead-ends at Cooke Road. (Map D–50)

Since there is little automobile traffic along the heavily wooded drive, it is a veritable sanctuary. Large numbers of spring and fall landbird migrants are drawn there by the creek, with scouring rushes along its banks, the shrubbery and tangles of underbrush, and the hundreds of towering trees.

Nesting birds include the Mourning Dove, Common Flicker, Downy Woodpecker, Great Crested Flycatcher, Eastern Phoebe, Eastern Wood-Pewee, Blue Jay, Common Crow, Carolina Chickadee, Tufted Titmouse, White-breasted Nuthatch, House and Carolina wrens, Gray Catbird, Wood Thrush, Blue-gray Gnatcatcher, Cedar Waxwing, Red-eyed Vireo, Common Yellowthroat, Louisiana Waterthrush, Northern Oriole, Northern Cardinal, Indigo Bunting, American Goldfinch, Rufous-sided Towhee, Chipping Sparrow, and Song Sparrow. All of these breeding birds—and probably a considerable number of others—are of especial interest because Overbrook Drive is in the midst of urban Columbus.

Overbrook Drive West

From I-71 in north Columbus take Cooke Road to High Street, turn south and go several blocks to Overbrook Drive which is on the east side of the street. (Map D–51)

This is one of the best places in central Ohio to find the rare Brewster's and Lawrence's warblers, hybrids of the Blue-winged and Golden-winged warblers. These two birds show up infrequently during the first two weeks in May with the Brewster's being seen most often. The Lawrence's is extremely rare, but it has been seen several times at Overbrook in the past ten years.

Immediately off High Street, a small glen on the north side of the drive extends back about fifty yards on either side of a drainage ditch. This is a good spot for Gray-cheeked Thrushes in spring migration, along with Veeries; Philadelphia Vireos; Black-throated Blue, Hooded, Wilson's and Canada warblers; and American Redstarts.

Farther along Overbrook Drive, scan the treetops for additional warblers, Scarlet Tanagers, Rose-breasted Grosbeaks, and troupes of Purple Finches, Pine Siskins, and American Goldfinches. Occasionally in May, a northward-bound flock of Evening Grosbeaks can be found feeding on maple and box-elder seeds and buds.

Other May migrants to look for are Yellow-billed and Black-billed cuckoos; Yellow-bellied and Least flycatchers; Swainson's Thrushes; Ruby-crowned Kinglets; Yellow-throated Vireos; Black-and-White, Tennessee, Nashville, Northern Parula, Magnolia, Cape May, Yellow-rumped, Black-throated Green, Blackburnian, Chestnut-sided, Bay-breasted, Blackpoll, and Palm warblers; Ovenbirds; Northern

Waterthrushes; Northern Orioles; and White-crowned and Lincoln's sparrows.

Nesting birds include the Yellow-billed Cuckoo, Great Crested Flycatcher, Carolina Chickadee, House and Carolina wrens, Wood Thrush, Northern Yellowthroat, and Louisiana Waterthrush.

Pickerington Pond Nature Preserve (Wright Road Pond)

On the east side of Columbus, exit I-70 south onto Brice Road; bear left onto Gender Road, then east onto Wright Road for about two miles to Bowen Road. (Map D–52)

This pond, marsh, and woodland were saved from the maw of encroaching development through the efforts of the Nature Conservancy. It is an excellent place to look for birds from March through May and during the extended fall migration from late July all the way to December. Good views of the pond can be obtained from either Wright or Bowen roads.

Puddle ducks favor the far shore and sometimes feed in numbers on green duckweed at the east end of the pond, while diving birds are more apt to be in the center. Marshy areas are close-at-hand on either side of Bowen Road.

Waterbirds seen with a fair degree of frequency include the Common Loon, Horned and Pied-billed grebes, Tundra Swan, Canada Goose, Ring-billed and Bonaparte's gulls, and Common, Caspian, and Black terns. Modest numbers of puddle and diving ducks are usually present during migration, especially in March and April. Transient Ospreys sometimes remain for a day or two, and Double-crested Cormorants have been seen more frequently in recent years.

Grassy edges and mudflats yield up Great Blue and Green-backed herons, an occasional Cattle or Great egret, and shorebirds—Semipalmated Plovers, Greater and Lesser yellowlegs, Solitary and Spotted sandpipers, Common Snipes, Semi-palmated, Least, and Pectoral sandpipers, and Dunlins—in small numbers when conditions are right.

Large numbers of Chimney Swifts, Tree, Bank, Northern Rough-winged, and Barn swallows, Purple Martins and, infrequently, a few Cliff Swallows converge on the pond on cool days in April and May. Flocks of Water Pipits ply back and forth between mudflats and nearby ploughed fields, and newly arrived Yellow and Yellow-rumped warblers are apt to be heard singing in willow trees along Bowen Road.

Noteworthy species that have nested include the Pied-billed Grebe, Green-backed Heron, Canada Goose, Blue-winged Teal, Sora, Amer-

ican Coot, and Marsh Wren. Rare species seen in migration are the
Glossy Ibis (in nearby fields), Little Blue Heron, Louisiana Heron,
Least Bittern, Mute Swan, Snow Goose, Eurasian Wigeon, Greater
Scaup, Virginia Rail, Red Knot, and Franklin's Gull.

Possum Creek Reserve

On Ohio 48 in the northwest part of Dayton. (Map C–53)

Four small ponds and a lake are set amidst woods, fields, and patches
of marsh at this Dayton-Montgomery County Park District reserve.
Possum Creek Farm is at the southern edge of the park and features
a farmhouse, barnyard, farm equipment, and animals. Beyond the
barn are an orchard, a farm pond, pastures, and a trail leading to a
woods, a stream, and a small marsh.

In early spring and fall, a variety of waterfowl—Mallards, Blue-
winged Teals, American Wigeons, Wood Ducks, and Ring-necked
Ducks—can be seen on the lake and ponds. Great Blue and Green-
backed herons are present during the warm months, and Ospreys are
sometimes spotted as they investigate the ponds. Wet spots and
marshland attract Greater and Lesser yellowlegs, Solitary and Spotted
sandpipers, and small peeps such as the Semi-palmated and Least
sandpipers.

Counted among the breeding birds are the Eastern Kingbird,
Willow Flycatcher, Barn Swallow, Carolina Wren, Eastern Bluebird,
Warbling Vireo, Northern Oriole, and Field Sparrow.

Rush Run State Wildlife Area

In Preble County five miles southeast of Camden on Northern Road. (Map C–54)

This enjoyable spot combines a 1,183-acre tract of oak-hickory-beech
woods, brushy patches, several small ponds, and a fifty-four-acre lake.
This diversity of habitat attracts a wide variety of birds.

Species commonly seen in summer include the Green-backed
Heron, Mallard, Wood Duck, Turkey Vulture, Red-tailed Hawk,
Northern Bobwhite, Ring-necked Pheasant, Killdeer, Spotted Sand-
piper, American Woodcock, Yellow-billed Cuckoo, Belted Kingfisher,
Red-headed Woodpecker, Eastern Kingbird, Acadian Flycatcher,
Northern Rough-winged and Barn swallows, Purple Martins, House
Wrens, Gray Catbirds and Brown Thrashers, Eastern Bluebirds, Wood
Thrushes, Yellow and Cerulean warblers, Common Yellowthroats,
Northern Orioles, Indigo Buntings, American Goldfinches, Rufous-
sided Towhees, and Chipping, Field, and Song sparrows.

During spring and fall, the lake and ponds attract Pied-billed Grebes, American Wigeons, Northern Shovelers, Blue-winged Teals, Redheads, Ring-necked Ducks, Lesser Scaups; Soras in wet overgrown edges; American Coots, Greater and Lesser yellowlegs; Solitary sandpipers, and occasional Common and Black terns.

After a heavy nocturnal migration during late April and the first two weeks in May, the wooded edges, groves of trees, and brushy areas are sometimes alive with a multitude of flycatchers, vireos, warblers, finches, and sparrows.

Sewerage Treatment Plant *See City of Columbus Sewerage Treatment Plant/American Aggregates Quarry.*

Sharon Woods Metropolitan Park *Drive north on Cleveland Avenue in Columbus after exiting from I-270 and go just past Schrock Road. (Map D–55)*

The park embraces 760 wooded acres of oak, ash, sycamore, and maple trees, as well as recreational parkland and a small lake. The Edward S. Thomas Nature Preserve, a 320-acre tract of undisturbed woodland, is included within the park.

Eleven-acre Schrock Lake attracts small numbers of waterbirds in the spring and fall including an occasional Common Loon, Horned and Pied-billed grebes, Mallards, Gadwalls, Blue-winged Teals, Wood Ducks, Redheads, Ring-necked Ducks, Lesser Scaups, Buffleheads, and Ruddy Ducks. A group of five Surf Scoters stopped over one spring.

Horned Larks and Eastern Meadowlarks are found in the grassy fields. During migration periods, flocks of swallows fly over the lake, and good numbers of landbirds can be found along the edges of the woods. A representative sample of nesting birds includes the Northern Bobwhite, Ring-necked Pheasant, Killdeer, American Woodcock, Red-bellied and Red-headed woodpeckers, Eastern Kingbird, Great Crested Flycatcher, Barn Swallow, House Wren, Northern Mockingbird, Gray Catbird, Brown Thrasher, Eastern Bluebird, Blue-gray Gnatcatcher, Cedar Waxwing, Red-eyed Vireo, Yellow Warbler, Common Yellowthroat, Northern Oriole, Northern Cardinal, Indigo Bunting, American Goldfinch, Rufous-sided Towhee, and Chipping, Field, and Song sparrows.

Stage's Pond State Nature
Preserve

Take U.S. 23 south from Columbus
about 14 miles beyond I-270; turn
east onto Hagerty Road and drive
1.6 miles to the entrance and
parking area. (Map D–56)

Stage's Pond is a glacial relict called a kettlehole, formed about eleven thousand years ago by a huge chunk of Wisconsinan glacier ice. As the ice melted, deposits of glacial till gravitated into the kettlehole, which was a by-product of the end moraine about three miles east of the pond.

The 45-acre pond is surrounded by over seventy acres of trees, grasses, and aquatic vegetation. Several hundred yards to the south, spring rains collect in a series of gentle depressions that often attract more waterbirds than the pond. An observation blind overlooks these sloughs and can be reached by following the trail due west of the parking lot bulletin board.

Soon after winter ice melts, a few ducks appear; accompanying the first Mallards and American Black Ducks are Northern Pintails, Gadwalls, Green-winged Teals, American Wigeons, Northern Shovelers, Redheads, Ring-necked Ducks, Canvasbacks, and Lesser Scaups. By mid-March, Blue-winged Teals, Wood Ducks, and Hooded Mergansers are usually present, along with American Coots.

Great Blue and Green-backed herons are present during all the warm months, and other herons and egrets should be looked for during migration periods, including Least and American bitterns. Greater and Lesser yellowlegs, Solitary and Spotted sandpipers, Common Snipes, and Pectoral Sandpipers are commonly found in the spring. Northern Harriers are frequently found hunting over the sloughs and surrounding fields from November to April.

The main system of trails leads through the woods north of the parking lot and one trail descends into grassy bottomlands and follows the west shore of Stage's Pond. Tree Swallows nest in dead trees around the pond; Soras can be found in grassy spots during spring migration, and congregations of post-breeding season Wood Ducks are a common sight in late summer and fall.

Summering birds around the pond and the surrounding woods and fields include the Great Blue and Green-backed herons, Mallard, Wood Duck, Turkey Vulture, Red-tailed Hawk, American Kestrel, Northern Bobwhite, Ring-necked Pheasant, American Coot, Killdeer, American Woodcock, Spotted Sandpiper, Mourning Dove, Yellow-billed Cuckoo, Eastern Screech Owl, Barred Owl, Chimney Swift,

Ruby-throated Hummingbird, Belted Kingfisher, Common Flicker, Red-bellied, Red-headed, Hairy, and Downy woodpeckers, Eastern Kingbird, Willow Flycatcher, Eastern Wood-Pewee, Horned Lark, Tree, Northern Rough-winged, and Barn swallows, Purple Martin, Blue Jay, Common Crow, Carolina Chickadee, Tufted Titmouse, House and Carolina wrens, Northern Mockingbird, Gray Catbird, Brown Thrasher, American Robin, Eastern Bluebird, Blue-gray Gnat-catcher, Cedar Waxwing, Red-eyed and Warbling vireos, Yellow War-bler, Common Yellowthroat, Yellow-breasted Chat, Eastern Meadowlark, Red-winged Blackbird, Northern Oriole, Common Grackle, Brown-headed Cowbird, Northern Cardinal, Indigo Bunt-ing, American Goldfinch, Rufous-sided Towhee, and Field, Chip-ping, and Song sparrows.

In April, surrounding ploughed fields and wet spots commonly yield flocks of Lesser Golden Plovers and Pectoral Sandpipers, occa-sional Upland Sandpipers, and Water Pipits.

Tawawa Forest   *Located just north of Wilberforce and Central State universities northeast of Xenia on Ohio 42. (Map C–57)*

Magnificent American beech trees, oaks, and maples still stand in this splendid virgin woods which was damaged by the tornado of 1974. However, resultant clearings have provided habitat for such edge-loving species as Yellow-billed Cuckoo, Ruby-throated Hummingbird, Brown Thrasher, Eastern Bluebird, Common Yellowthroat, Yellow-breasted Chat, Summer Tanager, Indigo Bunting, and Field and Song sparrows.

Taylorsville Reserve   *Take I-75 north of Dayton; exit at Ohio 40 and proceed to Brown School Road, or east and north along Ohio 40 to the several parts of the park. (Map C–58)*

Segments of the Buckeye Trail pass through the area which also includes remnants of the Miami-Erie Canal, sycamore- and cotton-wood-lined trails along the Great Miami River, a dam, upland woods, and extensive recreational parkland.

Great Blue and Green-backed herons, Mallards, Wood Ducks, and Belted Kingfishers occur along the river; a pair of Red-shouldered Hawks has nested nearby, and Great Horned, Eastern Screech, and Barred owls are resident breeders along with Pileated,

Red-bellied, and Hairy woodpeckers, Eastern Kingbirds, Willow Flycatchers, Carolina Chickadees, Tufted Titmice, White-breasted Nuthatches, House Wrens, Northern Mockingbirds, Red-eyed and Warbling vireos, Blue-winged and Yellow warblers, Common Yellow-throats, Yellow-breasted Chats, and Northern Orioles.

Twin Lakes

Cross O'Shaughnessy Dam at the Columbus Zoo and go north on Ohio 745 for about 1.5 miles and turn left into the park just south of the inlet. (Map D–59)

There are trails running north and south along the stream at the west end of the park, which is reached by a cinder road paralleling the lagoon. When water levels are low in late summer and fall, shorebirds are sometimes found on the resulting mudflats. In winter and early spring, small flocks of ducks might be present, along with Herring and Ring-billed gulls.

Some of the nesting birds are the Red-tailed Hawk, Yellow-billed Cuckoo, Eastern Screech and Great Horned owls, Common Flicker, Red-headed Woodpecker, Eastern Kingbird, Eastern Wood-Pewee, House Wren, Gray Catbird, Eastern Bluebird, Yellow-throated and Red-eyed vireos, Yellow Warbler, Common Yellowthroat, Northern Oriole, Scarlet Tanager, Northern Cardinal, Indigo Bunting, and Chipping, Field, and Song sparrows.

Union Cemetery

Take Olentangy River Road in Columbus to the cemetery, which is just north of Dodridge Avenue on the east side of the street. (Map D–60)

This is a good place to bird in both spring and fall. Large trees and plantings line the Olentangy River and a fine wooded trail extends south to Dodridge Avenue. During the warm months, look for Green-backed Herons, Mallards, Wood Ducks, Spotted Sandpipers, Chimney Swifts, Belted Kingfishers, and Northern Rough-winged and Barn swallows on or over the water. During the spring and fall migrations, most of the arboreal species can be seen to good advantage. The wooded area above Dodridge Avenue is especially good in May for Ovenbirds and Kentucky, Connecticut, Mourning, Hooded, Wilson's, and Canada warblers.

Walden Wildlife Refuge

See Blendon Woods Metropolitan Park.

Walter C. Tucker Nature
Interpretive Center

See Blacklick Woods Metropolitan
Park.

Whetstone Park

On North High Street in Columbus
watch for the Park of Roses sign a
few blocks south of Henderson Road
and turn west on Hollenback Drive.
(Map D–61)

This is an excellent place to observe migratory landbirds because of the park's proximity to the Olentangy River and the varied habitat of fields, woods, a creek, and a ravine. Occasional shorebirds such as the Solitary and Common Spotted sandpipers can be seen along the river, in addition to Green-backed Herons, Mallards, Wood Ducks, and Belted Kingfishers. Among the rare birds that have been observed here are the Western Kingbird; Bell's Vireo; and Golden-winged, Brewster's, Connecticut, and Mourning warblers.

Paths lead through a wooded corridor at the southwest corner of the park and continue south along the river to the smaller Northmoor Park—which can also be reached by car from North Broadway by turning north on Hennepin Road, then west on Kenworth Road, and north on Olentangy Boulevard. Another path meanders through the wooded ravine east of the small bridge.

Permanent residents include the American Kestrel, Eastern Screech Owl, Downy Woodpecker, Blue Jay, Common Crow, Carolina Chickadee, Tufted Titmouse, White-breasted Nuthatch, Northern Cardinal, and Song Sparrow.

Summer nesting birds commonly seen are Yellow-billed Cuckoos, Common Flickers, Great Crested Flycatchers, Eastern Wood-Pewees, Northern Rough-winged Swallows, House Wrens, Gray Catbirds, Wood Thrushes, Cedar Waxwings, Red-eyed Vireos, Warbling Vireos, Yellow Warblers, Common Yellowthroats, Northern Orioles, Indigo Buntings, American Goldfinches, and Chipping Sparrows.

Wright Road Pond

See Pickerington Pond Nature
Preserve.

Young Road Area

Take I-71 south of Columbus to the
intersection with Ohio 665, turn
right, then take the next left onto
Young Road and drive south.
(Map D–62)

From November through April, the farm fields in this region some-times attract good numbers of raptors. Species most often seen are the Cooper's, Red-tailed, and Rough-legged hawks, Northern Har-riers, and American Kestrels. During years of heavy rodent infesta-tion, Short-eared Owls move into the area and can be found perched on fence posts. During the winter months, also look for flocks of Horned Larks which might contain lesser numbers of Lapland Long-spurs and Snow Buntings.

March and April are the months to search for migrating flocks of Lesser Golden Plovers in the newly cultivated fields. They are often on the wing, so it is a good idea to look over every flock of unidenti-fied flying birds. At such times look for the rare Smith's Longspur, which has been found several times along Young Road in recent years. This bird seems to prefer fields of short stubble plant growth and is frequently associated with Horned Larks and migrant Savannah and Song sparrows.

PART III

The Southern and Eastern Unglaciated Counties

LAKE ERIE

STARK
COLUMBIANA

CARROLL

HOLMES

COSHOCTON

TUSCARAWAS

G
HARRISON

JEFFERSON

MUSKINGUM
GUERNSEY
BELMONT

PERRY
NOBLE
MONROE

FAIRFIELD

MORGAN

HOCKING
WASHINGTON

OHIO RIVER

BUTLER
WARREN
CLINTON
ROSS

ATHENS

F

VINTON

HAMILTON

E

CLERMONT
HIGHLAND

PIKE
JACKSON

MEIGS

BROWN
ADAMS

GALLIA

SCIOTO

LAWRENCE

OHIO
RIVER

THERE ARE 35 counties in the unglaciated region, which extends from the rolling highlands of eastern Ohio and the hills and bluffs above the Ohio River to the urban sprawl of Cincinnati and beyond to Indiana. Northward the region juts almost to the center of the state. This vast area is the Allegheny Plateau, typified by river and mining towns, sleepy hamlets, industrial centers—and a reassuring number of city and state parks, nature preserves, wildlife areas, and some just plain wonderful spots that have escaped the onslaught of "civilization."

The southwestern counties, shown on Map E, are Adams, Brown, Butler, Clermont, Clinton, Hamilton, Highland, and Warren. Map F shows the south-central counties: Athens, Fairfield, Gallia, Hocking, Jackson, Lawrence, Meigs, Monroe, Morgan, Noble, Perry, Pike, Ross, Scioto, Vinton, and Washington. Map G covers the east-central section: Belmont, Carroll, Columbiana, Coshocton, Guernsey, Harrison, Holmes, Jefferson, Muskingham, Stark, and Tuscarawas counties. Descriptions of, and directions to, the sites are presented in alphabetical order.

Adams Lake State Park   *On Ohio 41 several miles north of West Union. (Map E–1)*

This 90-acre tract contains a 47-acre impounded lake, patches of woods, nature trails, and a picnic area. Established to protect a small relict prairie, the preserve is owned and operated by the Ohio Department of Natural Resources.

Among the nesting birds and summer visitors, look for the Green-backed Heron; Turkey Vulture; Red-tailed and Red-shouldered hawks; Ruffed Grouse; Northern Bobwhite; Killdeer; Yellow-billed and Black-billed cuckoos; Great Horned Owl; Whip-poor-will; Hairy and Downy woodpeckers; Eastern Kingbird; Eastern Phoebe; Northern Rough-winged and Barn swallows; Purple Martin; Carolina Chickadee; Bewick's (rare) and Carolina wrens; Northern Mockingbird; Gray Catbird; Brown Thrasher; Eastern Bluebird; White-eyed, Yellow-throated, Red-eyed, and Warbling vireos; Blue-winged, Yellow, Cerulean, Prairie, and Kentucky warblers; Louisiana Waterthrush; Common Yellowthroat; Yellow-breasted Chat; Orchard Oriole; Indigo Bunting; Rufous-sided Towhee; and Chipping, Field, and Song sparrows. Cruise nearby roads to find numerous Grasshopper Sparrows,

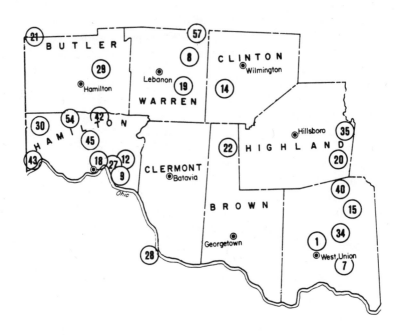

MAP E

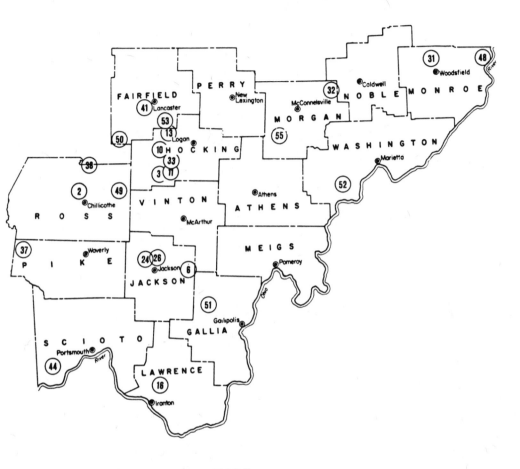

MAP F

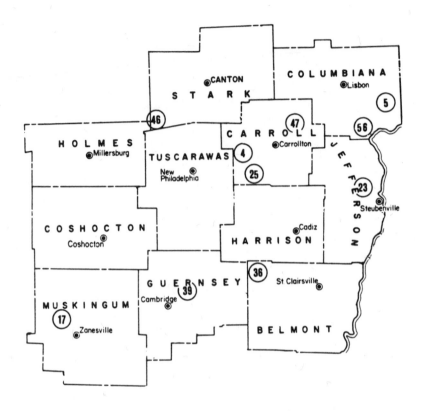

MAP G

4 Atwood Lake
5 Beaver Creek State Park
17 Dillon State Park and Reservoir
23 Jefferson Lake State Park
25 Leesville Lake
36 Piedmont Lake
39 Salt Fork State Park
46 Stark Wilderness Center
47 Still Fork Swamp (Specht Marsh)
56 Yellow Creek State Forest

a few Henslow's Sparrows and, perhaps, a pair or two of the rare Lark Sparrow.

Adena State Memorial   *On Ohio 104 to Allen Avenue,*
                                    northwest of Chillicothe. (Map F–2)

The early nineteenth-century home of Thomas Worthington, Ohio's founding father, this 300-acre estate is administered by the Ohio Historical Society. Open daily except Mondays, April through October, the mansion is situated on a hill with a view of the surrounding hills. Besides the beautiful house with its large barn, gardens, and orchard, there are acres of woodland and a ravine.

Typical spring and summer birds include the Turkey Vulture, Red-tailed Hawk, Northern Bobwhite, Yellow-billed Cuckoo, Chimney Swift, Ruby-throated Hummingbird, Red-bellied Woodpecker, Eastern Kingbird, Eastern Phoebe, Barn Swallow, Purple Martin, Carolina Chickadee, Tufted Titmouse, House Wren, Gray Catbird, Brown Thrasher, Wood Thrush, Eastern Bluebird, Blue-gray Gnatcatcher, Cedar Waxwing, White-eyed and Red-eyed vireos, Blue-winged, Yellow, and Cerulean warblers, Ovenbird, Common Yellowthroat, Eastern Meadowlark, Northern Oriole, Summer Tanager, Northern Cardinal, Indigo Bunting, American Goldfinch, Rufous-sided Towhee, and Chipping, Field, and Song sparrows. During the spring and fall, many warblers and other migrant passerine birds can be found on the grounds and in the surrounding countryside.

Ash Cave State Park   *Take U.S. 33 in Hocking County to*
                                 Ohio 664, which is several miles
                                 north of Logan. Drive west for about
                                 fifteen miles to the park entrance
                                 near the intersection with Ohio 56.
                                 (Map F–3)

Part of the Hocking State Forest, the park's wooded hillsides of mixed hardwoods are accented by towering hemlocks. Centerpiece is a horseshoe-shaped sandstone overhang some ninety feet high and seven hundred feet wide with a stream plunging from the top into a pool.

This area can produce an impressive list of breeding warblers and other specialties of the hills in May and June. These nesting birds include the Ruffed Grouse, Yellow-billed and Black-billed cuckoos, Great Horned Owl, Ruby-throated Hummingbird, Red-bellied Woodpecker, Acadian Flycatcher, Wood Thrush, Yellow-throated

Vireo, Black-and-White, Northern Parula, Black-throated Green, and Cerulean warblers, Ovenbird, Louisiana Waterthrush, Kentucky Warbler, Hooded Warbler, American Redstart, and Scarlet Tanager.

Atwood Lake

In Carroll County southwest of Carrollton between Ohio 39 and Ohio 542. (Map G–4)

A part of the Muskingham Watershed Conservancy District, this impounded 1,540-acre lake is set amidst dense woodlands, planted pine plantations, and rolling fields. Trails cross through the remote haunts of the Ruffed Grouse. The males celebrate the spring with their weird drumming—an accelerating series of thumps produced with their wings—surely one of the great sounds of nature.

Green-backed Herons nest and small groups of waterfowl are seen in spring and fall; Great Horned and Barred owls are resident, and all six species of Ohio's commonly nesting woodpeckers are present. There are camping areas, cabins, and a beautiful state lodge.

Beaver Creek State Park

In southeastern Columbiana County on Ohio 7 about eight miles north of East Liverpool. (Map G–5)

Natural scenery abounds in this 2,405-acre tract which contains a rushing creek, forested hills, and a deep gorge with hemlocks and Canadian yew. There are also extensive pine plantings, the remnants of an old canal, and a restored grist mill.

Warbling Vireos and Northern Orioles nest in sycamores and cottonwoods in open areas along the creek. The repetitious calling of Whip-poor-wills can be heard at night, along with the basso hooting of Great Horned Owls.

Sharp-shinned, Cooper's, and Red-tailed hawks nest, as do Belted Kingfishers, Pileated Woodpeckers, Acadian Flycatchers, Yellow-throated Vireos, Cerulean Warblers, Ovenbirds, Louisiana Waterthrushes, Kentucky Warblers, and Scarlet Tanagers, especially in the area around the gorge.

Buckeye Furnace

Take Ohio 35 to Ohio 124 in Jackson County; go east to County Road 58, then south to Township Road 167 and southwest to the furnace. (Map F–6)

This 270-acre site features a restored charcoal furnace used to smelt iron ore in the late nineteenth century. One of the two nature trails winds around the abandoned ore pits and old roads once used in the operation of the furnace.

In the spring, migrant birds of many species may be seen along the nature trails and around the site itself. Among the nesting birds are Yellow-billed and Black-billed cuckoos, Red-bellied Woodpeckers, Great Crested Flycatchers, Eastern Phoebes, Eastern Wood-Pewees, Carolina Wrens, Eastern Bluebirds, Blue-gray Gnatcatchers, White-eyed, Yellow-throated, and Red-eyed vireos, Yellow, Cerulean, and Kentucky warblers, Ovenbirds, Louisiana Waterthrushes, Common Yellowthroats, Yellow-breasted Chats, Northern Orioles, Scarlet and Summer tanagers, Indigo Buntings, and Chipping, Field, and Song sparrows.

Buzzardroost Rock

Drive east of West Union in Adams County to the village of Lynx. Turn south on Tulip Road (County Road 9). About a mile down this road, turn right at the first gravel road and go west for about one and a half miles to the village of Mahogany. Continue west for one-third mile to a small parking area near the Copas' home. (Map E–7)

Operated by the Cincinnati Museum of Natural History, this nature preserve is also known as the Christian and Emma Goetz Nature Preserve. Prairie, Appalachian, and southern plant species are found here, as well as those typical of Ohio. Rugged wooded hillsides, patches of prairie, a stream, and a waterfall are found on the 152-acre site.

Turkey Vultures soar overhead while below the forest canopy Ruffed Grouse, Yellow-billed and Black-billed cuckoos, Whip-poor-wills, Pileated Woodpeckers, and Cerulean Warblers reside. In more open spaces, there are Eastern Kingbirds, Eastern Bluebirds, Blue-winged and Prairie warblers, Common Yellowthroats and Yellow-breasted Chats, Eastern Meadowlarks, Red-winged Blackbirds, Orchard Orioles, Northern Cardinals, Indigo Buntings, and American Goldfinches. On the preserve or along nearby country roads, look for the following nesting sparrows: Grasshopper, Henslow's, Vesper, Lark, Chipping, Field, and Song.

Caesar Creek Gorge Wildlife Area

In Warren County, about two miles north of Oregonia between Corwin and O'Neall roads. (Map E–8)

A gorge created by tremendous glacial meltwaters, in some places the walls rise to 180 feet above the valley. Relatively untouched, the area is densely wooded with beech, maple, oak, and walnut trees. Prairie plants grow on the shallow soils of the cliffs.

Cooper's and Red-tailed hawks nest in the area, along with Eastern Screech and Great Horned owls, Yellow-billed Cuckoo, Red-bellied and Red-headed woodpeckers, Eastern Phoebe, Acadian Flycatcher, Cerulean Warbler, Ovenbird, Louisiana Waterthrush, Scarlet Tanager, and Rufous-sided Towhee.

Nearby is Caesar Creek Lake, a 2,830-acre reservoir created by the U.S. Army Corps of Engineers between 1971 and 1978. Park facilities and wildlife areas are maintained by the Ohio Department of Natural Resources.

Loons, grebes, ducks, and geese are present in season. Ospreys have been known to summer; Northern Harriers and Short-eared Owls frequent surrounding fields.

California Woods

Take U.S. 52 east from Cincinnati; the entrance is about a mile past the Little Miami River bridge at 5400 Kellog Avenue. (Map E–9)

Situated at the confluence of the Little Miami and Ohio river valleys, this woodland features an interpretive nature center, trails, and seasonal nature programs. Habitat includes a remnant bottomland hardwood forest through which Lick Run flows. Over fifty species of trees have been identified on the tract; four of the trees are believed to be over four hundred years old. Wildflowers abound in spring and summer and include ginseng, goldenseal, bent trillium, Canada lily, and lily-leaved twayblade. The creek is rich in fossils from the Ordovician period.

Nesting specialties include Great Horned Owls, Yellow-billed Cuckoos, Acadian Flycatchers, Eastern Wood-Pewees, Blue-gray Gnatcatchers, Red-eyed Vireos, Prothonotary, Worm-eating, Cerulean, and Yellow-throated warblers, Louisiana Waterthrushes, Common Yellowthroats, Northern Orioles, Scarlet and Summer tanagers, Indigo Buntings, and Rufous-sided Towhees.

Cantwell Cliffs State Park

Take U.S. 33 north of Logan in Hocking County to Ohio 374 and drive east about six miles. (Map F–10)

The northernmost component of the Hocking Hills State Park system, this site features a huge, horseshoe-shaped precipice 150 feet high. Trails go along the brink, descend into the valley, and thread the slopes. Plantations of red, white, and Scotch pines have been planted on the high ground, while mixed hardwoods and hemlocks grow in the valley and along the slopes.

A rich variety of breeding birds is found in the area during late May, June, and early July. Prominent among these are the Ruffed Grouse, Barred Owl, Whip-poor-will, Ruby-throated Hummingbird, Common Flicker, Pileated, Red-bellied, Hairy, and Downy woodpeckers, Eastern Kingbird, Great Crested and Acadian flycatchers, Eastern Phoebe, Eastern Wood-Pewee, Blue Jay, and American Crow.

Some of the above birds can be seen around the parking lot, in addition to the Carolina Chickadee, Tufted Titmouse, White-breasted Nuthatch, House and Carolina wrens, Gray Catbird, Common Yellowthroat, Northern Oriole, Brown-headed Cowbird, Summer Tanager, Northern Cardinal, Indigo Bunting, American Goldfinch, and Chipping and Song sparrows.

Down the wooded trail leading to the precipice, look and listen for the Wood Thrush, Yellow-throated and Red-eyed vireos, Black-and-White, Worm-eating, Northern Parula, Black-throated Green, and Cerulean warblers, Ovenbird, Louisiana Waterthrush, Kentucky and Hooded warblers, American Redstart, Scarlet Tanager, and Rufous-sided Towhee.

During winter months, Evening Grosbeaks, Pine Siskins, and an occasional Red or White-winged Crossbill can be found. In late spring and summer, Henslow's and Grasshopper sparrows can often be found in hilltop fields along the unimproved road off Ohio 374 about half a mile north of the park.

Cedar Falls State Park

Take U.S. 33 to the junction with Ohio 664 at Logan in Hocking County; go about twelve miles to the park entrance. (Map F–11)

The wilderness atmosphere of this Hocking Hills State Park makes a visit here a memorable experience. Beneath the deeply grooved face of Cedar Falls is a wooded gorge of hemlocks, one of which, at 149 feet, is probably the tallest tree in the state. Early settlers mistook the towering trees for cedars—hence the name Cedar Falls. A three-mile section of the Buckeye Trail follows a succession of valleys rich in birdlife to Old Man's Cave State Park.

In recent years, breeding records have been established for five species—the Brown Creeper, Hermit Thrush, Veery, Solitary Vireo, and Blackburnian Warbler—which are beyond the normal limits of their ranges. Twelve other warbler species that nest are the Black-and-White, Worm-eating, Northern Parula, Black-throated Green, Cerulean, Ovenbird, Louisiana Waterthrush, Kentucky, Common Yellowthroat, Yellow-breasted Chat, Hooded, and American Redstart.

Mixed hardwoods are integrated with hemlocks on the slopes and cover the uplands. In these various habitats nesting species include the Ruffed Grouse, Wild Turkey, Yellow-billed and Black-billed cuckoos, Eastern Screech and Barred owls, Whip-poor-will, Pileated and Red-bellied woodpeckers, Eastern Phoebe, Acadian Flycatcher, House and Carolina wrens, Gray Catbird and Brown Thrasher, the Summer Tanager around forest openings and edges, and the Scarlet Tanager in denser woods.

Cincinnati Nature Center

Exit from I-275 onto Ohio 32, go east to Gleneste-Williamsville Road, then north to a three-way intersection. Turn east (right) and go about two blocks. (Map E–12)

This 680-acre center has a hardwood forest, ravines, brushy fields, and several ponds, making it a delightful place to hike and go birding. The nature interpretive center has exhibits, a members' library, and up-to-date bird records. The center is open to the public on weekdays all year round. Weekends are reserved for members and their guests, but permission for a weekend visit may be obtained by writing or phoning the Cincinnati Nature Center, 4949 Tealtown Road, Milford, Ohio 45150, phone: (513) 831-1711.

During spring and fall a few waterfowl visit the ponds; however, the big attraction is the large number of landbirds that can be seen any time of the year. Spring is the most exciting with the mix of migrant warblers, tanagers, grosbeaks, and all their allies changing on a daily basis. Feeders bring many birds up close and, in winter, woodpeckers, Carolina Chickadees, Tufted Titmice, White-breasted and Red-breasted nuthatches, occasional Evening Grosbeaks, Purple Finches, Pine Siskins, American Goldfinches, Dark-eyed Juncos, and

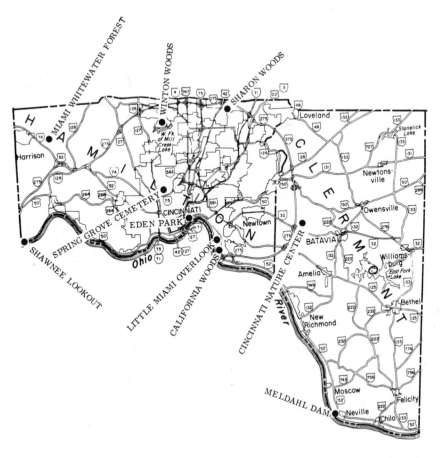

American Tree, Field, White-throated, and Song sparrows fly to-and-fro in close view.

Birds that nest or spend the summer in the area include the Green-backed Heron, Wood Duck, Turkey Vulture, Red-tailed, Red-shouldered, and Broad-winged hawks, American Kestrel, Northern Bobwhite, Yellow-billed Cuckoo, Eastern Screech, Great Horned, and Barred owls, Pileated and Red-bellied woodpeckers, Acadian Flycatcher, Willow Flycatcher, Northern Rough-winged and Barn swallows, Carolina Wren, Northern Mockingbird, Eastern Bluebird, Yellow-throated, White-eyed, and Red-eyed vireos, Blue-winged, Yellow, Cerulean, and Yellow-throated warbler, Kentucky Warbler, Common Yellowthroat; Yellow-breasted Chat, Northern Oriole, Scarlet and Summer tanagers, Northern Cardinal, and Rufous-sided Towhee.

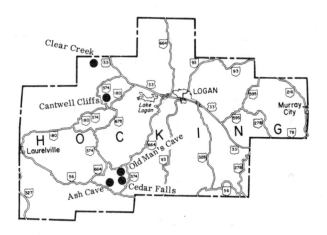

Clear Creek Valley

*In Hocking County, take U.S. 33 to
the Clear Creek road, which is 8.8
miles south of Lancaster.
(Map F–13)*

The unglaciated portion of this lovely valley is approximately seven
miles long and is bounded by outcroppings of rugged Black Hand
conglomerate sandstone (see p. 75) for much of its length. Resting on
glacial wash, the valley is a tapestry of tree-lined stream banks, swaths
of scouring rushes, grasses, patches of brush, and strips of fallow
fields. At its narrowest, the wooded slopes descend to the stream; in
the wider parts of the valley, there are intervening meadows and a
few cultivated fields. A profusion of native and introduced wildflowers flourish along the road and in the woods. Some trees typical of
the valley are the dogwood, redbud, wild plum, sour gum, tulip,
hemlock, sassafras, sourwood, pitch pine, Kentucky coffee, sweet birch,
sycamore, willow; scarlet, black, and chestnut oaks; red maple, black
walnut, and American beech. Vines and bushes common to the valley
include the mountain laurel, wild grape, green briar, witch hazel,
Virginia creeper, and bittersweet.

Once on the Clear Creek road, from mid-April to July, scan the
meadow to the south for Barn and Cliff swallows, American Goldfinches, and Field and Song sparrows. Overhead, scrutinize the swirls
of Turkey Vultures for individuals of the scarce Black Vulture, a few
of which nest in the vicinity. Keep a sharp lookout to the sky for
transiting Green-backed Herons, Pileated and Red-headed woodpeckers, Eastern Bluebirds, Cedar Waxwings, and companies of
Northern Rough-winged, Cliff, and Barn swallows and Purple Mar-

tins. Listen for the rollicking yodel of the Carolina Wren, the repetitious burry notes of the Yellow-throated Vireo, the *churry churry* of the Scarlet Tanager, and the egg-beater-like song of the Cerulean Warbler.

At the first of two houses on the right side of the road, turn into the driveway on the east side. It leads up a hill to Neotoma, a long wooded hollow. This site was extensively studied for many years by Edward S. Thomas, Curator Emeritus of the Ohio State Museum, members of the Wheaton Club—an organization of Ohio field naturalists—and researchers from The Ohio State University. It is now administered by the Metropolitan Park District of Columbus and Franklin County, which must be contacted for permission to enter the tract.

The birdlife at Neotoma during the nesting season is always of interest. Around the old cabin, look and listen for the Yellow-billed and Black-billed cuckoos, Acadian Flycatcher, Carolina Chickadee, Wood Thrush, Blue-gray Gnatcatcher, Black-and-White, Northern Parula, Cerulean, and, rarely, Pine warblers. Ovenbirds, American Redstarts, and Scarlet Tanagers visit the clearing; a pair of Summer Tanagers frequently nest near the cabin.

Several trails lead down the wooded hollow, which follows a small stream. Here there are Pileated and Red-bellied woodpeckers, Yellow-throated Vireos, Worm-eating and Kentucky warblers, several pairs of Louisiana Waterthrushes, and Rufous-sided Towhees. At the head of the valley and below the cabin, listen for Willow Flycatchers, Blue-winged Warblers, Common Yellowthroats, and Yellow-breasted Chats. At dusk, listen for the Whip-poor-will.

Two and a half miles down the Clear Creek road from U.S. 33, pull off the road and park near the wooded hollow on the right. A pair of Canada Warblers frequently nest back up the cool hemlock-covered slope. Eastern Wood-Pewees, Acadian and Great Crested flycatchers, Blue-gray Gnatcatchers, White-eyed, Yellow-throated, Red-eyed, and Warbling vireos, Northern Orioles, Scarlet Tanagers, Indigo Buntings, Rufous-sided Towhees, Song Sparrows, and a fine assortment of warblers also nest here. Among the latter are the Black-and-White, Worm-eating, Blue-winged, Northern Parula, Yellow, Magnolia (rare), Black-throated Green, Cerulean, Yellow-throated, Ovenbird, Louisiana Waterthrush, Common Yellowthroat, Yellow-breasted Chat, and American Redstart. Pileated Woodpeckers and a pair of Broad-winged Hawks nest nearby, and a short walk down the road in either direction will reveal Kentucky and Hooded warblers. A pair of scarce Bewick's Wrens nested in the hollow several years ago. The richness and diversity of birdlife in this one spot is probably due to the closeness of the creek to the wooded hollow with its giant hemlocks, roadside clearings, and adjoining slopes of mixed deciduous trees.

A little over four miles from Route 33 is an impressive part of the valley; steep wooded hillsides, a dramatic bluff, brushy tangles, and a sweeping view of a gentle draw on the opposite side of the creek make this an outstanding place for observing an abundance of birds. Species regularly recorded here include the Red-tailed and Red-shouldered hawks; Northern Bobwhite; Yellow-billed and Black-billed cuckoos; Ruby-throated Hummingbird; Belted Kingfisher; Eastern Phoebe; Acadian Flycatcher; Eastern Wood-Pewee; Northern Rough-winged and Barn swallows; Carolina Chickadee; Tufted Titmouse; House and Carolina wrens; Blue-gray Gnatcatcher; White-eyed, Yellow-throated, and Red-eyed vireos; Black-and-White, Blue-winged, Yellow, Yellow-throated, Chestnut-sided (scarce), and Prairie warblers; Ovenbird; Louisiana Waterthrush; Common Yellowthroat; Yellow-breasted Chat; American Redstart; Scarlet Tanager; Northern Cardinal; Indigo Bunting; American Goldfinch; Rufous-sided Towhee; and Chipping, Field, and Song sparrows.

Continuing along the road, at 4.8 miles from U.S. 33 is Written Rock, a graffiti-covered sandstone cliff at the edge of the road. Hundreds of initials are inscribed here, most of the recent ones with spray paint that unfortunately obscures some of the chiseled inscriptions, many of which are well over a hundred years old. A pair of Eastern Phoebes and several pairs of Northern Rough-winged Swallows sometimes nest in crannies on the face of the cliff. Sycamores along the creek attract nesting Eastern Kingbirds, Warbling Vireos, Northern Orioles and an occasional pair of Orchard Orioles. Other birds to look for in the vicinity, including the field across the creek, are the Red-tailed Hawk, Ruby-throated Hummingbird, Belted Kingfisher, Red-bellied Woodpecker, Willow Flycatcher, Barn Swallow, Eastern Bluebird, White-eyed, Yellow-throated, and Red-eyed vireos, Northern Parula (in the hemlocks high atop Written Rock), Yellow and Yellow-throated warblers, Common Yellowthroat, Yellow-breasted Chat, and Summer Tanager.

From Written Rock continue westward to the entrance of Barneby Center, an environmental station operated by The Ohio State University. Permission to bird on this extensive tract of wooded hills, which includes a small lake, can be obtained from supervisory personnel at the lodge at the upper end of the driveway. The Solitary Vireo has nested here, along with such birds as the Red-tailed and Broad-winged hawks, Yellow-billed and Black-billed cuckoos, Belted Kingfisher, Acadian and Willow flycatchers, Eastern Phoebe, Wood Thrush, Scarlet and Summer tanagers, Northern and Orchard orioles, Rose-breasted Grosbeak, and the following warblers: Black-and-White, Worm-eating, Blue-winged, Northern Parula, Yellow, Black-throated Green, Cerulean, Pine, Prairie, Ovenbird, Louisiana Waterthrush, Kentucky, Common Yellowthroat, Yellow-breasted Chat, Hooded, and American Redstart.

About a mile farther down the Clear Creek road an old iron bridge crosses the creek. Near the bridge look for the Blue-gray Gnatcatcher; Cedar Waxwing; Blue-winged, Cerulean, and Yellow-throated warblers; Ovenbird; Common Yellowthroat; Yellow-breasted Chat; Scarlet Tanager; Indigo Bunting; Rufous-sided Towhee, and Song Sparrow. Green-backed Herons, Belted Kingfishers, and Northern Rough-winged Swallows can frequently be seen flying along the creek. Listen for Northern Bobwhites in nearby fields.

The part of the valley between Rich Hollow Road and an old covered bridge farther on provides a final encore to the wonderful birdlife of this region. Many of the birds seen in other parts of the valley can be seen here, and it is a particularly good place to see the Yellow-throated Warbler.

A few Eastern Screech Owls and one or two pairs of Great Horned and Barred owls inhabit the valley, but are difficult to find except at night with the help of tape recorders. Eight to ten pairs of Whip-poor-wills can be heard calling on territory each year. In a 10-year population study of the valley, the author recorded 105 species of nesting birds. And there is some evidence that the Hermit Thrush and Veery might be added to the list.

Cowan Lake State Park   *Take Ohio 350 southwest of Wilmington in Clinton County to the park entrance. (Map E–14)*

This 700-acre lake attracts flocks of migrant waterfowl in March and April, and again in October and November. Mallards, American Wigeons, Ring-necked Ducks, and Redheads are usually most numerous. A few Common Loons, Horned and Pied-billed grebes are also apt to be present at such times.

Summering birds include the Green-backed Heron; Turkey Vulture; Red-shouldered Hawk (scarce); American Kestrel; Eastern Bobwhite; Killdeer; Spotted Sandpiper; Yellow-billed Cuckoo; Eastern Kingbird; Willow Flycatcher; Northern Rough-winged and Barn swallows; Wood Thrush; Yellow-throated, Red-eyed, and Warbling vireos; Yellow Warbler; Yellow-breasted Chat; Common Yellow-throat; and Northern Oriole.

Cumberland Mine Area   *See Ohio Power Recreation Area.*

Davis (Edwin H.) State   *Take Ohio 41 to the south edge of*
Memorial   *Peebles, go east on Steam Furnace*
                                        Road, then southeast about 2.3 miles
                                        to Township Road 129. Go east on
                                        this road for about 2.5 miles.
                                        (Map E–15)

This 88-acre tract, administered by the Ohio Historical Society, affords birders the opportunity to observe a good cross-section of southwestern Ohio birds in a setting of rugged dolomite cliffs, a cave, a canebrake, prairie openings, a stream, and a woodland composed of arborvitae, Virginia pine, red cedar, red and chestnut oaks, tulip, and sugar maple trees. Some of the birds found in these varied habitats include the Red-shouldered Hawk, Ruffed Grouse, Whip-poor-will, Barred Owl, Eastern Wood-Pewee, Wood Thrush, Red-eyed Vireo, Cerulean and Kentucky warblers, Ovenbird, Louisiana Waterthrush, Scarlet Tanager, Rufous-sided Towhee, and Chipping Sparrow. Along the South Trail—one of two nature trails—typical breeding birds are the Carolina Wren, Gray Catbird, Brown Thrasher, Yellow-throated Vireo, Summer Tanager, Indigo Bunting, and Field Sparrow. There is always a chance of finding the rare Bachman's Sparrow on the site or along nearby country roads.

Dean State Forest and Lake   *Take Ohio 93 in Lawrence County*
Vesuvius Recreation Area   *north from Ironton: seven miles to*
                                        Lake Vesuvius, fifteen miles to Dean
                                        State Forest. (Map F–16)

Both areas combine rugged wooded hills, streams, fallow fields, and hiking trails. Cooper's, Red-tailed, and Broad-winged hawks nest at both sites, as do Ruffed Grouse, Whip-poor-wills, and Pileated Woodpeckers. Breeding warblers include the Black-and-White, Worm-eating, Yellow, Cerulean, Prairie, Ovenbird, Louisiana Waterthrush, Kentucky, Common Yellowthroat, Yellow-breasted Chat, Hooded, and American Redstart.

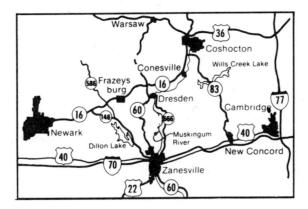

Dillon State Park and Reservoir   *Take Ohio 146 north of Zanesville about eight miles to the park entrance. (Map G–17)*

There is a diversity of habitat at this site including substantial areas of marshy shoreline, a large impounded lake, wooded hillsides, ravines, and brushy fields. Ohio 146 parallels the lake most of its length with a number of access roads leading to the shore. Common Loons, Horned and Pied-billed grebes, occasional Double-crested Cormorants and Tundra Swans, and sizeable assemblages of ducks and geese rest and feed here during their seasonal migrations. Great Blue Herons are present in all but the coldest months; Green-backed Herons can be found from late April to mid-September, and rarer wading birds such as the Little Blue Heron, Cattle and Great egrets, and small flocks of Black-crowned Night Herons are sometimes found in spring and late summer.

A few of the breeding bird specialties include the Wood Duck, Red-tailed and Red-shouldered hawks, Ruffed Grouse, Black-billed Cuckoo, Eastern Screech, Great Horned, and Barred owls, Whippoor-will, Pileated Woodpecker, Marsh Wren, Yellow-throated Vireo, Yellow Warbler, Cerulean Warbler, Ovenbird, Scarlet and Summer tanagers, and Rufous-sided Towhee.

Eden Park   *From downtown Cincinnati take U.S. 22 (Gilbert Avenue) east a short distance to the entrance. (Map E–18)*

This lovely park overlooks the Ohio River and features groves of mature trees, plantings, shrubs, walkways, and winding drives that lead to some of the cultural gems of the Queen City: the Cincinnati Museum of Natural Science, a conservatory, a repertory theatre, and the Cincinnati Art Museum. On early mornings in late April and May, an abundance of newly arrived warblers and other arboreal birds brighten the treetops with their color and song. On a red-letter day at least fifty species can be seen in several hours of birding.

Fort Ancient State Memorial

Take I-71 to the Lebanon exit, proceed southeast a short distance on Ohio 123, then turn left onto Ohio 350 and drive about five miles to the entrance. (Map E–19)

Approximately fifteen hundred years ago the Hopewell Indians built these earthworks, which circle the crest of a 270-foot-high bluff over the Little Miami River. Centuries later, the Fort Ancient Indians occupied the same site. A museum displays many of the artifacts of both cultures. Forested ravines and streams extend from the earthworks to the river valley below. Dominant trees include the American beech; sugar maple; white, scarlet, red, and chestnut oaks; hickory and, in the river bottom, sycamore and cottonwood. There are trails that lead to scenic overlooks, past brushy fields, and through extensive parklands.

Summer birds include the Turkey and Black vultures; Cooper's, Red-tailed, and Red-shouldered hawks; American Kestrel; Northern Bobwhite; Black-billed Cuckoo; Bewick's Wren (rare); Northern Mockingbird; Wood Thrush; Eastern Bluebird; White-eyed, Yellow-throated, Red-eyed, and Warbling vireos; Orchard and Northern orioles; Scarlet and Summer tanagers; Rufous-sided Towhee; Chipping, Field, and Song sparrows; and the following warblers: Black-and-White, Blue-winged, Yellow-throated (in sycamores), Cerulean, Ovenbird, Louisiana Waterthrush, Kentucky, Common Yellowthroat, Yellow-breasted Chat, and Hooded.

Fort Hill State Memorial

In eastern Highland County on County Road 256, which can be reached from Ohio 41. (Map E–20)

This 1,197-acre tract, a property of the Ohio Historical Society, includes remnants of prehistoric Indian earthworks in rugged terrain that ranges from dense forest and cool wooded slopes to hot arid hillsides and brushy bottomlands. Wild cherry and white and red oaks are abundant, and there are some sugar maples and tulip trees over 100 feet tall. A moist limestone gorge harbors such uncommon plants as the Canadian yew, *Sullivantia,* walking fern, and Canby's mountain lover. On the slopes are moss phlox, dwarf larkspur, wood-sorrel, and a splendid mosaic of other wildflowers and ferns.

Breeding and summer birds include the Wood Duck, Turkey Vulture, Sharp-shinned, Cooper's, Red-tailed, and Broad-winged hawks, American Kestrel, Northern Bobwhite, Yellow-billed and Black-billed cuckoos, Eastern Screech and Barred owls, Whip-poor-will, Ruby-throated Hummingbird, Belted Kingfisher, Common Flicker, Pileated, Red-bellied, Red-headed, Hairy, and Downy woodpeckers, Eastern Kingbird, Great Crested Flycatcher, Eastern Phoebe, Acadian Flycatcher, Eastern Wood-Pewee, Northern Rough-winged and Barn swallows, Purple Martin, Blue Jay, and American Crow.

Other typical breeding species are the Carolina Chickadee, Tufted Titmouse, White-breasted Nuthatch, House and Carolina wrens, Northern Mockingbird, Gray Catbird, Brown Thrasher, Wood Thrush, Eastern Bluebird, Blue-gray Gnatcatcher, Cedar Waxwing, White-eyed, Yellow-throated, and Red-eyed vireos, Black-and-White, Worm-eating, Blue-winged, Northern Parula, Yellow, Cerulean, Yellow-throated, and Prairie warblers, Ovenbird, Louisiana Waterthrush, Kentucky Warbler, Common Yellowthroat, Yellow-breasted Chat, American Redstart, Orchard and Northern orioles, Scarlet and Summer tanagers, Northern Cardinal, Indigo Bunting, American Goldfinch, Rufous-sided Towhee, and Chipping, Field, and Song sparrows. The scarce Bewick's Wren and Bachman's Sparrow have also been known to nest in the area.

Greenbelt Nature Preserves   *See Winton Woods.*

Goetz (Christian and Emma)   *See Buzzardroost Rock.*
Nature Preserve

Hueston Woods State Park   *In southern Preble County on Ohio*
177. Part of the park lies in Butler
County. (Map E-21)

A 3,584-acre tract of forest—much of it virgin woodland—and 625-acre Acton Lake complement recreational areas, a modern guest lodge, boating and fishing facilities, and miles of trails for hiking and horseback riding. Sledding, skating, ice fishing, ice boating, and cross-country skiing are available during the winter months.

Acton Lake induces modest numbers of waterbirds to feed and rest during spring and fall migrations, including the Common Loon, Horned Grebe, occasional herons and egrets, scatterings of puddle ducks, and rafts of diving ducks. A few shorebirds are sometimes found in inlets and along muddy edges.

A few of the representative breeding birds are the Cooper's, Red-tailed, and Red-shouldered hawks, Yellow-billed Cuckoo, Eastern Screech, Great Horned, and Barred owls, Pileated Woodpecker, Acadian Flycatcher, Carolina Wren, Eastern Bluebird, Blue-gray Gnatcatcher, Cedar Waxwing, Yellow-throated Vireo, Yellow and Cerulean warblers, Ovenbird, Common Yellowthroat, Yellow-breasted Chat, Scarlet and Summer tanagers, and Rufous-sided Towhees.

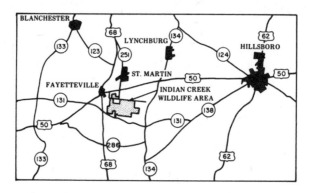

Indian Creek State Wildlife Area

In Brown County on Ohio 50 one mile east of Fayetteville. (Map E–22)

Birdlife and small mammals abound in this 1,540-acre tract of rolling hills, ponds, streams, bits of marsh, and oak-hickory woods. Mallards and Wood Ducks nest in wet areas and a few migratory species such as American Wigeons and Blue-winged Teals are present during the spring months. Greater and Lesser yellowlegs and Spotted and Solitary sandpipers can be found in the spring, late summer, and fall. During the spring months, wooded and brushy areas sometimes teem with transient flycatchers, vireos, warblers, finches, and sparrows.

Just a few of the nesting birds are the Green-backed Heron, Red-tailed Hawk, Ring-necked Pheasant, American Woodcock, Belted Kingfisher, Red-headed Woodpecker, Eastern Kingbird, Willow Flycatcher, Eastern Bluebird, Cedar Waxwing, Warbling Vireo, Yellow Warbler, and Northern Oriole.

Jefferson Lake State Park

In Jefferson County on Ohio 43 about four miles west of Richmond. (Map G–23)

A fine oak-hickory forest graces this 933-acre site which features rolling hills and ravines around a lovely lake, and lake-associated marsh. Bird life is profuse and nesting birds alone include some four score species.

Wood Ducks nest in boxes set out for them. Northern Bobwhites were plentiful before the severe winters in the late 70s and are still fairly common; Ruffed Grouse occur sparingly, and Spotted Sandpipers sometimes nest. Other nesting birds include the Eastern Screech and Great Horned owls, Whip-poor-will, Ruby-throated Hummingbird, Belted Kingfisher, five species of woodpeckers, Eastern Kingbird, Great Crested Flycatcher, Eastern Phoebe, Acadian Flycatcher, Eastern Wood-Pewee, Northern Rough-winged and Barn swallows, Purple Martin, Carolina Chickadee, Tufted Titmouse, and White-breasted Nuthatch.

Bewick's Wren is a possibility in brushy areas; House Wrens are common in similar places and around human habitations. Blue-gray Gnatcatchers and Cedar Waxwings are widespread and fairly common. Also look for Yellow-throated and Red-eyed vireos, Black-and-White, Blue-winged, Yellow, and Cerulean warblers, Louisiana Waterthrushes, Kentucky Warblers, Common Yellowthroats, Yellow-breasted Chats, Northern Orioles, Scarlet Tanagers, and Grasshopper and Vesper sparrows in surrounding fields.

Lake Katherine (Edwin A. Jones & James J. McKitterick Memorial Wildlife Sanctuary)

In Jackson County, take U.S. 35 about 3.3 miles north of Jackson; turn west on County Road 59, cross Little Salt Creek, go one mile to County Road 59A and turn south. (Map F–24)

A kaleidoscopic array of habitats are preserved in this 1,467-acre preserve through the foresight of two longtime business partners, Edwin A. Jones and the late James J. McKitterick, who donated the land to the Ohio Department of Natural Resources.

The sheer rock faces of high sandstone bluffs festooned with gnarled Virginia pines drop abruptly into the lake. Ferns, mosses, a myriad of wildflowers and rare plants—*Sullivantia* and several endangered species of Ohio orchids—make this a botanist's paradise. Hemlocks, mountain laurel, and sweet birch in the bottoms vie for attention with several hundred bigleaf magnolias and an undisturbed forest of oaks, maples, and beech trees.

Sharp-shinned, Cooper's, Red-tailed, and Broad-winged hawks

and Eastern Screech, Great Horned, and Barred owls nest in the area regularly. Other breeding species are the Turkey Vulture, American Kestrel, Ruffed Grouse, Northern Bobwhite, Black-billed Cuckoo, Whip-poor-will, Pileated Woodpecker, and the following warblers: Black-and-White, Yellow, Cerulean, Ovenbird, Louisiana Water-thrush, Kentucky, Common Yellowthroat, Yellow-breasted Chat, and Hooded.

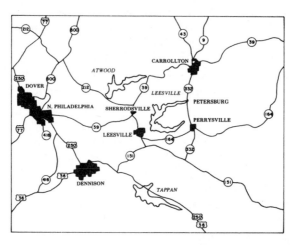

Leesville Lake

In southern Carroll County north of the village of Leesville. Roads lead to the lake from Ohio 212 and Ohio 164. (Map G–25)

This 1,000-acre lake and its wooded shoreline is part of the Mus-kingham Watershed Conservancy District. Although large numbers of waterfowl seldom gather here, there are pleasant forest trails which provide an opportunity to flush Ruffed Grouse, catch a glimpse of a Pileated Woodpecker, and hear the melancholy notes of the Black-billed Cuckoo. Belted Kingfishers nest, and a colony of Great Blue Herons is located on a wooded ridge bordering the lake.

Leo Petroglyph State Memorial

From U.S. 35 about five miles north of Jackson, take County Road 28 east for about two miles. (Map F–26)

Prehistoric Indians carved images of birds, fish, a bear, footprints, and animal tracks on a large stone outcropping at this twelve-acre site owned by the Ohio Historical Society. Trails meander beneath tall oaks and through cool moist spots carpeted with a fine variety of wildflowers, ferns, and mosses.

Turkey Vultures and a pair of Red-tailed Hawks are frequently seen soaring overhead. In the wooded areas in spring and summer, there are Yellow-billed Cuckoos, Whip-poor-wills, Red-bellied Woodpeckers, Great Crested and Acadian flycatchers, Eastern Wood-Pewees, Carolina Chickadees, Wood Thrushes, Red-eyed Vireos, Cerulean Warblers, Ovenbirds, Louisiana Waterthrushes, Scarlet Tanagers, and Rufous-sided Towhees.

In more open spaces, look and listen for Eastern Phoebes, House and Carolina wrens, Eastern Bluebirds, Blue-winged and Yellow warblers, Common Yellowthroats, Yellow-breasted Chats, Northern Orioles, Indigo Buntings, and Chipping and Song sparrows.

Little Miami River Overlook   *Drive east in Cincinnati on U.S. 52 to Reservoir Road and turn right toward the Ohio River to a parking lot and marina. (Map E–27)*

A variety of ducks can be seen here from late October to April. Look for Mallards, American Black Ducks, Northern Pintails, American Wigeons, Redheads, Canvasbacks, Common Goldeneyes, and Common, Red-breasted, and Hooded mergansers. At such times, Herring, Ring-billed, and Bonaparte's gulls are sometimes present. Small flocks of Common, Black, and a few Caspian terns are sometimes encountered in April and May and in late summer. Broadwinged Hawks, Ospreys and some of the other raptors have a tendency to follow the Little Miami River north during their spring migrations. In early May, the willows and shrubs in the area should yield good numbers of warblers and other transients.

Meldahl (Anthony) Dam   *Take U.S. 52 southeast of Cincinnati to Moscow (about thirty miles). Just beyond town turn right toward the Ohio River. (Map E–28)*

An excellent assortment of waterbirds can be seen from the dam or the parking lot from October through April. Look for the Common Loon, Horned and Pied-billed grebes, Canada Goose, Mallard, American Black Duck, Gadwall, Northern Pintail, Green-winged Teal, American Wigeon, Redhead, Canvasback, Lesser Scaup, Common Goldeneye, and all three mergansers. Gulls of several species are frequently present and, in spring, small companies of terns can be

seen flying over the water. A few Ospreys are recorded each spring
and fall. To compensate for the distance to the river, a spotting scope
is a necessity for birding at this site. Congregations of shorebirds on
a large gravel bar below the dam can best be seen from the Kentucky
shore. To get there, take I-75 across the river at Cincinnati, exit onto
Kentucky 8 and drive east for about 30 miles.

Miami and Erie Canal Park   *From Middletown in Butler County,*
take Canal, Headgate, or Reigart
roads southwest toward Hamilton.
(Map E–29)

This 170-acre park features several recreation areas, a hiking trail,
woodland, and restored portions of the old canal. Several scenic vistas
overlooking the Miami River are excellent places to look for migrating warblers and other arboreal species during the spring migration.

Birds commonly seen in early summer include the Green-backed
Heron, Spotted Sandpiper, Belted Kingfisher, Yellow-billed Cuckoo,
Common Flicker, Red-bellied Woodpecker, Eastern Kingbird, Northern Rough-winged Swallow, Carolina Chickadee, House and Carolina wrens, Gray Catbird, Cedar Waxwing, Yellow-throated, Red-eyed,
and Warbling vireos, Yellow and Cerulean warblers, Common Yellowthroat, and Northern Oriole.

Miami Whitewater Forest   *Take I-74 west of Cincinnati; at the*
Dry Fork exit go north for about two
miles. (Map E–30)

One of the older preserved forest areas in the state, this 2,000-acre
tract once knew the tread of Indian feet and, during the Civil War,
sheltered Morgan's Raiders. White-tailed deer roam the woods and
fields. There is a braille trail, as well as a trail to Reservoir Overlook
with views of Ohio, Indiana, and Kentucky.

Among the breeding birds are the Wood Duck, Cooper's and
Red-tailed hawks, Northern Bobwhite, American Woodcock, Yellow-
billed Cuckoo, Eastern Screech, Great Horned, and Barred owls, Pi-
leated, Red-bellied, Red-headed, and Hairy woodpeckers, Great Crested
Flycatcher, Eastern Phoebe, Acadian and Willow flycatchers, Eastern
Wood-Pewee, Carolina Chickadee, Tufted Titmouse, White-breasted
Nuthatch, House and Carolina wrens, Northern Mockingbird, Gray
Catbird, Brown Thrasher, Wood Thrush, Eastern Bluebird, Cedar
Waxwing, and White-eyed, Yellow-throated, Red-eyed, and Warbling
vireos.

Warblers that nest are the Black-and-White, Worm-eating, Blue-winged, Yellow, Cerulean, Ovenbird, Louisiana Waterthrush, Kentucky, Common Yellowthroat, Yellow-breasted Chat, and Hooded. Northern Orioles, Scarlet and Summer tanagers, an abundance of Northern Cardinals and Indigo Buntings, Rufous-sided Towhees, and Chipping, Field, and Song sparrows are all characteristic breeding birds.

Monroe Lake State Wildlife Area
In Monroe County on Ohio 800 five miles north of Woodsfield.
(Map F–31)

Densely wooded slopes descend to 39-acre Monroe Lake on this 1,332-acre tract of forest, pine plantings, streams, cultivated fields, and roadside thickets. A nature trail that circles the lake provides vantage points for observing small groups of transient waterfowl. About 70 species of birds nest in the area, including Ruffed Grouse and Pileated Woodpeckers. Many other species—including Ospreys—are seen in migration.

Neotoma
See Clear Creek Valley.

Newberry Wildlife Sanctuary
See Winton Woods.

Ohio Power Recreation Area (Cumberland Mine Area)
Located largely in Morgan County, sections spill over into Guernsey, Noble, and Muskingham counties. Best reached by taking Ohio 83 south from New Concord or Ohio 146 and Ohio 284 southeast from Zanesville.
(Map F–32)

Once stripped for coal, this vast area embracing 100,000 acres is largely reclaimed land and boasts 320 stocked lakes and ponds, 34 million planted tree seedlings, campsites, shelters, and picnic areas. Literature, maps, and camping permits may be obtained by stopping at any Ohio Power Company office, or writing to Ohio Power Company, P.O. Box 328, McConnelsville, Ohio 43756, or the Publication Center, Ohio Department of Natural Resources, Fountain Square, Building C, Columbus, Ohio 43224.

Bird species that have returned or adapted to the area are as numerous as the varied habitats, which include ravines, marshes, streams, extensive fields, and farmland. The most successful of these are birds of the open countryside.

Old Man's Cave State Park   *Take U.S. 33 to Ohio 374 or Ohio*
664 and proceed southeast for about
fifteen miles to the park entrance.
(Map F–33)

This dramatic park combines awesome overhangs of Black Hand sandstone (see p. 75), a gorge with tunnels, rock stairways, waterfalls, precipitous ledges and cliffs, and trails that ultimately lead to the Devil's Bathtub and Old Man's Cave. A canopy of mixed hardwoods and conifers cloak the hills and gorges creating a cool, damp environment for wildflowers, ferns, and mosses.

Resident and breeding birds are essentially the same as those listed for Ash Cave and Cantwell Cliffs State parks, with the exception of Yellow-throated Warblers, which nest in sycamores near the parking lot.

In April, early May, and again in late September and early October, this is a fine place to find such transients as the Broad-winged Hawk; Yellow-bellied Sapsucker; Red-breasted Nuthatch; Winter Wren; Hermit, Swainson's, and Gray-cheeked thrushes; Veery; Solitary Vireo; Nashville, Magnolia, Cape May, Yellow-rumped, Blackburnian, and Bay-breasted warblers; Northern Waterthrush; Wilson's and Canada warblers; and Rose-breasted Grosbeak.

Ohio Brush Creek   *Take Ohio 125 in Adams County*
about seven miles east of West
Union; go north on Waggoner Riffle
Road for five miles and park at the
side of the road. (Map E–34)

This region is famous among birders as one of the northernmost nesting outposts of the Chuck-will's-Widow. The birds can be heard after dark—along with numerous Whip-poor-wills—from early May to July. By cruising nearby roads before dark, Blue-winged, Yellow, and Prairie warblers, Yellow-breasted Chats, Scarlet and Summer tanagers, and Grasshopper, Henslow's, and the rare Lark and Bachman's sparrows might be seen or heard.

Paint Creek Reservoir and State   *Take U.S. 50 about five miles west of*
Park   *Bainbridge and turn north following*
the signs to the park. (Map E–35)

In 1973 Paint Creek was impounded about five miles below the confluence of Paint and Rattlesnake creeks. The habitat at the lake is diverse, including the 1,200-acre lake, streams, floodplain, heavily wooded hillsides, and agricultural land.

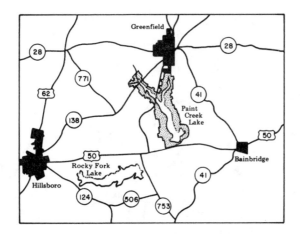

The chances for encountering waterfowl are good between late February and the first of May and from October through December. A few Common Loons and Pied-billed Grebes are usually seen each season; small numbers of ducks make brief stops, and up to a hundred or more American Coots are often present. The majority of shorebirds are usually seen in late summer and fall when there are a few mudflats. American Avocets have been recorded, and a few Ospreys put in an appearance each spring and fall.

Nesting species include the Green-backed Heron; Wood Duck; Turkey Vulture; Red-tailed Hawk; American Kestrel; Northern Bobwhite; Spotted Sandpiper; American Woodcock; Yellow-billed Cuckoo; Eastern Screech, Great Horned, and Barred owls; Ruby-throated Hummingbird; Belted Kingfisher; Red-bellied and Red-headed woodpeckers; Eastern Kingbird; Eastern Phoebe; Acadian Flycatcher; Northern Rough-winged and Barn swallows; Northern Mockingbird; Wood Thrush; Eastern Bluebird; Cedar Waxwing; White-eyed, Yellow-throated, Red-eyed, and Warbling vireos; Blue-winged, Yellow, and Cerulean warblers; Ovenbird; Kentucky Warbler; Common Yellowthroat; Yellow-breasted Chat; Orchard and Northern orioles; Scarlet and Summer tanagers; Rufous-sided Towhee; and Chipping, Field, and Song sparrows. There is some evidence that Tree Swallows and Prothonotary Warblers nest in small numbers.

Piedmont Lake

Take U.S. 22 to Smyrna or Piedmont and take any one of several county roads south to the lake, which is in northwestern Belmont County. (Map G–36)

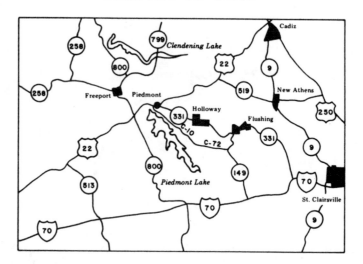

This Muskingham Conservancy District lake comprises 2,270 acres with an additional 4,330 acres of wooded parkland. Beech-maple and oak-hickory woods border the lake and cover the surrounding hills. Additional acres have been planted in pines. The dam across Stillwater Creek is near the village of Piedmont.

Rafts of diving ducks composed of Redheads, Ring-necked Ducks, Canvasbacks, and Lesser Scaups congregate on the lake in March, early April, and again in late October and November. Modest numbers of surface-feeding ducks—Mallards, American Black Ducks, Gadwalls, Northern Pintails, American Wigeons, and Northern Shovelers—occur along with the divers. Flocks of Canada Geese are rather common in November and December and late February and early March. A few Tundra Swans sometimes appear, usually in mid-March.

Some of the breeding birds to be found include Cooper's and Red-tailed hawks; Ruffed Grouse; Black-billed Cuckoo; Eastern Screech, Great Horned, and Barred owls; Whip-poor-will; Ruby-throated Hummingbird; Belted Kingfisher; Red-bellied and Hairy woodpeckers; Great Crested and Acadian flycatchers; Worm-eating (rare), Yellow, and Cerulean warblers; Ovenbird; Kentucky Warbler; American Redstart; Orchard and Northern orioles; Scarlet and Summer tanagers; and Rufous-sided Towhees.

Pike State Forest and Pike Lake State Park *In Pike County south of U.S. 50 on Ohio 41. (Map F–37)*

The 13-acre lake is in the northeast section of the forest and attracts small numbers of migrant waterfowl and occasional wading birds in all but the winter months. Roads and trails give access to the 10,586-acre forest, and another trail circles the lake.

Breeding bird specialties are the Broad-winged Hawk, Ruffed Grouse, Whip-poor-will, Pileated Woodpecker, White-eyed Vireo, and the following warblers: Black-and-White, Worm-eating, Blue-winged, Prairie, Louisiana Waterthrush, Kentucky, Hooded, and American Redstart. Orchard Orioles and Summer Tanagers can be found in clearings and around houses, and there is always a chance of turning up a scarce Bachman's Sparrow.

Ross-Pickaway County Line Road

Follow U.S. 23 south through Circleville and about six miles beyond to the Cole Brothers Nursery sign; turn right onto the road just north of a highway overpass. Follow this road south past the nursery to the intersection with the county line road, which passes over Route 23 and continues east to Kingston and Adelphi-Laurelville. (Map F–38)

One of the best places in Ohio to see raptors during the winter season is along this road in south-central Ohio. Most of the action starts in November and continues through March. On a Christmas Bird Count on December 19, 1976, participants recorded 25 Turkey Vultures; 20 Black Vultures; 1 Northern Goshawk; 2 Sharp-shinned Hawks; 5 Cooper's Hawks; 65 Red-tailed Hawks; 49 Rough-legged Hawks; 68 Northern Harriers; 1 Merlin; 132 American Kestrels; 2 Barn Owls; 1 Eastern Screech Owl; 4 Great Horned Owls, and 4 Short-eared Owls. Look for hawks perched in trees, on utility wires and fences, and in the air, both high and low.

The section of the road east of Kingston is especially productive for birds of prey. In late afternoon, the fields east of Whistler Road sometimes play host to extraordinary numbers of Northern Harriers which roost during the night in the clumps of tall grasses. During the twilight hours, sometimes twenty or even thirty or more of these beautiful birds can be seen gyrating about in the approaching darkness. Conclaves of Short-eared Owls are also known to frequent the Whistler Road area around sundown. Sometimes as many as two dozen of these owls gather together during the cold months.

In winter, it is not uncommon to find large numbers of Horned Larks; flocks of Eastern Bluebirds; a few Water Pipits; an occasional Loggerhead Shrike; groups of Eastern Meadowlarks; a few Savannah

Sparrows; large assemblages of American Tree Sparrows and, rarely, a few Lapland Longspurs and Snow Buntings.

The County Line Road can be interesting at other times of the year because of its wide fertile fields and its proximity to the hills of Ross, Hocking, and Vinton counties. Abundant rainfall in the spring creates sky ponds that frequently attract flocks of Lesser Golden Plover, Common Snipes, Greater and Lesser yellowlegs, Upland and Pectoral sandpipers, and a variety of peeps. A few pairs of Upland Sandpipers nest in the vicinity.

Other breeding birds include the Red-tailed Hawk, Northern Harrier, American Kestrel, Northern Bobwhite, Ring-necked Pheasant, Killdeer, Mourning Dove, Short-eared and Barn owls (both rare), Common Flicker, Red-headed Woodpecker, Eastern Kingbird, Horned Lark, American Crow, Northern Mockingbird, Eastern Bluebird, Yellow Warbler, Common Yellowthroat, Bobolink, Eastern Meadowlark, Red-winged Blackbird, Common Grackle, Brown-headed Cowbird, Northern Cardinal, Indigo Bunting, American Goldfinch, and Grasshopper, Henslow's (erratic), Vesper, Chipping, Field, and Song sparrows.

Salt Fork State Park   *On Ohio 22 about eight miles*
northeast of Cambridge in Guernsey
County. (Map G–39)

This 20,000-acre state park contains a 2,052-acre lake with bits of marsh in the upper ends, and integrated woodlots, fallow fields, and farms. A large state lodge, cabins, and recreational facilities are available.

In spring and fall, most of the commonly found species of Ohio waterfowl are found on the lake, in addition to occasional wading birds, a few rails and bitterns in the marsh habitat, small gatherings of shorebirds and, rarely, Peregrine Falcons and Bald Eagles. Breeding birds include such disparate species as the Green-backed Heron, Wood Duck, Red-shouldered Hawk, Ruffed Grouse, American Woodcock, Black-billed Cuckoo, Pileated Woodpecker, American Redstart, and Summer Tanager.

Serpent Mound State Memorial   *In northern Adams County on Ohio*
73 four miles northwest of Locust
Grove. (Map E–40)

This attractive park on the east bluff of Ohio Brush Creek contains the largest known effigy mound in the United States. One-quarter mile long with seven deep curves, the serpent is in the act of uncoiling; in its open jaws lies a small mound—possibly representing an egg. The Adena Indians built this ceremonial earthworks sometime between 1000 B.C. and A.D. 400. Both the mound and a five-mile-wide crater may be seen from the observation tower.

A few of the nesting birds of the area include the Whip-poor-will, Ruby-throated Hummingbird, Eastern Phoebe, Blue-gray Gnat-catcher, Carolina Wren, Wood Thrush, Yellow-throated Vireo, Yellow and Blue-winged warblers, Common Yellowthroat, Yellow-breasted Chat, Northern Oriole, Scarlet and Summer tanagers, Indigo Bunting, American Goldfinch, and Chipping and Song sparrows.

Shallenberger Nature Preserve   *In Fairfield County, take U.S. 22 three miles southwest of Lancaster and turn onto Beck Knob Road for 0.2 mile. (Map F–41)*

This 87-acre site is dominated by Allen Knob, a promontory of Black Hand sandstone (see p. 75) rising 270 feet above a creek on its north side. Chestnut oaks, mountain laurel, and remnants of American chestnuts clothe the knob, and mixed deciduous trees cover the lower slopes.

Breeding birds include American Kestrels, Black-billed Cuckoos, Great Crested and Acadian flycatchers, Eastern Wood-Pewees, Wood Thrushes, Yellow-throated Vireos, Black-and-White and Cerulean warblers, Ovenbirds, Louisiana Waterthrushes, Common Yellowthroats, Yellow-breasted Chats, and Scarlet Tanagers.

Sharon Woods County Park   *Take I-275 north of Cincinnati to U.S. 42 and drive south to the park entrance. (Map E–42)*

This 740-acre Hamilton County Park District tract includes a creek and waterfalls; a lake; a climax forest of oak, beech, and maple; a gorge famed for rare fossils; an Indian mound; and many hiking trails.

Modest numbers of waterbirds—Pied-billed Grebes, Mallards, American Black Ducks, Blue-winged Teals, American Wigeons, Wood Ducks, Redheads, Ring-necked Ducks, Lesser Scaups, and American Coots—are attracted to the pond, especially in the spring. During late April and May, large numbers of transient landbirds swarm through the area and listing fifty or sixty species in a single morning isn't unusual. Over fifty species have nested within the park.

Shawnee Lookout County Park   *Take I-74 west of Cincinnati for*
about 12 miles; turn south on I-275
and exit at Kilby Road, then drive
south and turn west onto U.S. 50.
(Map E–43)

This 1,010-acre Hamilton County Park District site at the mouth of
the Great Miami River features a fort built by Indians about two
thousand years ago and later used as a lookout by the Shawnees. One
of the best all-round places to go birding in southwestern Ohio, the
park attracts shorebirds, waterfowl, birds of prey, and large numbers
of landbirds. It is one of the few places in Ohio where the Black
Vulture nests.

Along the river, in early spring, look for Canada Geese, Mallards,
American Black Ducks, Gadwalls, Northern Pintails, Green-winged
and Blue-winged teals, American Wigeons, Northern Shovelers, Redheads, Ring-necked Ducks, Canvasbacks, Lesser Scaups, Common
Goldeneyes, Buffleheads, Ruddy Ducks, and all three merganser
species.

Breeding bird species include the Turkey Vulture, Cooper's and
Red-tailed hawks, Northern Bobwhite, Yellow-billed Cuckoo, Great
Horned Owl, Ruby-throated Hummingbird, Belted Kingfisher, Red-
bellied and Red-headed woodpeckers, Great Crested Flycatcher,
Eastern Phoebe; Carolina Chickadee, Tufted Titmouse, White-breasted
Nuthatch; House and Carolina wrens, Northern Mockingbird, Gray
Catbird, Brown Thrasher, Eastern Bluebird, White-eyed, Yellow-
throated, Red-eyed, and Warbling vireos, Prothonotary, Blue-winged,
Yellow, and Cerulean warblers, Ovenbird, Common Yellowthroat,
Yellow-breasted Chat, Kentucky Warbler, American Redstart, North-
ern Oriole, Scarlet and Summer tanagers, Northern Cardinal, Indigo
Bunting, and Rufous-sided Towhee.

Across the Great Miami River from Shawnee Lookout Park is an
old oxbow-shaped area that is a fine place to find shorebirds and a
variety of waterbirds. Spring visitors include the Horned and Pied-
billed grebes, occasional Double-crested Cormorants, Great Blue,
Green-backed, and Black-crowned Night herons, Ring-billed and Bonaparte's gulls, and Common, Caspian, and Black terns. Shorebirds
to look for are the Semi-palmated Plover, Killdeer, Lesser Golden and
Black-bellied plovers, Greater and Lesser yellowlegs, Spotted Sandpiper, Common Snipe, Semi-palmated, Least, White-rumped, Baird's,
Pectoral, and Stilt sandpipers, Dunlin and, rarely, Buff-breasted sandpipers. Many of the shorebirds are seen only in late summer and fall.

Shawnee State Forest and State Park

Take U.S. 52 west from Portsmouth about seven miles and turn onto Route 125; continue northwest about four miles. (Map F–44)

With 58,165 acres of rugged woodland, this sprawling tract north of the Ohio River is the largest forest in the state. Three lakes—Bear, Turkey Creek, and Roosevelt—attract occasional Common Loons, Pied-billed Grebes, small rafts of ducks, and American Coots. There is also a small pond that is sometimes good for waterbirds on U.S. 52 a short distance west of Ohio 125 just past the Friendship School.

Wild Turkeys can be seen in the vicinity of Bear Creek Reservoir; Broad-winged Hawks soar over the wooded hills, and Yellow-throated Warblers frequent the sycamores along many of the creeks. Pine Warblers are common in the stands of red and white pines, especially along Forest Road 1 off Route 125. Make a circuit of the Panoram-McBride-Shawnee roads for some good birding. Ruffed Grouse can be found in any of the wooded areas.

Bird specialties to look for in spring and summer include both cuckoos, Whip-poor-wills, Ruby-throated Hummingbirds, Eastern Kingbirds, Great Crested Flycatchers, Eastern Phoebes, Acadian Flycatchers, Eastern Wood-Pewees, Barn and Northern Rough-winged swallows, Purple Martins, House Wrens, Bewick's Wren (rare), Wood Thrushes, Blue-gray Gnatcatchers, Cedar Waxwings, and White-eyed, Yellow-throated, Red-eyed, and Warbling vireos—the latter in cottonwoods along the streams.

Breeding warblers also include the Black-and-White, Worm-eating, Golden-winged (rare), Blue-winged, Northern Parula (in hemlocks), Yellow, Black-throated Green, Cerulean, Prairie, Ovenbird, Louisiana Waterthrush (in ravines and along creeks), Kentucky, Common Yellowthroat, Yellow-breasted Chat, Hooded, and American Redstart.

Eastern Meadowlarks are common in the fields, and Orchard and Northern orioles are fond of clearings, groves of trees, and roadside streams. Northern Cardinals, Indigo Buntings, and American Goldfinches are abundant everywhere but in the deepest woods. There is always a chance of finding the rare Bachman's Sparrow in habitats of sparsely planted pines and fallow fields, and the equally rare Lark Sparrow on eroded hillsides.

Birds found in winter may include the Turkey Vulture; Cooper's, Red-tailed, and Red-shouldered hawks; Eastern Screech, Great Horned, Barred, and Long-eared (rare) owls; all of the woodpeckers regular in Ohio; Eastern Phoebe; Blue Jay; American Crow; Carolina Chickadee; Tufted Titmouse; White-breasted and Red-breasted nuthatches; Brown Creeper; Hermit Thrush; Eastern Bluebird; Cedar Waxwing; Yellow-rumped Warbler; Evening Grosbeak (erratic); Pine Siskin; American Goldfinch; Rufous-sided Towhee; Dark-eyed Junco; and American Tree, Field, White-crowned, White-throated, Fox (scarce), and Song sparrows.

Spring Beauty Dell   *See Winton Woods.*

Spring Grove Cemetery   *Take the Mitchell Avenue exit from*
I-75 in Cincinnati; drive north to
Spring Grove Avenue, go left on it
for half a mile. (Map E–45)

An excellent place to go birding for spring migrants, this site combines large parklike areas with smaller niches of natural habitat including wooded ravines and native stands of beech, oak, and maple.

In late April and May, large numbers of birds stop over, rest and feed a day or two, and then are on their way again. On a red-letter day, the trees are alive with Least Flycatchers and other *Empidonax,* a variety of vireos, and warblers such as the Black-and-White, Blue-winged, Golden-winged, Tennessee, Nashville, Magnolia, Cape May, Black-throated Blue, Yellow-rumped, Black-throated Green, Blackburnian, Chestnut-sided, Bay-breasted, Blackpoll, Palm, and American Redstart. Heavily wooded and brushy areas yield such species as the Swainson's and Gray-cheeked thrushes, Veery, Worm-eating Warbler, Northern Waterthrush; Kentucky, Connecticut (rare), Mourning (rare), Hooded, Wilson's, and Canada warblers. Sometimes one tree will be full of warblers plus Scarlet Tanagers, Northern Orioles, and Rose-breasted Grosbeaks.

A surprising number of these new arrivals remain to nest along with the resident birds. A partial list of breeding birds would include the Wood Duck; American Kestrel; Yellow-billed Cuckoo; Eastern Screech and Barred owls; Ruby-throated Hummingbird; Common Flicker; Hairy and Downy woodpeckers; Great Crested Flycatcher; Eastern Wood-Pewee; Blue Jay; Carolina Chickadee; Tufted Titmouse, White-breasted Nuthatch; House and Carolina wrens; Northern Mockingbird; Gray Catbird; Brown Thrasher; American Robin; Wood Thrush; Cedar Waxwing; Red-eyed Vireo; Yellow and Cerulean warblers; Common Yellowthroat; Kentucky Warbler; Northern Oriole; Scarlet Tanager; Indigo Bunting; American Redstart; and Chipping and Field sparrows.

Because of the numerous hemlocks, spruce, pines, sweet gum,

and alder trees, Spring Grove is an excellent place in winter to find such visitors as the Red-breasted Nuthatch, Evening Grosbeak, Purple Finch; American Goldfinch; Pine Siskin; and Red-winged and White-winged crossbills.

Spring Valley State
Wildlife Area

In Warren County, on U.S. 42 2.5 miles south of the village of Spring Valley, turn east on Roxanna-New Burlington Road, go 1.4 miles to Pence Jones Road; follow the signs to the parking lot.
(Map E-57)

This superb area includes an 80-acre lake, extensive marshes and overgrown channels, underbrush, fields, and an upland woods. Wide trails circle the lake and afford access to every nook and corner.

Loons, grebes, swans, geese, and all the common ducks can be seen here during migrations.

Nesting species include the Pied-billed Grebe, Least and American bitterns, Canada Goose, Mallard, Blue-winged Teal, Wood Duck, Virginia Rail, Sora, Common Moorhen, American Coot, Eastern Screech Owl, Belted Kingfisher, Red-bellied Woodpecker, Eastern Kingbird, Willow Flycatcher, Tree Swallow, Marsh Wren, Yellow-throated and Warbling vireos, Prothonotary Warbler, Yellow Warbler, Northern Oriole, and Swamp Sparrow.

Rarities have included Mute Swan, Oldsquaw, Sandhill Crane, King Rail, Yellow Rail, and Purple Gallinule.

Stark Wilderness Center

On U.S. 250 in Stark County one mile northwest of Wilmot.
(Map G-46)

Trails radiate out from a nature interpretive center to lead the birder through three woods, across fields, along creeks, and past a marsh and two ponds. Sigrist Woods boasts oaks 400 years old, in addition to mature beech and maple trees.

The center was founded in 1964 by the Canton Audubon Society in cooperation with the National Audubon Society and with grants from large corporations, foundations, and other interested organizations. Hunting, fishing, trapping, and camping are prohibited.

Waterfowl have responded to the protection they receive here and increasing numbers of geese and ducks feed and rest on the largest pond, especially in the spring. Pied-billed Grebes, Green-backed

Herons, occasional American Bitterns and Soras, and groups of American Coots are found at the lake or in the marsh.

Typical breeding birds are the Red-headed Woodpecker, Eastern Kingbird, Great Crested Flycatcher, Eastern Phoebe, Barn Swallow, Black-capped Chickadee, Wood Thrush, Red-eyed Vireo, Yellow and Cerulean warblers, Ovenbird, Northern Oriole, Scarlet Tanager, and Rufous-sided Towhee.

Still Fork Swamp (Specht Marsh)

In Carroll County, follow an improved county road north 1.5 miles from Mechanicstown, then turn west for about three miles to just beyond Watheys. (Map G–47)

This 125-acre marsh was obtained by the Nature Conservancy and is administered by Kent State University. Forest W. Buchanan has done extensive fieldwork in the area from which most of the data presented here are derived.

Plant species include swamp rose, wool-grass, marsh fern, cattail, giant bur-reed, arrowhead, duckweed, pondweed, spatterdock, and pickerelweed. Alders and several species of ash grow in and around the marsh.

Buchanan has established or verified the following breeding records for the marsh: Least Bittern, American Bittern, American Black Duck, Blue-winged Teal, Wood Duck, Northern Harrier, Virginia Rail, Sora, American Woodcock, Willow Flycatcher, Marsh Wren, Yellow Warbler, and Swamp Sparrow.

Sunfish Creek State Forest

On Ohio 7 in Monroe County four miles north of Clarington. (Map F–48)

Forested hills and wooded overlooks along the Ohio River descend to the meandering configurations of Sunfish Creek. Turkey Vultures and Cooper's and Red-tailed hawks nest in forest areas, along with Eastern Screech, Great Horned, and Barred owls. Other woodland breeders are the Ruffed Grouse, Yellow-billed and Black-billed cuckoos, Whip-poor-wills, Pileated and Red-bellied woodpeckers, Acadian Flycatchers, Wood Thrushes, and Scarlet Tanagers.

Eastern Phoebes, House and Carolina wrens, Gray Catbirds, Eastern Bluebirds, Blue-gray Gnatcatchers, and Warbling Vireos nest along the creek and in clearings.

Tar Hollow State Forest   *Take Ohio 56 southeast to Adelphi in*
southeastern Pickaway County; pick
up Ohio 327 and go south about ten
miles to the access road. (Map F–49)

This beautiful 16,126-acre tract is an enjoyable place to go birding
any time of the year. A dammed stream has created a lake, and there
are extensive wooded hills—most of them oak-hickory and beech-
maple—with sizeable plantings of pine. Deer are abundant, along
with many smaller mammals.

During the spring, birds are conspicuous all the way along Route
327 to the park, especially during the early morning hours when
newly arrived swifts twitter across the sky, Barn Swallows dip and dart
over the road, and every patch of woods and brush seems to harbor
a host of singing birds. Listen for the *turtle-turtle-turtle* song of the
Kentucky Warbler, and the more emphatic *teacher-teacher-teacher* song
of the Ovenbird. On a good May morning, warblers of many species
and the entire entourage of birds that move north with them can be
seen and heard along the park roads, around the lake and its attendant stream, and on the hillsides.

Typical breeding birds are the Turkey Vulture; Cooper's, Red-
tailed, and Broad-winged hawks; American Kestrel; Ruffed Grouse;
Northern Bobwhite; Yellow-billed and Black-billed cuckoos; Eastern
Screech, Great Horned, and Barred owls; Whip-poor-will; Ruby-
throated Hummingbird; Belted Kingfisher; Pileated, Red-bellied, and
Red-headed woodpeckers; Eastern Kingbird; Great Crested Fly-
catcher; Eastern Phoebe; Acadian Flycatcher; Eastern Wood-Pewee;
Carolina Chickadee; Tufted Titmouse; White-breasted Nuthatch;
House and Carolina wrens; Northern Mockingbird; Gray Catbird;
Brown Thrasher; Wood Thrush; Eastern Bluebird; Blue-gray Gnat-
catcher; Cedar Waxwing; and White-eyed, Yellow-throated, Red-eyed,
and Warbling vireos.

Warblers that nest are the Black-and-White, Worm-eating, Blue-
winged, Northern Parula, Yellow, Cerulean, Yellow-throated, Pine,
Prairie, Ovenbird, Louisiana Waterthrush, Kentucky, Common Yellowthroat, Yellow-breasted Chat, Hooded, and American Redstart.

Other breeders include the Orchard and Northern orioles, Scarlet and Summer tanagers, Indigo Bunting, American Goldfinch,
Rufous-sided Towhee, and Field and Song sparrows.

In nearby farmland look for Bobolinks, Eastern Meadowlarks,
and Grasshopper and Henslow's sparrows. Wintering birds, in addition to resident species, frequently include the Yellow-bellied Sap-

sucker, Red-breasted Nuthatch, Black-capped Chickadee, Brown Creeper, Golden-crowned and Ruby-crowned (rare) kinglets, Yellow-rumped Warbler, Pine Siskin, Red and White-winged crossbills (rare and erratic), Dark-eyed Junco, and American Tree, Field, White-crowned, White-throated, and Song sparrows.

Tarlton Cross Mound   *Southeast of Circleville, take Ohio 159 to the village of Tarlton; turn west and go several blocks to Redding Street (County Road 12); turn north and go half a mile to the entrance on the left side of the road. (Map F–50)*

This pleasant 16-acre tract is the site of an unusual cross-shaped Hopewell Indian ceremonial earthwork. A footbridge crosses a small stream and one trail leads to the mound; others meander through the oak-maple woods. Birds present in the spring and summer are the Yellow-billed Cuckoo, Common Flicker, Great Crested and Acadian flycatchers, Eastern Wood-Pewee, Blue Jay, Tufted Titmouse, White-breasted Nuthatch, Wood Thrush, Blue-gray Gnatcatcher, Yellow-throated and Red-eyed vireos, Yellow Warbler, Ovenbird, Louisiana Waterthrush, Kentucky Warbler, American Redstart, Scarlet Tanager, Northern Cardinal, and Rufous-sided Towhee.

In the sycamores along the creek, look for a pair or two of Yellow-throated Warblers. In the brushy areas along the creek and around the perimeter of the small park, there are House Wrens, Gray Catbirds, Yellow-breasted Chats, Indigo Buntings, American Goldfinches, and Chipping Sparrows. On the far western side of the woods is a shallow gully with a few sycamores, willows, cottonwoods, and shrub-dotted upland. Here Brown Thrashers, White-eyed Vireos, Prairie Warblers, and Field Sparrows can be found.

Trillium Trails   *See Winton Woods.*

Tycoon Lake State Wildlife Area   *Take Ohio 554 in Gallia County several miles northeast of Rio Grande to the access road on the left. (Map F–51)*

The lake and attendant marsh, woodland, brushy areas, fields, and surrounding farmland provide mixed habitats for an abundance of diversified bird species.

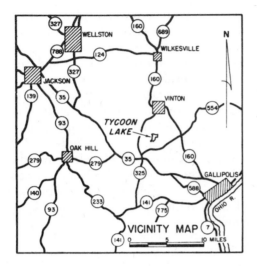

Green-backed Herons, Wood Ducks, migrant Soras, Solitary and Spotted sandpipers, and Common Snipe inhabit the marsh. Red-tailed Hawks nest nearby. Ruffed Grouse are sometimes encountered; the Northern Bobwhite was plentiful before 1976 and is making a comeback. Some of the frequently found breeding birds are the Yellow-billed Cuckoo, Barred Owl, Whip-poor-will, Ruby-throated Hummingbird, Pileated Woodpecker, Willow Flycatcher, Northern Mockingbird, Wood Thrush, Eastern Bluebird, Cedar Waxwing, Kentucky and Hooded warblers, Scarlet and Summer tanagers, Rufous-sided Towhee, and the possibility of the rare Bachman's Sparrow.

Vesuvius, Lake   *See Dean State Forest.*

Veto Lake State Wildlife Area   *On Ohio 339 about eight miles*
                                      northwest of Belpre in Washington
                                               County. (Map F–52)

Mallards, Blue-winged Teals, American Wigeons, Northern Shovelers, Redheads, Ring-necked Ducks, and Lesser Scaups are typical of the waterfowl attracted in spring to this 160-acre lake set in a tract of mixed hardwoods. In April, all of the swallows seen in Ohio can be found skimming over the water and, by the end of the month, the surrounding woods and countryside resound with the songs of a multitude of newly arrived birds. Look for Eastern Kingbirds; Swainson's Thrushes; Ruby-crowned Kinglets; Red-eyed Vireos; Blue-winged, Tennessee, Nashville, Magnolia, Yellow-rumped, Blackburnian, and

Wilson's warblers; and White-crowned and White-throated sparrows. Lincoln's Sparrows lurk in brushy areas, and an occasional Swamp Sparrow can be flushed from wet tangles. On big migration days in May, Orchard and Northern orioles, Scarlet and Summer tanagers, and Rose-breasted Grosbeaks are abundant.

Marshy spots along the lake shore attract Great Blue and Green-backed herons, and occasional shorebirds such as the Greater and Lesser yellowlegs, Solitary and Spotted sandpipers, and Common Snipe. Breeding birds commonly present are the Red-tailed Hawk, Northern Bobwhite, Black-billed Cuckoo, Red-bellied Woodpecker, Eastern Phoebe, Willow Flycatcher, Barn Swallow, House Wren, Eastern Bluebird, Yellow-throated Vireo, Yellow Warbler, Common Yellowthroat, Yellow-breasted Chat, Summer Tanager, Indigo Bunting, and Field and Song sparrows.

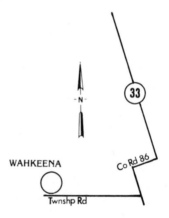

Wahkeena State Memorial

Take U.S. 33 six miles south from Lancaster and turn right onto County Road 86, then left onto Pumping Station Road and go about two miles to the entrance.
(Map F–53)

Mr. and Mrs. Frank Warner bequeathed this 150 acres of wooded hills, a small lake, and lodge to the Ohio Historical Society to be used as an outdoor nature laboratory. Black Hand sandstone outcroppings provide a scenic backdrop to many of the trails. Native trees include hemlock, pitch, scrub, and white pines, flowering dogwood, redbud, common alder, chestnut, black walnut, tulip, black cherry, mocker-nut hickory, shingle, pin, rock chestnut, and white oaks, sassafras, red maple, sourwood, red elm, sweet birch, bigtooth aspen, white ash, black locust, American beech, and ironwood.

Wahkeena is a delightful place to study spring wildflowers. A few of the many to be found are creeping phlox, fire-pink, wild columbine, bluebells, bluets, Jacob's ladder, long-spurred violet, common periwinkle, wild cranesbill, speedwell, swamp buttercup, hairy Solomon's seal, kidney-leaf crowfoot, marsh marigold, spring avens, bloodroot, bulbous bitter cress, false Solomon's seal, large-flowered trillium, May-apple, rue anemone, spring beauty, striped white violet, wild strawberry, showy orchis, and pink lady's slipper.

Rhododendron and mountain laurel are plentiful, and the cool, wooded hillsides and rocky damp spots provide fine habitat for many species of ferns, among them the ostrich, Christmas, wood, marginal shield, fragile, common polypody, ebony spleenwort, interrupted, sensitive, cinnamon, upland lady, rattlesnake, marsh, broad beech, maidenhair, silvery spleenwort, New York, evergreen wood, bulblet, blunt-lobed woodsia, and water clover, or pepperwort.

There are birds aplenty, too. A pair of Wood Ducks nest every year in a box at the northeastern end of the lake. Pied-billed Grebes, Mallards, Blue-winged Teals, and Northern Shovelers sometimes show up; a pair of Spotted Sandpipers sometimes nest somewhere nearby, and Belted Kingfishers are resident as long as the water is open. Most years, a pair of Green-backed Herons nest in the trees near the lake.

Red-tailed Hawks are seen year-round and, in summer, a pair of Broad-winged Hawks are frequently noted soaring overhead. During spring and fall migrations, a full spectrum of flycatchers, thrushes, vireos, warblers, orioles, tanagers, and finches are sometimes present after a big migration wave and they can be found in the trees and shrubbery about the lawn and in thickets and willows around the lake. The lake is also a favorite feeding place for groups of swallows, transients, and summer residents.

Nesting species readily seen and heard around the lodge and lake include the Ruby-throated Hummingbird, Common Flicker, Downy Woodpecker, Eastern Phoebe, Blue Jay, Carolina Chickadee, Tufted Titmouse, White-breasted Nuthatch, Carolina Wren, Gray Catbird, Brown Thrasher, American Robin, Blue-gray Gnatcatcher, Cedar Waxwing, White-eyed and Warbling vireos, Blue-winged and Yellow-throated warblers, Common Yellowthroat, Yellow-breasted Chat, Northern Oriole, Summer Tanager, Northern Cardinal, Indigo Bunting, American Goldfinch, and Song Sparrow.

Birds that usually nest in the deeper woods are the Ruffed Grouse, Eastern Screech and Barred owls, Red-bellied and Hairy woodpeckers; Great Crested and Acadian flycatchers, Eastern Wood-Pewee, Wood Thrush, Yellow-throated and Red-eyed vireos, Black-and-White, Worm-eating, and Cerulean warblers, Ovenbird, Louisiana Water-thrush, Kentucky and Hooded warblers, American Redstart, Scarlet Tanager, and Rufous-sided Towhee.

Hiking along the trails at Wahkeena is invigorating at any time of the year, and winter is no exception. An occasional Pileated Wood-pecker is sometimes heard or seen flying across a clearing; Yellow-bellied Sapsuckers and Hairy Woodpeckers are frequently present, and Black-capped Chickadees, Red-breasted Nuthatches, Pine Sis-kins, Dark-eyed Juncos, and White-throated Sparrows join their resi-dent compatriots at the feeders around the lodge.

Winton Woods (Greenbelt Nature Preserves, Newberry Wildlife Sanctuary, Spring Beauty Dell and Trillium Trails)

From I-275 north of Cincinnati, exit south onto Winton Road. (Map E–54)

Located on the edge of the municipality of Greenhills, this series of parks and nature preserves embraces some 2,000 acres. Newberry Wildlife Sanctuary can be reached by following Springdale Road west from U.S. 27 and proceeding northwest to Bhreh and Sheits roads. Spring Beauty Dell can be reached from Winton Road. Trillium Trails is immediately east of Winton Woods.

Red-tailed Hawks, Eastern Screech, Great Horned, and Barred owls, Pileated Woodpeckers, and many songbirds nest, and large numbers of migrating spring warblers can be found in late April and May.

Wildflowers in the various habitats include goldenseal, Jack-in-the-pulpit, Indian pipe, Dutchman's breeches, nodding trillium, Virginia bluebell, yellow trout lily, bloodwort, and Solomon's seal. Among the many animals that are found in the area are white-tailed deer, red fox, woodchuck, mink, muskrat, raccoon, opossum, and red, gray, and flying squirrels.

Wolf Creek Wildlife Area

Both Ohio 78 and Ohio 555 in Morgan County lead to the area, which is just south and east of Ringold. (Map F–55)

The rolling terrain of this 3,500-acre scenic area combines forests, pastures, cropland, fallow fields, and brushy stream edges, providing a rich ecological mix for a diversity of birdlife. A three-tier nine-acre lake just off Ohio 78 near County Road 13 attracts small numbers of waterbirds.

In areas of scrubby growth, forest and stream edges, from late April through most of the summer, look for these nesting birds: Northern Bobwhite, Eastern Kingbird, Eastern Phoebe, Horned Lark, Northern Rough-winged, Barn, and Cliff swallows, Northern Mockingbird, White-eyed and Warbling vireos, Blue-winged, Yellow, and Prairie warblers, Common Yellowthroat, Yellow-breasted Chat, Orchard and Northern orioles, Summer Tanager, and Indigo Bunting.

Species nesting in wooded situations include the Cooper's and Red-tailed hawks, Ruffed Grouse, American Woodcock, Yellow-billed Cuckoo, Eastern Screech and Great Horned owls, Whip-poor-will, Pileated Woodpecker, Great Crested Flycatcher, Wood Thrush, Yellow-throated Vireo, Cerulean Warbler, Louisiana Waterthrush, Kentucky Warbler, American Redstart, and Scarlet Tanager.

In winter, a number of half-hardy species—American Robin, Eastern Bluebird, Yellow-rumped Warbler, Eastern Meadowlark, Purple Finch, American Goldfinch, Rufous-sided Towhee, and Field, White-crowned, White-throated, Swamp, and Song sparrows—are frequently encountered.

Yellow Creek State Forest   *On Ohio 39 in southern Columbiana*
County about ten miles east of
Salineville. (G–56)

Hemlocks, pitch pines, and red cedars shade the deep ravines of this 756-acre retreat, while oaks, tulip trees, and maples clothe the upland hills. Ruffed Grouse and Whip-poor-wills are found in the woods; Great Horned Owls occur, and the Long-eared Owl has been known to nest nearby. The Sharp-shinned Hawk is a rare breeding bird, and there is a record of the Brown Creeper nesting in the vicinity. Warblers that nest are the Black-and-White, Worm-eating, Yellow, Cerulean, Ovenbird, Louisiana Waterthrush, Kentucky, Common Yellowthroat, Yellow-breasted Chat, and Hooded.

PART IV

The Birds of Ohio

THERE FOLLOWS an annotated list of every species of bird known to have occurred in Ohio. Of these, 196 have at one time nested in the state; 192 are migrants or visitors and include rarities beyond their normal ranges. Twenty-four of the latter are considered hypothetical either because there is no specimen or photograph or because the bird in question was not observed and documented by at least three veteran birders. Nevertheless, the hypothetical records are important and—noted as such—they are included in the general check-list. In addition, seven species have been extirpated from Ohio, three of which are extinct; two forms are hybrids, and 18 species are considered exotics—most likely escapes from aviaries or the cages of bird fanciers.

A total, then of 413 species may be considered the number recorded in historical times in Ohio, 390 of which have been recorded and properly documented as wild birds occurring within the borders of the state in this century.

The species accounts that follow are in accord with the sequence and nomenclature of the American Ornithologists' Union Check-List of North American Birds, Sixth Edition (1983). A number of name changes have been incorporated into this work in accordance with the new A.O.U. designations. They are

Former Name	*Present Name*
American Flamingo	Greater Flamingo
Whistling Swan	Tundra Swan
Fulvous Tree Duck	Fulvous Whistling-Duck
Common Pintail	Northern Pintail
Common Bobwhite	Northern Bobwhite
Common Gallinule	Common Moorhen
Northern Phalarope	Red-necked Phalarope
European Woodcock	Eurasian Woodcock
Greater Black-backed Gull	Great Black-backed Gull
Black-headed Gull	Common Black-headed Gull
Little Tern	Least Tern
Common Screech Owl	Eastern Screech Owl
Saw-whet Owl	Northern Saw-whet Owl
Black-backed Three-toed Woodpecker	Black-backed Woodpecker
Eastern Pewee	Eastern Wood-Pewee

Rough-winged Swallow	Northern Rough-winged Swallow
Northern Raven	Common Raven
Northern Parula Warbler	Northern Parula
Gray-crowned, Black, and	
Brown-capped Rosy Finch	Rosy Finch
Northern Junco, or Slate-colored	
Junco	Dark-eyed Junco

An attempt has been made to define the various terms of abundance used in the annotated list. The terms, of course, are arbitrary and can only serve as guides to the relative abundance of given species. There are also bound to be many variables because of the constant changes in bird populations, movement, the progression of the seasons, weather, time of day, ease or difficulty of observation, and the skills and patience of the individual birder.

The following table has been devised to at least provide some indication of the numerical status of each species. The first seven categories are a guide to probable population densities at a particular time of year. A "locality" can be defined as an ecologically appropriate habitat for a given species which can be investigated on foot and by car in a time period of several hours. The final three categories refer to the statewide historical status of a given species.

Very abundant	over 1000 per day per locality (often in large flocks)
Abundant	201–1000 per day per locality
Very common	51–200 per day per locality
Common	21–50 per day per locality
Fairly common	7–20 per day per locality
Uncommon	1–6 per day per locality
Rare	1–6 per season
Very rare	over 25 records, but very infrequent
Casual	11–24 records
Accidental	1–10 records

The upper-case letters in parentheses that follow the species write-ups represent average periods of migration and residence and are intended to supplement other information already provided. These indicators are omitted in the case of vagrants and other rare species or where this information has already been discussed.

- R   Resident (year-round)
- WR   Winter Resident or visitor (October-November through March-April)
- SR   Summer Resident (variable, usually from April-May until September-October)

LSV   Late Summer Visitor (July through September)
ESM   Early Spring Migrant (March through April)
SM   Spring Migrant (April through May)
LSM   Late Spring Migrant (mid-May to mid-June)
EFM   Early Fall Migrant (July to September-October-November)
FM   Fall Migrant (mid-August to mid-October)
LFM   Late Fall Migrant (October to early January)
I   Irregular

A brief glossary of terms used in the annotated list, plus an explanation or two, are as follows:

Accidental or vagrant	A species beyond its normal range.
Extinct	A species that does not survive anywhere.
Extirpated	A species that may occur elsewhere, but is no longer found in Ohio.
Exotic	An individual of a species not native to Ohio that has escaped from a zoo, aviary, or the cage of a bird fancier. Sometimes referred to as an escape.
Migrant	Species that regularly shift populations, usually to the north or northwest in spring, to the south or southeast in fall, frequently for great distances.
Resident	A species that maintains a permanent population in Ohio although there may be largely undetected shifts in population, i.e., Blue Jays and Robins that nest in Ohio may move farther south in winter; others from Michigan and Canada may move into Ohio.
Summer or winter resident	The first is a species that includes Ohio within its breeding range, migrates into and out of the state in the spring and fall, and is largely absent in the winter. The second is a species such as the American Tree Sparrow which winters in Ohio, migrates south into the state in the fall and north again in spring.

Abbreviations used are as follows:

CBC   Refers to the Christmas Bird Counts made by the National Audubon Society. In each, volunteers record the kinds and numbers of birds seen in one day in an area roughly 15 miles in diameter. Counts are usually done sometime between December 18 and January 2. Over 1350 CBCs a year are now made in North America, fifty some of them in Ohio by over 1300 observers.

et al. Refers to additional observers.

fide Means "in faith" or on the authority of, usually used in referring to details of an observation related to a veteran ornithologist.

m. obs. Means many observers.

Max. Maximum numbers of individuals observed.

NWR National Wildlife Refuge, used exclusively to refer to the Ottawa National Wildlife Refuge, a complex of marshes between Port Clinton and Toledo. The headquarters is immediately west of Crane Creek State Park, which embraces Magee Marsh.

Obs. u. Observer unknown.

Whenever possible, credit has been given for records cited, although in some cases it was impossible to ascertain who initially discovered and identified a particular bird or birds. The author's records are designated by (T). Birds that have nested in Ohio are marked by an asterisk.

One final thought. If the reader aspires to a serious study of birds, a list should be kept of each trip afield and the number of individuals of each species observed should be counted or carefully estimated. Records are virtually useless without this vital information. Field notes regarding behavior, song, plumage, and other features of a bird's appearance such as eye, bill, and leg color are essential to the proper documentation of a rare species. Additional data, such as association with other bird species, habitat, weather conditions, and personal impressions add to the value of a journal.

ORDER GAVIIFORMES

Family Gaviidae: Loons

☐ **Red-throated Loon**, *Gavia stellata*. Rare migrant and winter visitor on lakes, quarries, and deep rivers. Seldom more than two seen at one time.

☐ **Arctic Loon**, *Gavia arctica*. Accidental-hypothetical. One sight record of an individual 8–29 November 1970 at Mehldahl Dam in Clermont County (Randle, Honshopp).

☐ **Common Loon**, *Gavia immer.* Uncommon migrant, infrequently very common to abundant, especially in late fall on Lake Erie from Huron east to Mentor. Rare winter visitor and summer straggler. *Max.:* 600, 23 November 1978 offshore at Cleveland (T); 300 to 500, 15 November 1972 at Buckeye Lake (M. Trautman); and 250, 11 November 1979 at Alum Creek Reservoir (Peterjohn). (SM/ISR/FM/IWR)

ORDER PODICIPEDIFORMES

Family Podicipedidae: Grebes

☐ ***Pied-billed Grebe**, *Podilymbus podiceps.* Rare to common migrant and rare to fairly common winter straggler. Rare nesting bird in inland marshes; uncommon to fairly common in Lake Erie marshes. *Max.:* 50, 7 September 1947 in the Cedar Point Marsh, Lucas County (Campbell).

☐ **Horned Grebe**, *Podiceps auritus.* Rare to common migrant on lakes, quarries, and deep rivers. Sometimes very common along eastern Lake Erie, less often inland. On 26 November 1978, 693 were recorded at Cleveland, 958 were there 18 November 1979 (Klamm), and 800 were at Mosquito Creek Reservoir 16 April 1977 (C. Johnson). Rare in winter, accidental in summer. (ESM/LFM)

☐ **Red-necked Grebe**, *Podiceps grisegena.* Rare migrant and very rare winter visitor. Seldom more than two seen at one time, but six were on a borrow pit 5 November 1976 in Columbus (Counts).

☐ **Eared Grebe**, *Podiceps nigricollis.* Rare western visitor in spring, very rare in fall and winter. Three were seen 20 March 1972 on a quarry near Columbus (T).

☐ **Western Grebe**, *Aechmophorus occidentalis.* Casual visitor in spring and fall. Records on hand are: one collected 30 October 1913 in Mahoning County (*fide* Forcyce); one, 10 May 1958 at Buckeye Lake, Licking County (T); two, 30 March to 5 April 1959 at Pippin Lake, Portage County (m. obs.); one, 25 April to 13 May 1964 on a quarry at Columbus (E. S. Thomas); and one, 8–12 April 1975 at Clear Fork Reservoir, Richland County (R. Trautman, J. Herman).

ORDER PROCELLARIIFORMES

Family Procellariidae: Shearwaters and Fulmars

☐ **Black-capped Petrel**, *Pterodroma hasitata*. Accidental. One record of an individual found dead in Hamilton County, 5 October 1898 (Lindahl).

☐ **Sooty Shearwater**, *Puffinus griseus*. Accidental-hypothetical. One record of a bird on the Portage River south of Port Clinton, 13 November 1954 (Van Camp, Wirt).

Family Hydrobatidae: Storm Petrels

☐ **Wilson's Storm-Petrel**, *Oceanites oceanicus*. Accidental-hypothetical. One record of an individual at Lake St. Marys in 1907 (Henninger).

☐ **Leach's Storm-Petrel**, *Oceanodroma leucorhoa*. Accidental. One record of an individual found dead 16 May 1929 in Montgomery County (Blincoe).

ORDER PELECANIFORMES

Family Sulidae: Boobies and Gannets

☐ **Northern Gannet**, *Morus bassanus*. Very rare offshore migrant along Lake Erie, most often in November and December, from Huron east. One was seen 6 December 1980 in Maumee Bay (Kemp). *Max.:* One to five seen almost daily near the Cleveland Illuminating Plant between 6 December 1947 and 13 January 1948 (m. obs.).

Family Pelecanidae: Pelicans

☐ **American White Pelican**, *Pelicanus erythrorhynchos*. Very rare spring, summer, and fall visitor on lakes and ponds. Usually single individuals, but there is a record of six birds at Buckeye Lake 21 June 1933 (E. Prior) and four were seen during the fall of 1982 at the Oregon Power Plant and Little Cedar Point (m. obs.).

☐ **Brown Pelican**, *Pelecanus occidentalis*. Accidental-hypothetical. An individual on the Ohio River near Chilo, about 25 miles upstream from Cincinnati during the summer of 1963 (A. Merganthaler, *fide* A. Wiseman).

Family Phalacrocoracidae: Cormorants

☐ *Double-crested Cormorant*, *Phalacrocorax auritus*. Rare to uncommon migrant on lakes and quarries; rare winter visitor and summer straggler. *Max.:* 64, 21 October 1945 at Put-in-Bay, Ottawa County (C. Walker); 12, 12 May 1975 at Cincinnati (Perbix, A. Stamm); and 24, 13 April 1980 at Hudson, Summit County (Rosche). Formerly nested. (SM/LFM)

Family Anhingidae: Darters

☐ **Anhinga**, *Anhinga anhinga*. Accidental. An individual collected in Washington County in November 1885 (Jones).

Family Fregatidae: Frigatebirds

☐ **Magnificent Frigatebird**, *Fregata magnificens*. Accidental. Three records: one shot in Fairfield County, 1880 (*fide* Davie); one observed in Hamilton County, 29 September 1967, and one discovered at Clearfork Reservoir, Richland County, 30 September 1967 (T. Nye, collected by M. Trautman).

ORDER CICONIIFORMES

Family Ardeidae: Herons and Bitterns

☐ *American Bittern*, *Botaurus lentiginosus*. Rare to uncommon migrant and summer resident known to breed in 38 counties in the northern two-thirds of the state. *Max.:* 35 in the marshes of Lucas County, 4 August 1929 (Campbell). Very rare in winter. (SM/SR/FM)

☐ *Least Bittern*, *Ixobrychus exilis*. Locally rare to uncommon transient and summer resident known to nest in 40 counties, most commonly in the Lake Erie marshes. Not known as a breeding bird in 20 southeastern counties and large portions of western and northwestern Ohio. *Max.:* Nine, 27 June 1981 in Little Cedar Point Marsh (Counts, Alexander). (SM/SR/FM)

☐ *Great Blue Heron*, *Ardea herodias*. Uncommon to fairly common migrant and late summer wanderer. Very common in Lake Erie marshes from March to November, less numerous later depending on the severity of the winter. Nests locally in colonies of assorted sizes, from large ones at West Sister Island and Winous Point Marsh to smaller ones scattered over many of the unglaciated counties of the state. *Max.:* 595, 28 June 1976 in Ottawa County (Van Camp); and about 800, 9 April 1971 at Winous Point (T). (ESM/SR/EFM/WR)

☐ ***Great Egret**, *Casmerodius albus.* Locally rare to uncommon migrant and summer visitor, except in the Lake Erie marshes where it is very common to abundant from March to mid-October. Nests on West Sister Island and, sparingly, in marshes on the mainland. Casual in winter. *Max.:* 466, 21 September 1978 in the Ottawa-Magee complex of marshes (Fry). (SM/SR/FM)

☐ **Snowy Egret**, *Egretta thula.* Very rare transient and summer visitor. Somewhat more frequent in northern Ohio marshes. *Max.:* four, 29 September 1941 at Lake St. Marys (Clark); and eight at Ottawa NWR in late July 1982 (m. obs.).

☐ **Little Blue Heron**, *Egretta caerulea.* Rare transient and late summer nomad. An invasion of this species into Ohio during the late summer of 1930 resulted in the largest numbers ever recorded for the state: 85 on 9 and 10 August in the marshes of Lucas County (Campbell) and 77 at Buckeye Lake, Licking County, on 9 August (Trautman). (SM/EFM)

☐ **Tricolored Heron**, *Egretta tricolor.* Casual transient and summer visitor. Records include individuals seen 30 May 1971 at Sandusky Bay (Hammond), 16 May 1976 in the Cleveland area (Mahan), 23 May to 2 July 1979 at the Ottawa National Wildlife Refuge (Pogacnik), and 28 to 30 April 1981 at Pickerington Pond, Fairfield and Franklin counties (J. Fry).

☐ ***Cattle Egret**, *Bubulcus ibis.* First occurred in Ohio during the early 60s. It is now a locally rare to common migrant and summer visitor, especially in the marshes of Ottawa and Lucas counties. The first breeding record for the state was verified in 1978 when 20 nests were found in the Little Cedar Point section of the Ottawa National Wildlife Refuge. *Max.:* 51 at the above location 24 September 1978 (Peterjohn). (SM/SR/FM)

☐ ***Green-backed Heron**, *Butorides striatus.* Former name: Green Heron. Uncommon to fairly common migrant and summer resident nesting in almost every county. Especially numerous locally in late summer.

Black-crowned and Yellow-crowned Night Herons

Casual in winter. *Max.:* 31, 30 August 1974 at Hoover Reservoir, Delaware County (T). (SM/SR/EFM)

☐ ***Black-crowned Night Heron**, Nycticorax nycticorax.* Rare to fairly common migrant and summer visitor. Uncommon to common in Lake Erie marshes in summer. Less numerous than formerly. Nesting colonies exist on West Sister and North Bass islands, and small numbers probably nest in Great Blue Heron colonies in the larger marshes. Known to nest in 17 counties in central, southwest, and northwest Ohio. Sometimes found in winter. *Max.:* 2,000, 30 May 1942 at a heronry on West Sister Island (Campbell), and 205, 5 August 1979 at Ottawa NWR (Van Camp).

☐ ***Yellow-crowned Night Heron**, Nycticorax violaceus.* Locally rare to very rare migrant and summer resident. A few individuals are seen each year in the northern tier of counties; a pair nested in the Rocky River Valley, Cuyahoga County, in 1978 (Klamm). Other nesting records for Paulding, Logan, Montgomery, and Hamilton counties. Probably breeds most commonly along the Scioto River in Franklin and Delaware counties where eight or ten pairs nest annually. (SM/SR/FM)

Family Threskiornithidae: Ibises and Spoonbills

☐ **White Ibis**, *Eudocimus albus*. Accidental. An immature bird was present from 20 to 31 August 1964 at the Englewood Dam, Montgomery County. During its visit, it was seen and photographed by many persons. (Blincoe).

☐ **Glossy Ibis**, *Plegadis falcinellus*. Very rare migrant, most records from northern Ohio. *Max.:* 26, 21 April to 23 May 1962 at Magee Marsh (Campbell *et al.*), and 5 on 14 May 1973 at Cleveland's Burke Lakefront Airport (Klamm). Increasing populations and range expansions on the East Coast will probably result in more frequent sightings in Ohio.

☐ **White-faced Ibis**, *Plegadis chihi*. Accidental. One collected 1 October 1949 in Brown County (Kemsies, Randle) and a few sight records constitute the only occurrences. This and the preceding species are very difficult to separate in the field; notes should be taken of all field marks, especially eye, mandible, and leg color.

Family Ciconiidae: Storks

☐ **Wood Stork**, *Mycteria americana*. Accidental. Seven records: a young male collected near Cleveland in 1879 (Chubb); another taken near Cleveland in September 1981 (J. Bole); one captured alive by two boys at Todd's Fork near Wilmington, Clinton County, 23 July 1909; one at Gordon Park in Cleveland, July 1914 (J. Bole, Jr.); one captured at the same location 5 May 1946 (Hazard); two which flew into a field in Ashtabula County on 1 July 1955 and remained for 24 hours were photographed (A. Sheehan *et al.*), and a sight record of 13 in a tree on the east bank of the Maumee River at its mouth on 1 November 1964 (Crites, *fide* Campbell).

ORDER ANSERIFORMES

Family Anatidae: Swans, Geese, and Ducks

☐ **Fulvous Whistling-Duck**, *Dendrocygna bicolor*. Accidental, erratic visitor. Records on hand are:
  19 October 1962: one in the Metzger Marsh, Lucas County (L. Shafer).
  20 October 1962: three shot from a flock of nine in Ottawa County.

17 November 1963: one in a Sandusky County marsh (O. Davies).

21 November 1963: six near Ashland, Ashland County (B. Kahl).

12–13 April 1964: one near Amherst, Lorain County (Dolbear).

25 June 1967: two at Killdeer Plains Wildlife Area, Wyandot County (obs. u.).

24 November 1969: 12 seen flying over Buckeye Lake, Licking County (M. Trautman).

11 April 1974: four in Butler County (D. Osborne, M. Peters).

24–25 April 1975: nine near Carey, Wyandot County (A. Claugus).

5 April 1979: three at Pickerington Pond, Franklin County (C. Franz).

☐ **Tundra Swan**, *Olor columbianus*. Former name: Whistling Swan. Rare to fairly common migrant, but common to abundant in the Lake Erie marshes and flights over northeastern Ohio in March and November. A few are seen most winters. *Max.:* 5500, 15 March 1962 in Ottawa and Lucas counties (Bednarik, Hanson); 5000, 30 March 1930 in the Cedar Point Marsh (Campbell). Flocks totaling 1100 birds passed over Cleveland 22 November 1975 (Klamm). (ESM/LFM)

☐ **Trumpeter Swan**, *Cygnus buccinator*. Extirpated in this century. One collected out of four individuals on the Ohio River near Cincinnati, December 1876 (*fide* Lanfdon), and one collected 20 April 1891 at Lorain (McCormick, *fide* L. Jones).

☐ **Mute Swan**, *Cygnus olor*. This Eurasian species was first introduced into this country in southern New York state and eastern Long Island in 1910 and 1912. In the years since then it has become well established up and down the eastern seaboard and during the past 20 years has become a rare visitor to Ohio and other midwestern states. Most frequently seen in winter in the northern counties, but there are records throughout the state for almost every month. *Max.:* four, 29 December 1974 on the Logan CBC.

☐ **Greater White-fronted Goose**, *Anser albifrons*. This western species is a rare migrant sometimes occurring in fairly large flocks. Most often recorded near Lake Erie, but also in Franklin, Pickaway, Wyandot, Hamilton, Delaware, Mercer, Licking, and Wayne counties. Several winter records. *Max.:* 42, 30 March 1932 near Painesville, Lake County (Hadeler); 100, 11 November 1962 in flight over Kirtland Hills, Lake County (obs. u.); and 18, 26 October 1949 feeding in a cornfield in Kirtland Hills (Scheele).

☐ **Snow Goose**, *Chen caerulescens*. Rare to fairly common fall migrant, but during infrequent large flights it is abundant to very abundant.

Most consistently found in the marshes of Ottawa and Lucas counties. Rare to uncommon in spring. Most individuals seen in Ohio are the dark white-headed phase "Blue" goose. *Max.:* estimated 10,000 flying over Columbus in October 1939 (Hicks); 3,207 in Lucas County in November 1948 (Campbell); 620 flying over Columbus on 21 October 1969 (T), and 170 at Hoover Reservoir, Delaware County, 28 October 1965 (T).

Ross' Goose, *Chen rossii.* Accidental. One record: an individual feeding with Canada and Snow geese from 18 to 23 March 1982 in and around the Ottawa NWR (Pogacnik, Windnagel, *et al.*)

☐ **Brant**, *Branta bernicla.* Rare migrant; most records along Lake Erie. *Max.:* 36 feeding in a wet meadow 9 March 1924 near Painesville (Williams); 27 at Walnut Beach, Ashtabula County, 20 to 25 May 1956 (Savage), and 19 on the Firelands CBC (Erie and Huron counties) 19 December 1976.

☐ ***Canada Goose**, *Branta canadensis.* Fairly common to abundant migrant and winter resident where there is open water; very abundant at such times—as well as being an established breeding bird—in the Lake Erie marshes, Lake St. Marys, and Killdeer Plains, in addition to such large bodies of water as Mosquito Creek Lake. Small numbers, mostly individual pairs, sometimes attempt nesting in other locations. *Max.:* 9600 on 15 October 1964 at Killdeer Plains (M. Trautman); 10,000 on 26 December 1971 on the Ottawa NWR CBC, and 12,678 on 23 December 1979 on the Trumbull County CBC. (ESM/SR/LFM)

☐ ***Wood Duck**, *Aix sponsa.* Uncommon to fairly common migrant and nesting bird widespread through the state. Occasional concentrations in late summer and fall. Known to nest in 57 counties, but mostly absent from southwestern and east-central Ohio. *Max.:* 250, 11 September 1970 at Stage's Pond, Pickaway County (G. Warner). (EFM/SR/FM)

☐ ***Green-winged Teal**, *Anas crecca.* Uncommon to fairly common in migration except for larger concentrations in extensive marsh areas. Rare breeding bird in Ottawa and Lucas counties, and has been known to nest in Washington County. Sometimes winters in small numbers. *Max.:* 1,250, 23 November 1959 on Catawba Island, Ottawa County (M. Trautman). (ESM/FM)

☐ **Falcated Teal**, *Anas falcata.* Accidental–hypothetical. One was present on the Cleveland waterfront from 21 December 1963 to 1 January 1964 (J. Surman *et al.*).

☐ *American Black Duck*, *Anas rubripes*. Uncommon to fairly common except for local winter concentrations when it is sometimes abundant. Nests sparingly, mostly in northern Ohio. Less numerous in recent years. *Max.:* 16,715 on 1 January 1960, the Gypsum CBC. (ESM/SR/LFM/WR)

☐ *Mallard*, *Anas platyrhynchos*. Fairly common and widespread resident, locally abundant from October to March. Most numerous in the Lake Erie marshes. Nests primarily in the northern two-thirds of the state. *Max.:* 25,035 on 1 January 1960, the Gypsum CBC. (ESM/SR/LFM/WR)

☐ *Northern Pintail*, *Anas acuta*. Uncommon to common, except for local concentrations when it is sometimes more numerous. Nests rarely in Lake Erie marshes. Less numerous than formerly. *Max.:* 6,500, 27 November 1948, in Ottawa and Lucas counties (Campbell). (ESM/FM)

☐ *Blue-winged Teal*, *Anas discors*. Common migrant, sometimes abundant in refuges and along the marshy edges of reservoirs and lakes. Nests in 30 scattered counties from central Ohio north, plus a few records in Hamilton, Clermont, Butler, and Montgomery counties. Rare in winter. *Max.:* 930, 1 September 1975 in the marshes of western Lake Erie (T). (ESM/SR/EFM)

☐ Cinnamon Teal, *Anas cyanoptera.* Accidental. One collected 4 April 1895 in Fairfield County (Davie). At Lake St. Marys three records by Clark (1950, 1952, 1953), one by Sipe (1 July 1964), and another by Chambers (29 August 1964). At Magee Marsh one on 11 May 1980 (Fazio, Limes, Myer, T) and another on 5 October 1980 (*fide* Campbell).

☐ *Northern Shoveler*, *Anas clypeata*. Rare to fairly common migrant. Uncommon nesting bird in Ottawa, Lucas, Sandusky, and Erie counties. Has also been known to nest in Marion County. Rare in winter. *Max.:* 80, 14 April 1946 in the Little Cedar Point Marsh (Campbell). (ESM/FM)

☐ *Gadwall*, *Anas strepera*. Uncommon to locally very common migrant. Uncommon in winter. Rare to uncommon nesting bird in Lake Erie marshes. *Max.:* 200, 10 November 1948 in Ottawa and Lucas counties (Campbell). (ESM/LFM)

☐ Eurasian Wigeon, *Anas penelope*. Rare migrant with many records, mostly in spring.

☐ *American Wigeon*, *Anas americana*. Fairly common to very abundant in migration, more numerous locally in refuges and wildlife areas. Rare to uncommon in winter. A few nest in the Lake Erie marshes. *Max.:* 10,000 on 13 November 1948 at East Harbor, Ottawa County (Campbell). (ESM/LFM)

☐ ***Canvasback**, Aythya valisineria.* Uncommon to common migrant and winter resident; abundant locally on Lake Erie. Rare in summer. One breeding record for the state in Fairfield County. *Max.:* 10,206 ON 19 December 1976 on the Toledo CBC. (ESM/LFM/WR)

☐ ***Redhead**, Aythya americana.* Uncommon to common migrant, sometimes very common at favorite stopping places, but definitely declining in numbers over the past 20 years. A few pairs nest in the Ottawa County marshes. *Max.:* 2,000 at the Cleveland Municipal Power Plant in mid-February 1977 (Klamm). (ESM/LFM)

☐ **Ring-necked Duck**, *Aythya collaris.* Uncommon to formerly abundant, but now generally reduced in numbers except for infrequent concentrations. Uncommon in winter. *Max.:* 1200, 2 March 1975 on a quarry south of Columbus (T) (ESM/LFM).

☐ **Tufted Duck**, *Aythya fuligula.* Accidental. One record: an individual at Lorain 3–14 March 1980 (Tom LePage *et al.*).

☐ **Greater Scaup**, *Aythya marila.* Rare migrant and winter visitor, but regularly very common from Lorain east along Lake Erie in winter. Many inland records, usually of one or two birds. *Max.:* 3000, 22 December 1963, on the Lakewood CBC. (LFM/WR/ESM)

☐ ***Lesser Scaup**, Aythya affinis.* Uncommon to common in migration with occasional concentrations along Lake Erie and on some of the larger inland lakes. Uncommon in winter except locally along Lake Erie. Rare breeding bird in Lucas and Ottawa counties. Also known to have nested in Mercer, Franklin, and Carroll counties. *Max.:* 2500, 9 April 1971 at Bay View, Erie County (T). (ESM/LFM)

☐ **Common Eider**, *Somateria mollissima.* Very rare migrant and winter visitor along Lake Erie from Lorain east. However, an individual was seen in Maumee Bay on 12 October 1980 (*fide* Campbell).

☐ **King Eider**, *Somateria spectabilis.* Rare migrant and winter visitor along Lake Erie from Lorain east. Other records include one at the Hebron Fish Hatchery, Licking County, 25 May 1965 (T), and one shot by a hunter along the Ohio River near Cincinnati, 2 January 1971. *Max.:* five at Lorain Harbor, 22 December 1973 (Ward).

☐ **Harlequin Duck**, *Histrionicus histrionicus.* Accidental except along the Lake Erie shore from Lorain east where it is rare, but usually seen each winter. A male was seen 13 February 1949 on the Great Miami River near West Carrolton (B. Smith).

☐ **Oldsquaw**, *Clangula hyemalis*. Rare migrant and winter visitor; sometimes more plentiful along the Lake Erie shore east of Huron and on some of the larger lakes and reservoirs. *Max.:* 14, 28 December 1950 at Ashtabula (L. E. Hicks); 53, 15 April 1972 at La Due Reservoir, Geauga County (English). (ESM/LFM/WR)

☐ **Black Scoter**, *Melanitta nigra*. Rare to very rare migrant and winter visitor, slightly more numerous on Lake Erie. *Max.:* three, 18 April 1937 at Hinkley Lake, Medina County (F. Johnson, A. Williams); six, 30 October 1955 at Hoover Reservoir, Delaware County (M. Thomas); five, 5 December 1975 on the Mentor CBC; and four, 9 November 1977 at Hoover Reservoir (E. Limes). (ESM/LFM)

☐ **Surf Scoter**, *Melanitta perspicillata*. Rare to very rare migrant and winter visitor. *Max.:* 19, 5 November 1967 offshore at Cleveland (Klamm); six, 16 October 1975 at Findley Reservoir, Hancock County (B. Stehling); and four, 13 November 1969 at Hoover Reservoir, Delaware County (T). (ESM/LFM)

☐ **White-winged Scoter**, *Melanitta fusca*. Rare migrant and winter visitor, somewhat more numerous on Lake Erie. *Max.:* 13, 24 April 1977 on the Ohio River near Marietta (P. Murphy); nine, 19 October 1979 at Cleveland (Klamm); and 14, 7 December 1958 near Lakeside, Ottawa County (*fide* Campbell). (ESM/LFM/WR)

☐ **Common Goldeneye**, *Bucephala clangula*. Uncommon to common migrant and winter visitor. Concentrations sometimes encountered along Lake Erie and on the larger lakes and reservoirs. *Max.:* 1000, 28 February 1974 on the American Aggregates Company quarry at Columbus (T). (ESM/LFM/WR)

☐ **Barrow's Goldeneye**, *Bucephala islandica*. Accidental–hypothetical. Several 19th century records of the species being taken by hunters, and the following sight records: one at Holden Arboretum, Lake County, 24 March 1962 (obs. u.); one at the mouth of the Portage River at Port Clinton, 23 January 1966 (A. Claugus); two males near Cincinnati, 16 February 1967 (V. Watts, *fide* Wiseman), and one female in Lorain Harbor, 25 February 1967 (O. Davies).

☐ **Bufflehead**, *Bucephala albeola*. Uncommon to fairly common migrant. Rare to uncommon in winter. *Max.:* 300, 24 April 1967, on the Ohio River near Marietta (P. Murphy). (ESM/LFM)

☐ ***Hooded Merganser**, *Lophodytes cucullatus*. Uncommon to common migrant. In winter, rare to uncommon where there is open water. Nests sparingly in Ottawa and Lucas counties, and there are isolated breeding records for Mercer, Auglaize, Franklin, and Trumbull counties. *Max.:* 150, 27 November 1965 at Hoover Reservoir, Delaware County (T). (ESM/LFM)

☐ **Common Merganser**, *Mergus merganser*. Uncommon to common migrant inland; abundant in fall and early winter on Lake Erie from Cedar Point east. Present, but less common, later in winter throughout the entire state where there is open water. *Max.:* 2000, 18 November 1968 at Cedar Point (T); 2500, 1 January 1960 on the Gypsum CBC (counties on Sandusky Bay); and 9003, 23 December 1979 on the Ottawa NWR CBC. (ESM/LFM/WR)

☐ **Red-breasted Merganser**, *Mergus serrator*. Uncommon to common migrant inland; frequently very abundant in fall and early winter from Cedar Point east along Lake Erie. *Max.:* 250,000 on 12 November 1975, some rafted up, others flying east between Lorain and Cleveland (C. Dolbear, C. Ward); 250,000 on 19 November 1978 in the Huron area (J. Fry); and 75,000 on 24 November 1979 at Cleveland (Pogacnik). (SM/LFM)

☐ ***Ruddy Duck**, *Oxyura jamaicensis*. Uncommon to fairly common migrant inland; sometimes common to abundant along Lake Erie, including winter months when there is open water. *Max.:* 1100, 19 December 1971 on the Firelands CBC (Erie and Huron counties), and 5000, 5 November 1978 on Maumee Bay (E. Tramer). Isolated breeding records for Ottawa, Ashtabula, and Hamilton counties. Nonbreeding birds are sometimes found in summer. (ESM/LFM)

ORDER FALCONIFORMES

Family Cathartidae: American Vultures

☐ ***Black Vulture**, *Coragyps atratus*. Rare breeding bird in 14 southern counties and as far north as Licking and Fairfield counties. Frequently winters within its breeding range. Stragglers have been reported in Cleveland and Summit County. *Max.:* 90 wintered in a roost in northeast Licking County from December 1957 to March 1958 (C. Wagner). (ESM/SR/FM/WR)

☐ *Turkey Vulture, *Cathartes aura.* Locally uncommon to fairly common migrant—occasionally very common at a few spots along Lake Erie—and widespread summer resident, common to very common around roosting sites. Lawrence E. Hicks in the *Distribution of the Breeding Birds of Ohio,* Ohio Biological Survey Bulletin 32, 1935, states that he located 114 roosts and estimated 3650 birds for the state. *Max.:* 207 in migration 2 April 1980 at Magee Marsh (Pogacnik), and 279, 3 September 1975 at the Hoover Dam, Delaware County, roost (T). Frequent winter resident in southern third of state. (ESM/SR/FM)

Family Accipitridae: Kites, Hawks, and Harriers

☐ *Osprey, *Pandion haliaetus.* Widespread but rare migrant around lakes and rivers. Before 1900 nested rather regularly around the state, but the only breeding record for this century was at Lake St. Marys in 1913 (Henninger). Non-breeding birds sometimes found in summer. Several December records and one on 11 January 1978 in Columbus (Counts). *Max.:* five, 6 May 1977 at Magee Marsh (A. Adams). (SM/FM)

☐ American Swallow-tailed Kite, *Elanus forficatus.* Accidental–hypothetical. According to early ornithologists this species occurred in Ohio into the early 19th century and was "quite common" in Portage and Stark counties (Kirtland, 1838; Wheaton, 1882). Since that time thought to be extirpated from the state, but there is one recent sight record. An individual was observed on 26 May 1975 near Fremont, Sandusky County, and carefully documented by Ted Hilty.

☐ Mississippi Kite, *Ictinia misisippiensis.* Accidental–hypothetical. One possible record of an individual flying over Greenlawn Cemetery in Columbus on 13 May 1978 (F. Bader, L. Champney), and an immature bird observed 16 May 1982 in the Oak Openings, Lucas County (Kemp), and another immature, perhaps the same bird, the first week of June 1982 in Seneca County (Bartlett). This species should continue to be looked for since it now nests in southern Illinois and there are an increasing number of records for Indiana and western Kentucky.

☐ *Bald Eagle, *Haliaeetus leucocephalus.* Rare vagrant, usually seen near lakes and rivers, recorded throughout the state. About five pairs nest in Ottawa, Sandusky, and Erie counties. In 1980 these birds fledged three young plus one transplant. There are past breeding records for 16 additional counties, mostly in northern Ohio. *Max.:*

seven, 1 January 1960 on the Gypsum CBC; and four, 23 December 1979 on the Ottawa NWR CBC. (R)

☐ ***Northern Harrier**, *Circus cyaneus*. Rare to uncommon resident and winter visitor infrequently very common during local concentrations. Before 1950, it nested in 51 counties, but now it nests in less than half that number and in reduced numbers. *Max.:* 53, 27 December 1970 on the Cincinnati CBC; 75, 3 February 1974 at Killdeer Plains Wildlife Area, Wyandot County (J. Stahl); and 80, 28 December 1975 on the Kingston CBC (ESM/SR/LFM/WR)

☐ ***Sharp-shinned Hawk**, *Accipiter striatus*. Rare to uncommon migrant except at some points along Lake Erie where significant flights are sometimes observed. Has been known to nest in 50 counties, most often in unglaciated portions of the state, especially where gorges and mature hemlocks occur. *Max.:* 109, 26 April 1980 at Lorain (Pogacnik); 107, 27 April 1980 at Cleveland (Klamm); and 91, 6 April 1980 at Magee Marsh (Pogacnik). Rare in winter. (SM/SR/FM/WR)

☐ ***Cooper's Hawk**, *Accipiter cooperii*. Rare to uncommon migrant and resident apparently recovering from a 20-year population slump. Concentrations sometimes occur on good flight days along the shores of Lake Erie. It once nested rather commonly throughout the state but now nests most often in the forested hill counties of southern and eastern Ohio. Often found in winter. *Max.:* 65, 5 May 1946 at Bay Village, Cuyahoga County (*fide* A. Williams); and 211, 6 April 1980 in the Magee Marsh—Ottawa NWR area (Pogacnik). (ESM/SR/LFM/WR)

☐ **Northern Goshawk**, *Accipiter gentilis*. Rare migrant and winter visitor most often seen in northern Ohio. *Max.:* two, 17 December 1979 on the Cuyahoga Falls CBC, and two, 28 December 1958 on the Dayton CBC. (LFM/WR/ESM)

☐ **Harris' Hawk**, *Parabuteo unicinctus*. Accidental. One record: an individual collected 24 December 1917 in Pickaway County (Earl).

☐ ***Red-shouldered Hawk**, *Buteo lineatus*. Rare to uncommon migrant and resident. Concentrations occur at various points along Lake Erie—Little Cedar Point, Magee Marsh, Catawba Island, Bay Village, Clifton Park—during the spring migration. Formerly nested in most counties outside of the unglaciated hills, it now occupies but a fraction of its former range. *Max.:* 59, 9 March 1977 at Magee Marsh (A. Maley, Van Camp); and 52, 18 March 1978 at Ottawa NWR (B. Staehling). (ESM/SR/LFM/WR)

Red-shouldered Hawk

☐ ***Broad-winged Hawk**, *Buteo platypterus*. Locally common to abundant during large flights between mid-April and mid-May and again in mid-September. Rare to uncommon breeding bird in 34 counties, mostly in southeastern and northeastern Ohio. *Max.:* 400, 30 April 1973 at Perkins Beach in Cleveland (obs. u.); 700, 30 April and 1 May 1975 at Cleveland (A. Flanigan); 1500, 18 September 1976 at Tiffin, Seneca County (T. Bartlett), and 250, 17 September 1978 at Columbus (A. Reitter). (SM/SR/FM)

☐ **Swainson's Hawk**, *Buteo swainsoni*. Accidental–hypothetical. Two sight records; one, 31 December 1977 on the New Lexington CBC (Perry County); and one, 4 June 1978 at Ottawa NWR (Campbell).

☐ ***Red-tailed Hawk**, *Buteo jamaicensis*. Uncommon to very common migrant; uncommon but widespread resident breeding bird in all 88 counties. From late October to March, residents are augmented by considerable numbers of northern birds wintering in Ohio. *Max.:* 96, 14 March 1971 at Magee Marsh (T); 92, 26 December 1977 on the Wilmot CBC; 148, 17 March 1979 at Ottawa NWR (Pogacnik); and 50, 2 September 1979 at Ottawa NWR (Counts, Alexander). (ESM/SR/LFM/WR)

☐ **Ferruginous Hawk**, *Buteo regalis*. Acccidental–hypothetical. Two records: one, 19 to 24 April 1981 at Ottawa NWR (Campbell); and one, 29 November 1964 at Dayton (Hill, Johnson, La Pointe).

☐ **Rough-legged Hawk**, *Buteo lagopus*. Rare to uncommon migrant and winter visitor. Locally numerous in winter concentrations, less often in migratory flights. *Max.:* 20, 27 April 1919 at Painesville, Lake County (Doolittle); 72, 14 December 1974 on the Kingston CBC (Ross and Pickaway counties); 29, 22 December 1974 on the Ottawa NWR CBC; and 87, 28 December 1975 on the Kingston CBC. (WR)

☐ **Golden Eagle**, *Aquila chrysaetos*. Very rare visitor recorded somewhat more often in northeastern Ohio. About two dozen records, all of single birds.

Family Falconidae: Caracaras and Falcons

☐ ***American Kestrel**, *Falco sparverius*. Uncommon to fairly common widespread resident and nesting species over the entire state. Somewhat more numerous in winter and during migratory shifting of populations. Frequently seen hunting along freeways even in the largest cities, and sometimes nests in the open-ended pipes supporting the freeway signs. *Max.:* 122, 26 December 1976 on the Cincinnati CBC. (R)

☐ **Merlin**, *Falco columbarius*. Rare migrant, much more common before 1900. All recent records are of individual birds. Casual in winter. (SM/FM)

☐ **Peregrine Falcon**, *Falco peregrinus*. Almost extirpated from Ohio during the 1960s, this rare migrant is now making a comeback. Almost all records are of single birds. A few December records. (SM/FM)

☐ **Gyrfalcon**, *Falco rusticolus*. Very rare winter visitor. Except for one collected 30 January 1907 in Fayette County (Henninger), all records are from northern Ohio and of single birds.

ORDER GALLIFORMES

Family Phasianidae: Grouse and Ptarmigan

☐ *Gray (Hungarian) Partridge, *Perdix perdix*. About 9000 of these Eurasian birds were introduced throughout the state between 1909 and 1930. For a number of years the species flourished and nested in approximately 22 counties of west-central and northwestern Ohio. One of the last successful enclaves was in Madison County. Sixty birds were restocked between 1968 and 1969 in Wood (15); Champaign (6); Marion (20); Pickaway (13), and Greene (6) counties, but it is doubtful if any have survived recent severe winters.

☐ *Ring-necked Pheasant, *Phasianus colchicus*. First introduced in 1896 and repeatedly restocked through the years. Known to have nested in every county, but most common in western Ohio and, locally, in marshes. (R)

☐ *Ruffed Grouse, *Bonasa umbellus*. Uncommon resident known to nest in 43 counties east of a line drawn from Cuyahoga to Richmond to Fairfield to Adams counties. *Max.:* 14, 18 December 1977 on the Portsmouth CBC; 16, 16 December 1979 on the Steubenville CBC; and seven, 29 December 1979 on the Ashtabula CBC. (R)

☐ Greater Prairie Chicken, *Tympanuchus cupido*. Extirpated. Formerly an uncommon resident of open areas, most common in northwestern Ohio. A specimen was shot 16 November 1878 seven miles west of Columbus (Wheaton 1912, 446).

☐ Sharp-tailed Grouse, *Tympanuchus phasianellus*. Accidental–hypothetical. One record: an individual along a wooded driveway in Geauga County, April 20, 1973, was closely observed from a car for several minutes (Kremm). The normal range of this species extends halfway down the state of Wisconsin and into northern Michigan. In 1939 individuals of this species were released in Lucas County with unknown results.

☐ *Wild Turkey, *Meleagris gallopavo*. The original population was extirpated between 1850 and 1890, but wild birds have been reintroduced in recent years and it now breeds in a number of counties—most successfully in southeastern Ohio. *Max.:* 60 in February 1978 in Hocking County (*fide* E. S. Thomas). (R)

☐ *Northern Bobwhite, *Colinus virginianus*. Abundant resident except in northeastern Ohio where it is sometimes quite local or absent.

Recent severe winters have drastically reduced its numbers throughout the entire state. On the 1980–1981 CBCs only 269 individuals
were tallied on 51 counts. (R)

ORDER GRUIFORMES

Family Rallidae: Rails, Gallinules, and Coots

☐ *Yellow Rail, *Coturnicops noveboracensis.* Very rare migrant and
breeding bird known to have nested in three counties: Ashtabula,
Huron, and Pickaway. About 20 records of this scarce and elusive
species are on hand for the past 40 years, the majority in northern
Ohio.

☐ Black Rail, *Laterallus jamaicensis.* Very rare migrant. All records in
April and May with the exception of two in June and two in July, but
there is no evidence of nesting. It has been observed in Ottawa, Sandusky, Lake, Mercer, Licking, Franklin, and Montgomery counties.

☐ *King Rail, *Rallus elegans.* Rare migrant and summer resident once
rather widespread, but now greatly reduced in numbers. Accidental
in winter. (SM/SR/FM)

☐ *Virginia Rail, *Rallus limicola.* Rare migrant and summer resident
most often found in west Lake Erie marshes and small bogs and
marshes in the northern two-thirds of the state. Now absent from
much of its former range. (SM/SR/FM)

☐ *Sora, *Porzana carolina.* Rare to fairly common migrant and summer resident sometimes with local concentrations during migration.
Has nested in 33 scattered unglaciated counties. *Max.:* On 1 May
1976, over 100 responded to tape recordings on the Becker Trail of
Mentor Marsh, Lake County. (SM/SR/FM)

☐ *Purple Gallinule, *Porphyrula martinica.* Accidental. Twelve known
records, including a pair that nested and fledged five young in southern Franklin County in June 1962 (S. Glines, E. S. Thomas, M. Trautman, E. Knoder). The most recent occurrence was an individual at
the Spring Valley Wildlife Area, Warren County, 16–19 April 1983
(Mathena *et al.*).

☐ *Common Moorhen, *Gallinula chloropus.* Former name: Common
Gallinule. Rare to uncommon migrant and summer resident most
numerous in the Lake Erie marshes, but known to have nested in 34

counties. *Max.:* 22, 21 May 1977 at Mosquito Creek Lake (C. Johnson); and 23, 27 September 1970 at Magee Marsh and the Ottawa NWR (T). Accidental in winter. (ESM/SR/FM)

☐ *American Coot, *Fulica americana.* Locally common to very abundant during migration. Breeds in the marshes of Lucas, Ottawa, Sandusky, Erie and, irregularly, in 14 other counties. Uncommon in winter after January 1. *Max.:* 3500, 4 April 1948 at Little Cedar Point Marsh, Lucas County (Campbell); 2000, 11 October 1969 in Ottawa and Lucas counties (T); and 4050, 15 October 1976 at Alum Creek Reservoir, Delaware County (Counts, Alexander). (ESM/SR/LFM)

Family Gruidae: Cranes

☐ *Sandhill Crane, *Grus canadensis.* Rare in occurrence, but flocks in migration are sometimes composed of numerous individuals. Most records, however, are of just a few birds. Formerly bred in several northern counties: the last known record was of a pair that nested until 1926 in a southwest Huron County bog until one of the birds was shot. The survivor returned to the site each year from 1927 to 1931. There are about 50 records of the species being seen in migration since 1950. *Max.:* 34, 1 November 1959 in Delaware County (D. Mack); 23, 7 November 1970 flying over Madison County (A. Staffan); 94, 12 November 1977 flying over Paint Creek Reservoir, Ross County (Peterjohn); 54, 2 December 1979 heading south over Dayton (*fide* C. Mathena); and approximately 300 from 18–23 November 1982 at Indian Lake, Logan County (m. obs.). (ESM/LFM)

ORDER CHARADRIIFORMES

Family Charadriidae: Plovers

☐ Black-bellied Plover, *Pluvialis squatarola.* Uncommon to locally common migrant, often in newly ploughed fields in spring, and on mudflats in late summer and fall. Most numerous along Lake Erie. *Max.:* 225, 21 May 1972 at Little Cedar Point Marsh (T). (LSM/FM)

☐ Lesser Golden Plover, *Pluvialis dominica.* Uncommon to locally abundant migrant. Large flocks are sometimes found in ploughed fields in late March and April—usually in the western half of the state. Smaller numbers are found in late summer and fall on mudflats. *Max.:* 4000, 24 April 1954 in Ottawa County (T); 5000, 2 May 1950 in Lucas County (Campbell); 2500, 2 April 1967 in Pickaway County (I. Kassoy, E. S. Thomas); and 800, 3 October 1976 at Ottawa NWR (Van Camp). (ESM/FM)

☐ **Wilson's Plover**, *Charadrius wilsonia*. Accidental. An adult male was collected 17 June 1936 at Little Cedar Point Marsh, Lucas County (Campbell). Another was seen 3 June 1959 at the Hebron Fish Hatchery, Licking County (Claugus).

☐ **Semi-palmated Plover**, *Charadrius semipalmatus*. Uncommon to common migrant. *Max.:* 200, 24 May 1931 in Lucas County (Campbell); and 354, 5 September 1979 at Ottawa NWR (Pogacnik). (SM/EFM)

☐ ***Piping Plover**, *Charadrius melodus*. Rare migrant. Formerly nested in modest numbers along the beaches of Ashtabula, Lake, Lorain, Erie, Ottawa, and Lucas counties but there are no recent records. *Max.:* 15, 24 August 1963 at Lorain Harbor (obs. u.). (SM/EFM)

☐ ***Killdeer**, *Charadrius vociferus*. Uncommon to very common widespread migrant and summer resident. Winters rather regularly in reduced numbers, especially in southern Ohio. *Max.:* 203, 7 September 1941 at the Columbus Sewerage Disposal Plant (T). (ESM/SR/LFM/WR)

Family Recurvirostridae: Stilts and Avocets

☐ **Black-necked Stilt**, *Himantopus mexicanus*. Accidental. Three records: on 24 October 1881 one was shot in Berea, Cuyahoga County (Hall, *fide* Jones); a dead bird was found on the pavement in Cleveland Heights near Lower Shaker Lake, 15 August 1941 (Mueller), and one observed 18 July 1981 at Magee Marsh (Hocevar, Peterjohn).

☐ **American Avocet**, *Recurvirostra americana*. Rare migrant, but its occurrences are increasing—with over 30 statewide records in the 1970s. *Max.:* 42, 28 April 1974 near Sandusky (*fide* Campbell); eight, 29 April 1979 at Magee Marsh (Pogacnik); 16, 3 May 1980 in Fairfield County (Margery Thomas), and 14, 18 April 1976 at Paint Creek Reservoir (J. Skinner). (SM/EFM)

Family Scolopacidae: Sandpipers and Phalaropes

☐ **Greater Yellowlegs**, *Tringa melanoleuca*. Uncommon to common migrant, sometimes more numerous along western Lake Erie. Appears early in the spring and its southbound migration extends over most of the summer to late fall. *Max.:* 250, 2 May 1943 in Lucas County (Campbell); 50, 27 April 1969 in Pickaway County (I. Kassoy); and 140, 2 September 1979 at Ottawa NWR (Counts, Alexander). (ESM/EFM)

☐ **Lesser Yellowlegs**, *Tringa flavipes.* Uncommon to abundant migrant in spring around sky ponds and shorelines, in fall on mudflats. *Max.:* 500, 27 April 1929 and 12 August 1944 in Lucas County (Campbell); 130, 21 September 1957 at the Columbus Sewerage Disposal Plant (T); and 300, 4 May 1969 at Winous Point Marsh, Ottawa County (T). (ESM/EFM)

☐ **Spotted Redshank**, *Tringa erythropus.* Accidental–hypothetical. One record: An individual in breeding plumage was closely observed and documented 28 August 1979 at Huron (L. Rosche, E. Elder).

☐ **Solitary Sandpiper**, *Tringa solitaria.* Uncommon to locally common migrant along streams, ditches, and ponds. *Max.:* 53, 21 July 1941 at the Columbus Sewerage Disposal Plant (T); and 25, 6 August 1939 at Little Cedar Point Marsh, Ottawa County (Campbell). (SM/EFM)

☐ **Willet**, *Catoptrophorus semipalmatus.* Rare to fairly common migrant, especially along Lake Erie where it has occurred with considerable regularity the last 30 years. Adding the numbers seen on 74 separate occasions since the early 50s yields a total of at least 244, the largest concentration being 50, 21 August 1976 at Cleveland (the Hoffmans). Inland records include 12, 30 April 1966 near Barnesville, Belmont County (Chapman, Edgerton); 12, 5 July 1971 along the Little Miami River (Randle); and 12, 31 April 1979 in Franklin County (E. Reichelderfer).

☐ ***Spotted Sandpiper**, *Actitis macularia.* Uncommon to fairly common migrant and widespread summer resident nesting along streams and near lakes. Somewhat fewer in number than formerly, but migrating groups varying in size from six to 32 have been seen in one locality during the 70s. Several winter records. (SM/SR/FM)

☐ ***Upland Sandpiper**, *Bartramia longicauda.* Rare to uncommon migrant and summer resident, considerably less numerous than before 1950. Extremely local breeding species probably not occupying more than half the 76 counties where it once nested. *Max.:* 7, 17 August 1971 at Hoover Reservoir, Delaware County (T); and 12, 10 June 1979 at Bolton Field, Franklin County (T). (ESM/SR/EFM)

☐ **Eskimo Curlew**, *Numenius borealis.* This once very abundant bird was thought to have become extinct because of indiscriminate hunting in the 19th century—it was common until the 1870s—but several sightings along the Texas Gulf Coast in recent years have led to the hope that somehow the species will survive. Wheaton in his *Report on the Birds of Ohio*, Geol. Surv. 4, 1882, pp. 493–495, speaks of this curlew being taken in Cincinnati, and that it occurred in the vicinity of Cleveland. A specimen in the Ohio State Museum was collected before 1900 near Sandusky, Erie County.

☐ **Whimbrel**, *Numenius phaeopus*. Rare migrant encountered most often near Lake Erie. Seen regularly at Burke Lakefront Airport in Cleveland. *Max.:* 80, 20 May 1934 at Little Cedar Point Marsh (Campbell); 80, 23 May 1959 at Ashtabula (J. Ahlquist); and 75, 21 May 1976 at Magee Marsh (A. Newell). (SM/EFM)

Whimbrel

☐ **Long-billed Curlew**, *Numenius americanus*. Accidental–hypothetical. Possible records include seven at the Licking Reservoir, (Buckeye Lake), 31 May 1902 (Field); one at O'Shaughnessy Reservoir, Delaware County, 26 May 1926 (R. Geist, C. Walker, M. Trautman); plus three 19th century records from the vicinity of Cleveland. According to Dr. Trautman, it is probable that all of these sightings were of whimbrels.

☐ **Hudsonian Godwit**, *Limosa haemastica*. Very rare downstate, but sometimes fairly common to very common at Ottawa NWR and Magee Marsh, and rather frequent east along Lake Erie, but in small numbers. *Max.:* 63, 7 October 1967 at Ottawa NWR (Campbell, J. Hawkins); and 89 to 143, 28 September to 5 October 1975 at the same location (L. Carter, J. Herman). (FM)

☐ **Marbled Godwit**, *Limosa fedoa.* Rare migrant most often seen in Ottawa and Lucas counties, less frequently east along Lake Erie, and in smaller numbers. Accidental away from the lake. *Max.:* 8, 5 August to 1 October 1979 at Ottawa NWR (Pogacnik). (SM/EFM)

☐ **Ruddy Turnstone**, *Arenaria interpres.* Locally rare to very rare in migration except along Lake Erie where it is sometimes abundant, especially in spring. *Max.:* 350, 26 May 1956 at South Bass Island (M. Trautman); 500, 21 May 1965 in Lucas County (Campbell); 55, 10 August 1965 in Lucas County (Campbell); and 800, 24 May 1980 in Ottawa County (E. Limes). (LSM/EFM)

☐ **Red Knot**, *Calidris canutus.* Locally rare to uncommon migrant, mostly along Lake Erie. *Max.:* flocks of from 25 to 150 along western shores of Lake Erie, 24–26 May 1956 (A. Smith, M. Trautman); 49, 17 May 1980 at Ottawa NWR (L. Rosche *et al.*); and 11, 11 September 1979 at Huron (T. LePage). (LSM/FM)

☐ **Sanderling**, *Calidris alba.* Locally rare migrant downstate, fairly common along Lake Erie, and sometimes very common along the Maumee River rapids in fall, where 225 were counted on 17 October 1933 (Campbell). Sixteen were present 3 September 1976 at Ottawa NWR (Counts, Alexander); and 10, 8 October 1969 at Hoover Reservoir (T). (SM/EFM)

☐ **Semi-palmated Sandpiper**, *Calidris pusilla.* Locally uncommon to common migrant, sometimes abundant on mudflats in Lake Erie marshes. *Max.:* 1000, 11 August 1979 at Ottawa NWR (Peterjohn); and 1000, 22 May 1964 at Bay Point, Ottawa County, (M. Trautman). (SM/EFM)

☐ **Western Sandpiper**, *Calidris mauri.* Rare migrant from mid-July through September. Seldom seen in spring. *Max.:* four, 17 to 25 August 1963 at Hoover Reservoir, Delaware County (T); and four, 19 July 1975 at Cleveland (Hannikman). (SM/EFM)

☐ **Rufous-necked Stint**, *Calidris ruficollis.* Accidental. One record: An individual was observed and photographed 21–22 July 1962 at Walnut Beach, Ashtabula (A. Ahlquist, R. Browning, P. & L. Savage—photographs verified by A. Wetmore, D. Amadon, and H. Oberholser).

☐ **Least Sandpiper**, *Calidris minutilla*. Locally uncommon to very common migrant. *Max.:* 200, 3 August 1930 in Lucas County (Campbell); 173, 30 August 1974 at Hoover Reservoir, Delaware County (T). Several December and late February records. (SM/EFM)

☐ **White-rumped Sandpiper**, *Calidris fuscicollis*. Rare to common migrant, most common in late May and the first part of June in spring, from early July through much of October in fall. *Max.:* 200, 23 May 1971 at Magee Marsh (E. S. Thomas); 25, 29 October 1955 in Lucas County (Campbell); and 25, 27 May 1974 at Alum Creek Reservoir, Delaware County (T). Mid-June records might be non-breeding first-year birds. (LSM/EFM)

☐ **Baird's Sandpiper**, *Calidris bairdii*. Rare migrant most often seen in August and September. Accidental in spring. Unseasonal records include an individual photographed at Huron, 11 December 1979 (T. LePage); one on the Hoover Reservoir CBC, 19 December 1982 (Peterjohn, C. H. Gambill); and one at the Clarence J. Brown Reservoir 8 January 1983 (Counts, Alexander). *Max.:* six, 31 August 1963 at Hoover Reservoir, Delaware County (T); and two occasions in the fall when Lou Campbell observed 12 at Little Cedar Point Marsh, Lucas County. (EFM)

☐ **Pectoral Sandpiper**, *Calidris melanotos*. Rather common to locally abundant migrant. *Max.:* 500, 7 April 1951 at Stage's Pond, Pickaway County (H. Schuer, A. Claugus); 1200, 4 May 1969 in a field along the Sandusky River, Sandusky County (T); and 600, 12 April 1981 at Bolton Field, Franklin County (T). (ESM/EFM)

☐ **Purple Sandpiper**, *Calidris maritima*. Rare winter visitor along Lake Erie, recorded about 90 times in this century. Most records are of single birds in November, December, and January. *Max.:* six, 10 November 1952 at Starve Island (M. Trautman).

☐ **Dunlin**, *Calidris alpina*. Uncommon to locally abundant migrant, most numerous in late spring, not returning again in appreciable numbers until late September. *Max.:* 1500, 21 October 1973 in Ottawa County (M. Bolton, R. Osborne, T); and 2600, 24 May 1969 in the same county (E. Limes).

☐ **Curlew Sandpiper**, *Calidris ferruginea*. Accidental. One record: three observed 28 April 1974 at Neilson Marsh, Sandusky County (Campbell *et al.*).

☐ **Stilt Sandpiper**, *Calidris himantopus*. Rare to uncommon migrant in most areas, sometimes very common in Lucas and Ottawa counties.

Very rare in spring. *Max.:* 24, 11 September 1960 at Hoover Reservoir (T); 15, 4 August 1975 at White City, Cuyahoga County (Hannikman *et al.*); 70, 16 August 1978 at Ottawa NWR (m. obs.); 100, 15 September 1979 at Ottawa NWR (D. & J. Hoffman); 60, 10 July 1981 at the Bay Shore Power Plant, Lucas County (Counts, Alexander); and 80, 28 July 1982 at the latter location (J. McCormic). (SM/EFM)

☐ **Buff-breasted Sandpiper**, *Tryngites subruficollis*. Rare to uncommon migrant, somewhat more numerous in the Cleveland area—especially at Burke Lakefront Airport. Only two spring records at hand: one, 30 April 1929, and one, 28 April 1935, both in Licking County (E. V. Prior). *Max.:* five, 12 September 1948 at Mosquito Creek Lake (*fide* Williams); four, 17 September 1974 at the Hebron Fish Hatchery, Licking County (F. Griffith); six, 23–24 August 1975 Cleveland's Burke Lakefront Airport (Klamm); and 22, 11 September 1976 at the same location (*fide* Klamm). (SM/FM)

☐ **Ruff**, *Philomachus pugnax*. Casual migrant encountered somewhat more often in spring than fall, usually single birds. Records on hand are for the following counties: Licking(4); Ottawa (3); Wayne (1); Erie (1); Wooster (1), and Pickaway (1). *Max.:* three males, 7 July 1954 at Ottawa NWR, two in black plumage, one in orange (*fide* Campbell).

☐ **Short-billed Dowitcher**, *Limnodromus griseus*. Locally uncommon to abundant migrant. Most numerous from mid-July to October. *Max.:* 136, 17 September 1974 at Hoover Reservoir, Delaware County (T); at Ottawa NWR 540, 19 July 1975 (T), and 300, 2 September 1979 (P. Jack). (SM/EFM)

☐ **Long-billed Dowitcher**, *Limnodromus scolopaceus*. Rare migrant, usually in late summer and fall. *Max.:* 25, 10 August 1935 in Lucas County (*fide* Campbell); and 100, 23 October 1979 at Ottawa NWR (Peterjohn). (FM)

☐ ***Common Snipe**, *Gallinago gallinago*. Uncommon to common migrant and rare breeding bird in Lucas, Lorain, Ashtabula, Trumbull, Mahoning, Columbiana, Portage, and Carroll counties. Rare in winter. *Max.:* 150, 19 April 1980 near Cincinnati (D. Styer); and 81, 11 April 1981 in Franklin County (T). (ESM/SR/EFM)

☐ **Eurasian Woodcock**, *Scolopax rusticola*. Accidental. One local record: a specimen was shot 6 November 1935 in Newbury Township, Geauga County. The relatively large size of the bird induced the hunter to talk to Dr. John W. Aldrich, of the Cleveland Museum of Natural History. Although parts of the bird had been destroyed, Ald-

rich and H. Oberholser (Aldrich) were able to make a positive identification from what remained.

☐ *American Woodcock, *Scolopax minor*. Rare to uncommon migrant
and summer resident, nesting most regularly in southeast, central,
and northeast Ohio. Sometimes locally numerous in migration. Rare
in winter. *Max.:* 42, 12 March 1976, in brushy fields along a railroad
track in Columbus (Counts); 16 pairs of breeding birds in Cincinnati
area, 8 May 1975 (K. Maslowski), and 14, April 18, 1976, in woods
and fields around Paint Creek Reservoir, Highland County (J. Skinner). (ESM/SR/FM)

☐ *Wilson's Phalarope, *Steganopus tricolor*. Rare to fairly common in
Lucas and Ottawa counties, rare in other parts of the state. This
species has become more numerous in the past decade along the west
end of Lake Erie. The first breeding record for Ohio was established
at Ottawa NWR in June 1980 when a nest with four eggs was discovered, and a second nest might have been present. *Max.:* 47, 10 May
1978 at Magee Marsh (Van Camp); and 33 at Ottawa NWR 2 September 1979 (Pogacnik). (SM/EFM)

☐ **Red-necked Phalarope**, *Lobipes lobatus*. Former name: Northern
Phalarope. Rare migrant with records widely distributed around the
state. *Max.:* 10, 29 August 1974 at Lima, Allen County (D. Smith);
four, 20 October 1972 near Carey, Wyandot County (A. Claugus);
and 26, 7 August 1977 at Ottawa NWR (Van Camp). (LSM/FM)

☐ **Red Phalarope**, *Phalaropus fulicarius*. Rare migrant with the majority of records from northeastern Ohio along Lake Erie. Seen quite
often in winter. *Max.:* 30 or 35, 17 September 1963 on the Toledo
Ship Channel in Lake Erie (L. Shafer, R. Biggs); 3, 27 September
1968 at Buckeye Lake (M. Trautman). (LFM/WR)

SUBORDER LARI

Family Laridae: Jaegers and Skuas

☐ **Pomarine Jaeger**, *Stercorarius pomarinus*. Accidental inland; rare
offshore along Lake Erie from Lorain east between September and
December. An immature bird was collected at Lake St. Marys, 17
October 1964 (Kemsies, Ruthven, Key), and a mature bird was observed there 15 October 1966 (Ruthven, Zimmerman).

☐ **Parasitic Jaeger**, *Stercorarius parasiticus*. Rare to very rare offshore along Lake Erie from July to December with 13 out of 30 modern sightings in September. Accidental elsewhere. *Max.:* three, 16 November 1935 at the mouth of the Maumee River (Campbell).

☐ **Long-tailed Jaeger**, *Stercorarius longicaudus*. Accidental. Several records: an emaciated immature bird collected near Cranberry Island, Buckeye Lake, 5 September 1928 (C. Walker, M. Trautman); one found in a weakened condition, but still alive near Yellow Springs, Greene County, in the spring of 1950; an immature bird found alive (17 September 1960) but incapable of flight on a lawn in Parma, Cuyahoga County, later died at the Cleveland Zoo.

☐ **Great Skua**, *Catharacta skua*. Accidental. One record: an individual observed between 30 December 1979 and 1 January 1980 at the Darby section of the Ottawa NWR (Anderson, Campbell *et al.*, well documented).

Subfamily Larinae

☐ **Laughing Gull**, *Larus atricilla*. This rare "summer" gull first appeared in Ohio in the mid-fifties and continues to increase in the number of its occurrences. Seen most often on Lake Erie, it has also been recorded in Franklin (4), Delaware (1), Montgomery (1), and Hamilton (1) counties. Records span every month but December, January, and February. *Max.:* three, 7 July 1963 at Lorain (O. Davies, M. Stasko).

☐ **Franklin's Gull**, *Larus pipixcan*. Rare to uncommon migrant and irregular visitor. Most records in the Cleveland area, but there are at least 27 occurrences downstate. Recorded every month except February, with visitations increasing from May (4) through August (9), September (7), October (7), November (7) to December (13). *Max.:* seven, 12 September 1970 at Cleveland (Klamm); 11, 11 November 1975 at Findley Reservoir (B. Stehling); and 18, 16 October 1976 at Huron (Peterjohn).

☐ **Little Gull**, *Larus minutus*. Rare to uncommon fall and winter visitor along Lake Erie, mostly from Lorain to Cleveland; very rare in spring, and accidental in summer. No inland records except for an individual collected 7 November 1970 at Buckeye Lake (M. Trautman). *Max.:* twelve, 27 November 1979 at Cleveland (m. obs.).

Little Gulls

☐ **Common Black-headed Gull**, *Larus ridibundus*. Very rare along Lake Erie from Huron to Cleveland. Most records are of single birds in winter (November to March), but there are two summer records. One individual was observed in Cleveland from 23 July to 4 August 1978 (Klamm, Hannikman), and another at Lorain in mid-August 1981.

☐ **Bonaparte's Gull**, *Larus philadelphia*. Locally uncommon to common inland. On Lake Erie, populations build up to very abundant through November to about January 10, after which there is usually an exodus eastward. Flocks reappear in March and peak in April and May. Rare anywhere in summer, but there is a record of six birds at Ottawa NWR, 19 July 1975 (T). *Max.:* 41,000 on 30 December 1967 on the Elyria-Lorain CBC; 25,650 on 14 December 1974 on the Cleveland CBC; and 15,952 on 17 December 1979 on the Toledo CBC. (ESM/FM/WR)

☐ **Heerman's Gull**, *Larus heermanni*. Accidental. A second-year bird was photographed and seen by many observers from 12 February to 12 March 1980 at Lorain (Pogacnik, J. Fry, A. & E. Thompson).

☐ **Mew Gull**, *Larus canus*. Accidental. One record: a first-year bird carefully observed and photographed at Lorain, 28 November to 27 December 1981 (Peterjohn, Hannikman, Rosche).

☐ ***Ring-billed Gull**, *Larus delawarensis*. Ohio's most numerous gull is very abundant on Lake Erie, where populations peak in April and May and again in fall and early winter. From September through May, it is locally uncommon to abundant throughout the state. Small numbers nest on islands at the western end of Lake Erie at the Oregon Power Plant, and nonbreeding birds are frequently found throughout the state in summer. *Max.:* 79,000 on 2 December 1966 on the Elyria-Lorain CBC; 75,000 were estimated 17 November 1979 in Erie County (Pogacnik); and 38,652 on 17 December 1979 on the Toledo CBC. (ESM/SR/FM/WR)

☐ **California Gull**, *Larus californicus*. Casual to very rare winter visitor along Lake Erie in winter between Lorain and Cleveland. Most records date from 26 November 1966 when three were observed at Lakewood, Cuyahoga County (O. Davies). *Max.:* 17 immatures 22 December 1968, on the Lakewood, Cuyahoga County, CBC.

☐ ***Herring Gull**, *Larus argentatus*. Very abundant on Lake Erie in late fall and early winter as large numbers migrate east along the shore and return again in March and April. Modest numbers are found throughout the state, especially from October to April. Small numbers nest on islands at the western end of Lake Erie and on impoundments at the Oregon Power Plant. *Max.:* 30,000 on 10 and 11 January 1948 in Cleveland (R. Hill); and 63,104 on 21 December 1975 on the Toledo CBC. (ESM/SR/FM/WR)

☐ **Thayer's Gull**, *Larus thayeri*. Accidental. An immature female was collected 26 February 1946 at Put-in-Bay, Ottawa County (M. Trautman), and up to a half dozen have been identified the last several years at Lorain. It is difficult to distinguish this species from the Herring Gull, and it is possible that a few have been present each winter.

☐ **Iceland Gull**, *Larus glaucoides*. Rare to very rare winter visitor along Lake Erie. Five inland records are: one, 9 January 1938 at Buckeye Lake (A. Claugus); one at O'Shaughnessy Reservoir, Delaware County, 14 April 1941 (D. Borror); at Lake St. Marys, one on 12 April 1949 (Mayfield), one on 10 October 1955 (Clark), and one on 12 April 1949 (Kemsies, Randle). *Max.:* three, 18 January to 11 February 1979 at Cleveland (Pogacnik). An individual of the Kumlien's race of this species was present in Maumee Bay, 1–8 March 1981 (*fide* Campbell).

☐ **Lesser Black-backed Gull**, *Larus fuscus.* Casual winter visitor. First appeared along the Cleveland waterfront 20 January 1977, when three individuals were discovered. Since that time, two or three have been seen each winter at Cleveland or Lorain.

☐ **Glaucous Gull**, *Larus hyperboreus.* Rare winter visitor along Lake Erie, usually from December to March, but there are several off-season records including an individual 13 May 1961 at Little Cedar Point, Lucas County (T), and another 7 August 1977 at Cleveland (Klamm). *Max.:* 14, 15 February 1978 at Cleveland (the Hoffmans); 10, 23 January 1978 at Avon-on-the-Lake, Lorain County (J. Fry); and 13, 5 February 1980 at Lorain (Pogacnik).

☐ **Great Black-backed Gull**, *Larus marinus.* Fairly common to abundant in winter along the Lake Erie shore. It has become numerous only since mid-century. There are four records for Lake St. Marys: one, 5–12 November 1952 (Clark); one, 15 November 1954 (Clark); one, 24 October 1965 (Sipe); and one, 31 December 1966 (Kemsies). An immature bird in company with Herring and Ring-billed gulls was carefully observed 17 November 1962 at a quarry in Columbus (T). An adult was discovered at the Greenlawn Avenue Dam in Columbus 30 January 1983 (the Gambills). *Max.:* 350 in the Maumee Bay area in December 1967; and 350, 5 February 1978 at Cleveland (Klamm). (WR)

☐ **Black-legged Kittiwake**, *Rissa brevirostris.* Rare winter visitor along Lake Erie, most records from Lorain and Cleveland in November and December. Individual records from Dayton, Lake St. Marys, Columbus, and Delaware County. *Max.:* two during November 1967 in Cleveland; two, 19 and 20 November 1974 in Lucas County (*fide* Campbell); and two, 4 January 1976 on the Gypsum CBC.

☐ **Sabine's Gull**, *Xema sabini.* Accidental. All records from September to December, most from Cleveland. Inland records are: one, 9 September 1926 at Buckeye Lake, Licking County (M. Trautman); one, 20 October 1956 collected at Lake St. Marys (Clark); and one, 4 October 1970 at Hoover Reservoir, Delaware County (T).

☐ **Ivory Gull**, *Pagophila eburnea.* Accidental. Two records; one, 23 December 1966 at Cleveland (F. Gray, *fide* Davies); and one, 17 to 19 December 1975 along the waterfront near East 72nd Street in Cleveland, well documented and seen by many observers (J. Hoffman, Carrothers).

Subfamily Sterninae

☐ **Large-billed Tern**, *Phaetusa simplex*. Accidental–hypothetical. An individual of this tropical species was seen in company with Common and Caspian terns, 29 May 1954 at Evans Lake, south of Poland in Mahoning County (E. Dressel, W. Findley, V. McLaughlin). Well documented and sketched (see *American Birds*, Vol. 33, No. 5).

☐ **Gull-billed Tern**, *Gelochelidon nilotica*. Accidental–hypothetical. Mentioned by Wheaton (1882:553) as a "Rare visitor in the vicinity of Cleveland, where taken by Mr. Winslow." There are two modern sight records: one at Fairport Harbor, Lake County, in July 1938 (B. Bole, Jr., Z. Adams); and one, 17 October 1965 at Lake St. Marys (Randle, Wiseman).

☐ **Caspian Tern**, *Sterna caspia*. Locally rare to very common migrant, most numerous along Lake Erie, from April to November. A few December records. *Max.:* 16, 28 May 1924 at Buckeye Lake, Licking County (M. Trautman); 200, 31 August 1928 at Port Clinton, Ottawa County (Campbell); and 144, 21–25 April 1979 at Cleveland (Klamm). (ESM/SR–non-breeding–FM)

☐ **Roseate Tern**, *Sterna dougallii*. Accidental. Six records: one, 31 July 1919 near Fairport on Lake Erie (Doolittle); one, 24–26 April 1949 near Cincinnati (Randle); one, 7 May 1950 along the Great Miami River near Tipp City, Miami County (B. Smith, P. Greene, H. Lohmier); at Lake St. Marys two on 1 May 1955 (Clark), and one on 18 May 1958 (Kemsies); and one photographed 19 July 1971 at Hoover Reservoir, Delaware County (T).

☐ ***Common Tern**, *Sterna hirundo*. Uncommon to common migrant; locally very abundant along Lake Erie. Nests rather commonly at the western end of Lake Erie on islands, mud banks and, occasionally, on muskrat houses in the marshes. A few winter records. *Max.:* 8000, 4 September 1974 at Magee Marsh and Ottawa NWR (T); 3300, 21 September 1969 at the harbor breakwater on the Cuyahoga River (Klamm); 600, 24 August 1975 at Ottawa NWR (T); and 4000, 2 September 1979 in the same area (P. Jack). (SM/SR/LFM)

☐ **Arctic Tern**, *Sterna paradisaea*. Accidental. One record: an individual photographed 27 July 1980 at Huron (Peterjohn, m. obs.).

☐ **Forster's Tern**, *Sterna forsteri*. Rare to locally very commom migrant, most numerous in April through May and August through

November in the western Lake Erie marshes. Rare to uncommon elsewhere. One winter record on 14 January 1974 of 15 flying in from the northwest, then proceeding east along the shore at Lorain (T). *Max.:* 20, 26 April 1949 near Cincinnati (Kemsies, Randle); 200, 5 November 1958 in Lucas County (Campbell); and 215, 2 September 1979 at Ottawa NWR (P. Jack). (SM/LFM)

☐ **Least Tern**, *Sterna antillarum*. Casual summer visitor, most often recorded in Lucas and Ottawa counties. About 15 records in this century. *Max.:* two, 16 September 1934 at Little Cedar Point Marsh (Campbell); and three, 13 May 1956 at Painesville, Lake County (H. Schaefer).

☐ ***Black Tern**, *Chlidonias niger*. Locally rare to very common migrant inland around large lakes; fairly common to common along Lake Erie, and very common to abundant there in late summer and early fall. Modest numbers nest in the marshes of Lucas, Ottawa, and Sandusky counties. *Max.:* 1500, 19 July 1941 and 26 August 1944 in the above counties (Campbell); 200, 18 May 1952 at Lake St. Marys (Sipe); over 100, 12 May 1951 in Hamilton County (Kemsies, Randle); and 200, 13 September 1979 at Cleveland (D. & J. Hoffman). (SM/SR/FM)

Family Alcidae: Alcids

☐ **Thick-billed Murre**, *Uria lomvia*. Accidental. During the winter of 1894–95, in December 1896, and in December 1907 as many as two dozen of these birds were found in Ohio and Michigan waters of western Lake Erie, including Sandusky Bay. Two specimens are in the Ohio State Museum, Columbus.

☐ **Ancient Murrelet**, *Synthliboramphus antiquus*. Accidental. One record: two birds were retrieved from a fishing net in Sandusky Bay 28 March 1951 (H. Nielson).

☐ **Atlantic Puffin**, *Fratercula arctica*. Accidental. One record: On 18 November 1980 a live individual was found in a field near Toledo and taken to the zoo, where it later died.

ORDER COLUMBIFORMES

Family Columbidae: Pigeons and Doves

☐ ***Rock Dove**, *Columba livia*. This is the common pigeon, a widespread and common to very abundant transplant now firmly established as a wild breeding bird. *Max.:* 3356, 28 December 1974 on the Columbus CBC. Less common in northern Ohio, particularly in winter. (R)

☐ ***Mourning Dove**, Zenaida macroura.* Widespread, locally common to abundant resident, but highly variable in numbers, especially in winter when it is very susceptible to the effects of severe weather. *Max.:* 1786 (25-year high), 26 December 1971 on the Cincinnati CBC. (ESM/SR/LFM/WR)

***Passenger Pigeon**, Ectopistes migratorius.* Extinct. Former multitudes included flocks of a million or more birds, but by 1885 their numbers had been reduced to a handful by market hunters. Possibly the last bird shot was killed at Sargents, Pike County, on 24 March 1900. The last passenger pigeon, a bird named Martha, died 1 September 1914 at the Cincinnati Zoo. She was 29 years old.

ORDER PSITTACIFORMES

Family Psittacidae: Parrots

***Carolina Parakeet**, Conuropsis carolinesis.* Extinct. Flocks of these colorful birds are said to have been rather common at the beginning of the 19th century, especially in the southern half of the state. By 1850, the species was becoming rare. One of the last records was of 25 or 30 individuals seen in elms about the state capitol in Columbus in July 1862 (Sullivant: Dawson, 1903). Probably bred sparingly in river bottomlands in southern Ohio.

ORDER CUCULIFORMES

Family Cuculidae: Cuckoos, Roadrunners, and Anis

☐ ***Yellow-billed Cuckoo**, Coccyzus americanus.* Uncommon to fairly common migrant and widespread summer resident, less numerous in northeastern Ohio. Particularly numerous during outbreaks of the tent caterpillar (*Lasiocampidae*). *Max.:* 20, 4 September 1939 in Lucas County (Campbell); and 19, 1 June 1981 in the Clear Creek Valley, Hocking and Fairfield counties (T). (SM/SR/FM)

☐ ***Black-billed Cuckoo**, Coccyzus erythropthalmus.* Rare to uncommon migrant and summer resident, most numerous in eastern Ohio and in the Oak Openings of Lucas County. *Max.:* eight, 31 May 1958 at Little Cedar Point, Lucas County (T). (SM/SR/FM)

☐ **Groove-billed Ani**, *Crotophaga sulcirostris*. Accidental. Four records: one was observed 20 October 1963 at Magee Marsh, Ottawa County (Bednarik, Van Camp, J. Brown); an individual was discovered by Vernon Kline on his farm in Holmes County and remained from mid-October to mid-November 1972, when it was captured and placed in a Cleveland aviary; another was found near the Alum Creek Reservoir, Delaware County, 10 August 1980 (Peterjohn); and one at the home of Arlene and William Brown in Owensville, Clermont County, in October and November 1981 (m. obs.).

ORDER STRIGIFORMES

Family Tytonidae: Barn Owls

☐ *****Barn Owl**, *Tyto alba*. Locally rare resident, less numerous the last 30 years. According to Lawrence E. Hicks in the *Distribution of the Breeding Birds of Ohio*, 1935, this species has nested in 84 counties, but all indications are that it is now much less widespread. Laurel Van Camp banded the young of five Ottawa County nests in 1960. (R)

Family Strigidae: Typical Owls

☐ *****Eastern Screech Owl**, *Ottus asio*. Locally rare to uncommon resident, rather rare in northeastern Ohio, and probably absent from parts of its former range in other counties. Yet on the Whitehouse–Waterville CBC on 6 January 1982 112 individuals were recorded. (R)

☐ *****Great Horned Owl**, *Bubo virginianus*. Increasing in numbers over the past several decades, this species is a rare to uncommon resident throughout much of the state. Somewhat less numerous in the western third of the state. *Max.:* 16, 14 December 1974 on the Oxford CBC; and 15, 29 December 1979 on the Wilmot CBC. (R)

☐ **Snowy Owl**, *Nyctea scandiaca*. Rare to very rare winter visitor, periodically more numerous during invasion years, especially in Lake Erie counties. Most often seen from November through January, but there are records as early as mid-October and as late as May. On 24 May 1968, an individual was seen on The Ohio State University farms in Columbus (H. Burtt). (LFM/WR/ESM)

Snowy Owl

☐ **Northern Hawk Owl**, *Surnia ulula*. Accidental. One was collected 10 November 1927 in Pepper Pike Village, Cuyahoga County (R. Kula). Observations: One, 5 December 1940 at Holden Arboretum, Lake County (B. Bole, Jr.); another (possibly the same bird), from 24 December 1940 to 6 January 1941 at nearby Northfield (R. Kula); one on the ice off Clifton Beach in Cleveland, 2 March 1957; one, 1–5 January 1968 at Lorain (Wolfe); and one, 16 January 1978 north of Maumee, Lucas County (Campbell).

☐ **Burrowing Owl**, *Speotyto cunicularia*. Accidental–hypothetical. On 5 and 6 April 1981 near Toledo one closely observed was seen running across a field (S. Zenser).

☐ ***Barred Owl**, *Strix varia*. Rare to uncommon resident breeding in most counties except a few in northwestern and southwestern parts of the state. *Max.:* 11, 31 December 1978 on the Cincinnati CBC. (R)

☐ ***Long-eared Owl**, *Asio otus*. Rare migrant and winter resident. Has nested in 20 scattered counties, most of them northern, several southwestern. *Max.:* nine, February 1966 at a roost in Lucas County (Campbell); and three, 3 April 1955 in Greenlawn Cemetery, Columbus (T). (ESM/SR/LFM/WR)

☐ ***Short-eared Owl**, *Asio flammeus*. Locally rare or absent to infrequently common at winter gathering places in marshes or extensive areas of fallow fields. Often found at the Killdeer Plains Wildlife Area, Wyandot County, in winter. Has nested in nine scattered counties. *Max.:* 100, 20 January 1967 at Killdeer Plains (M. Trautman). (ESM/SR/LFM/WR)

☐ ***Northern Saw-whet Owl**, Aegolius acadicus.* Rare migrant and winter visitor usually found in dense evergreens and tangles. A frequent April visitor along the bird walk at Crane Creek State Park, Ottawa County. Has been found nesting in 18 scattered counties in the northern two-thirds of the state. *Max.:* five, 19 December 1976 on the Western Hamilton County CBC. (ESM/SR/WR)

Northern Saw-whet Owl

ORDER CAPRIMULGIFORMES

Family Caprimulgidae: Goatsuckers

☐ ***Common Nighthawk**, Chordeiles minor.* Uncommon spring migrant, but frequently very common to very abundant during the southward movement in late summer. Uncommon to fairly common resident in 75 counties, most numerous in urban areas. *Max.:* over 3000, 3 September 1976 in Columbus (T). (SM/SR/EFM)

☐ ***Chuck-will's-widow**, Caprimulgus carolinensis.* Rare nesting bird along a stretch of Ohio Brush Creek in Adams County. Accidental

Chuck-will's-widow

vagrant elsewhere with records from Cuyahoga (F. Ackerman, M. Stasko), Miami (R. Ramey), Lucas (M. Anderson), Clermont (Goodpaster), and Montgomery (Blincoe) counties. (SR)

☐ *Whip-poor-will*, *Caprimulgus vociferus*. Rare to uncommon migrant; uncommon to fairly common nesting bird in 69 counties, most numerous in the hilly unglaciated parts of the state. *Max.:* 18, 2 June 1971 in Hocking County (T). (SM/SR/FM)

ORDER APODIFORMES

Family Apodidae: Swifts

☐ *Chimney Swift*, *Chaetura pelagica*. Common to sometimes abundant migrant and widespread breeding bird occurring in every county. (SM/SR/FM)

Family Trochilidae: Hummingbirds

☐ *Ruby-throated Hummingbird*, *Archilochus colubris*. Rare to uncommon migrant and locally uncommon summer resident, most numerous in unglaciated counties. Has nested in all 88 counties, but is less common than formerly. Sometimes more numerous during migration along Lake Erie. *Max.:* 75, 25 August 1934 in Lucas County (Campbell). (SM/SR/FM)

ORDER CORACIIFORMES

Family Alcedinidae: Kingfishers

☐ *Belted Kingfisher, *Ceryle alcyon.* Uncommon but widespread summer resident, often remaining in winter as long as there is open water. Nests throughout the state. *Max.:* 35, 28 December 1975 on the Cincinnati CBC. (ESM/SR/LFM/WR)

ORDER PICIFORMES

Family Picidae: Woodpeckers and Wrynecks

☐ *Red-headed Woodpecker, *Melanerpes erythrocephalus.* Locally rare to fairly common resident, sometimes shifting populations in migratory movements. Has nested in all 88 counties, but rather variable from year to year. *Max.:* 268, 30 December 1956 on the Buckeye Lake CBC. (SM/SR/FM/WR)

☐ *Red-bellied Woodpecker, *Melanerpes carolinus.* Rare to locally uncommon resident in all but west-central and northwestern Ohio. Most numerous in the unglaciated counties. *Max.:* 265, 26 December 1974 on the Cincinnati CBC. (R)

☐ *Yellow-bellied Sapsucker, *Sphyrapicus varius.* Uncommon to common migrant, and accidental to very rare breeding bird in Lorain, Wayne, Geauga, Ashtabula, and Trumbull counties. *Max.:* 50, 5 April 1963, and 43, 30 April 1969, at Greenlawn Cemetery in Columbus (T). (ESM/LFM/WR)

☐ *Downy Woodpecker, *Picoides pubescens.* Ohio's most widespread woodpecker nests in all 88 counties and is found in urban and rural areas. Some migration is evident in spring and fall. *Max.:* 508, 26 December 1971 on the Cincinnati CBC. (R)

☐ *Hairy Woodpecker, *Picoides villosus.* Locally rare to uncommon resident. Most numerous in forested areas of unglaciated Ohio. Seldom more than two or three seen in a day by a single observer. *Max.:* 68, 29 December 1974, on the Cincinnati CBC. (R)

☐ **Red-cockaded Woodpecker**, *Picoides borealis*. Accidental. There is a specimen of a bird collected 15 March 1872, in Franklin County (Jones); one was seen on the 1965 Oxford (Butler County) CBC, and one was present from 22 April to 4 May 1975 at Old Man's Cave State Park, Hocking County (E. Brown, E. S. Thomas, M. Trautman, T.).

☐ **Black-backed Woodpecker**, *Picoides arcticus*. Casual winter visitor. All records from northern Ohio, usually of single birds, but three were at a suet feeder in Kirtland Hills, Lake County, 12 February 1962 (B. Boles, Jr.), and two were seen along the east branch of the Chagrin River near Chardon, Geauga County, 10 March 1940 (R. Eisle, W. Goodsell).

☐ **Northern Flicker**, *Colaptes auratus*. Fairly common to locally very common migrant; uncommon to fairly common summer resident nesting in every county. Winters regularly in modest numbers mostly from central Ohio south. *Max.:* 188, 30 December 1962 on the Cincinnati CBC; 185, 30 December 1956 on the Buckeye Lake (Licking County) CBC, and 80, 17 April 1963 at Greenlawn Cemetery in Columbus (T). (ESM/SR/FM/WR)

☐ ***Pileated Woodpecker**, *Dryocopus pileatus*. Locally rare or absent to uncommon resident, confined mostly to the forested hilly regions of southern, eastern, and northeastern Ohio, extending locally into central portions of the state. *Max.:* 24, 28 December 1974 on the Wilmot CBC; and 21, 29 December 1974 on the Portsmouth CBC. (R)

Ivory-billed Woodpecker, *Campephilus principalis*. Extirpated from Ohio, where it was probably a casual visitor in prehistoric times.

ORDER PASSERIFORMES

Family Tyrannidae: Tyrant Flycatchers

☐ ***Olive-sided Flycatcher**, *Contopus borealis*. Rare late spring and early fall migrant. One definite nesting record, 16 June 1932, in the old Pymatuning Bog, Ashtabula County (Hicks). There are a few summer records, including one on 4 July 1973 in Hocking County (T) and one, on 29 June 1979 at Akron (Tveekrem). (LSM/FM)

☐ ***Eastern Wood-Pewee**, *Contopus virens*. Uncommon to fairly common widespread migrant and summer resident breeding throughout the state. *Max.:* 20, 15 August 1937 in the Oak Openings of Lucas County (Campbell). (SM/SR/FM)

☐ **Yellow-bellied Flycatcher**, *Empidonax flaviventris*. Rare to uncommon migrant. Because it is difficult to distinguish this species from other *empidonax* flycatchers in the fall, most valid records are in the spring. *Max.:* 18 banded, 29 May 1980 at Magee Marsh, Lucas County (Pogacnik). (LSM/EFM)

☐ *****Acadian Flycatcher**, *Empidonax virescens*. Uncommon to common migrant and widespread summer resident. Nests in every county but Putnam, Hancock, and Allen. Most numerous in the unglaciated counties. *Max.:* 24, 21 May 1974 in Hocking County (T). (SM/SR/FM)

☐ *****Alder Flycatcher**, *Empidonax alnorum*. Casual migrant. Indistinguishable from the Willow Flycatcher except by its song, *fee-beé-o* rather than the *fitz-bew* of the former species. Several spring records in central Ohio (D. Borror, T), and on 2 June 1973 one was observed in northwestern Morrow County singing within 100 yards of two Willow Flycatchers (Little). Probably breeds in Ohio, but further fieldwork is needed to determine its status. (SM/SR/EFM)

☐ *****Willow Flycatcher**, *Empidonax traillii*. Locally rare to uncommon migrant and summer resident, frequently near swales, marshes, fallow fields with scattered small trees, and groves of alders. Nests sparingly in most counties except a handful in the southern part of the state along the Ohio River. *Max.:* nine, 28 May 1964 at the Hebron Fish Hatchery, Licking County (T). (SM/SR/EFM)

☐ *****Least Flycatcher**, *Empidonax minimus*. Uncommon to common migrant and locally rare to uncommon summer resident in five northeastern and three northwestern counties, plus records from Ashland and Delaware counties. *Max.:* 35, 15 May 1948 near Lakeside, Ottawa County (Campbell), and a migratory concentration of an estimated 300 birds, 14 May 1981 at Greenlawn Cemetery in Columbus (T). (SM/SR/FM)

☐ *****Eastern Phoebe**, *Sayornis phoebe*. Locally uncommon to fairly common migrant and summer resident nesting in all counties, but most common in unglaciated Ohio. A few sometimes winter in southern Ohio. *Max.:* 24, 5 June 1966 in the Clear Creek Valley, Fairfield and Hocking counties (T). (ESM/SR/FM/WR)

☐ **Vermilion Flycatcher**, *Pyrocephalus rubinus*. Accidental. One collected 21 September 1958 in Clark County (*fide* M. Trautman), and a sight record of two males 2 May 1973 at Avery, Erie County (Bodkin, Stickley).

☐ *Great Crested Flycatcher, *Myiarchus crinitus*. Uncommon to common migrant; uncommon summer resident. Nests in wooded areas in every county. *Max.:* 50, 15 May 1948 at Lakeside, Ottawa County (Campbell); and 20, 31 May 1958 at Little Cedar Point, Lucas County (T), (SM/SR/FM)

☐ *Western Kingbird, *Tyrannus verticalis*. Casual migrant in May, and in late August and early September. Recorded in Lucas, Cuyahoga, Lake, Summit, Holmes, Franklin, Delaware, and Hamilton counties. One nesting record: a female was feeding three juveniles at Reno-on-the-Lake, Lucas County, 29 July 1933 (Campbell).

☐ *Eastern Kingbird, *Tyrannus tyrannus*. Uncommon to fairly common migrant and summer visitor. Nests throughout Ohio, in the country and along streams. *Max.:* 32, 17 May 1975 in the marshes of western Lake Erie (T); 28, 20 August 1975 at Alum Creek Reservoir, Delaware County (Counts, Alexander); and 27, 27 August 1979 at Streetsboro, Portage County (L. Rosche). (SM/SR/EFM)

☐ Scissor-tailed Flycatcher, *Tyrannus forficatus*. Accidental–hypothetical. Three sight records: one, 3 May 1959 near Barberton, Summit County (obs. u.); one, 8 May 1966 in Adams County (E. Richard); and one during the fall of 1970 near Cincinnati (Honshopp).

Family Alaudidae: Larks

☐ *Horned Lark, *Eremophila alpestris*. Uncommon to abundant resident breeding throughout Ohio, most numerous during winter concentrations. *Max.:* 1202, 16 December 1972, on the Darbydale, Franklin County, CBC. (R/WR)

Family Hirundinidae: Swallows

☐ *Purple Martin, *Progne subis*. Fairly common to common spring migrant and summer resident nesting throughout the state. Locally very abundant during late summer concentrations before migration. *Max.:* 25,000 on 24 August 1964 roosting in the Ohio Penitentiary yard at Columbus (E. S. Thomas, Limes, Kassoy, D. Smith, T). (ESM/SR/ESM)

☐ *Tree Swallow, *Tachycineta bicolor*. Locally uncommon to very common migrant, sometimes very abundant, especially in the marshes of western Lake Erie. Nests abundantly in the marshes of Lucas, Ottawa,

Sandusky, and Erie counties, rather commonly in four other north-western counties, 13 northeastern counties, and sparingly in a scattering of locations in central Ohio. *Max.:* 15,000 on 30 September 1934 near Reno Beach, Lucas County (Campbell); 2000, 26 August 1976 at Lake St. Marys (Randle); and 1700, 8 April 1980 at Lorain (Pogacnik). (ESM/SR/LFM)

☐ **Violet-green Swallow**, *Tachycineta thalassina*. Accidental–hypothetical. One sight record of two birds 3 May 1970 at Mentor Marsh, Lake County, closely observed both at rest and in flight, which showed the distinctive white rump patches (Booth, Strock, Vallender).

☐ ***Northern Rough-winged Swallow**, *Stelgidopteryx serripennis*. Uncommon to very common migrant; fairly common summer resident throughout Ohio, somewhat more numerous in southern Ohio. *Max.:* 500, 8 May 1960 in central Ohio (T). (SM/SR/FM)

☐ ***Bank Swallow**, *Riparia riparia*. Uncommon to very common migrant; common to abundant around nesting colonies in 31 scattered counties. Most numerous in northern Ohio. *Max.:* 6686, 1 August 1976 at Ottawa NWR (Campbell). (SM/SR/FM)

☐ ***Cliff Swallow**, *Hirundo pyrrhonota*. Locally rare migrant and summer resident, sometimes absent from large areas, but nests in 45 scattered counties. Less numerous in western Ohio. *Max.:* 150, 26 May 1949 at Sand Beach, Ottawa County (C. Wagner). (SM/SR/EFM)

☐ ***Barn Swallow**, *Hirundo rustica*. Common to very abundant migrant and common summer resident nesting in all 88 counties. *Max.:* 3000, 8 May 1960 in central Ohio (T); and 1800, 28 July 1981, in Morgan County (Counts). (ESM/SR/FM)

Family Corvidae: Jays, Magpies, and Crows

☐ ***Blue Jay**, *Cyanocitta cristata*. Fairly common to common migrant and summer resident; sometimes very abundant along Lake Erie in migration. Nests throughout the state. *Max.:* 5500, 11 May 1974 at Little Cedar Point, Lucas County (T). (SM/SR/FM/WR)

☐ ***Black-billed Magpie**, *Pica pica*. Accidental. Five records (two may have been escapes) from Lucas County between 1937 and 1964; one, 31 December 1956, at O'Shaughnessy Reservoir, Delaware County, may have been an escape; two present the fall and winter of 1961 near Canton, and two pairs which attempted to nest at Sandusky, then disappeared. Photographs taken of one nest (*fide* Davies).

☐ *__American Crow__, *Corvus brachyrhynchos.* Fairly common to very common migrant and resident; very abundant near some roosts. Nests throughout the state. *Max.:* 21,410 on 23 December 1956 on the Toledo CBC; and 10,000, 18 December 1977 on the Mansfield CBC. (SM/SR/FM/WR)

☐ __Common Raven__, *Corvus corax.* Extirpated. Once rather common in northeastern Ohio, especially along Lake Erie.

Family Paridae: Titmice, Verdins, and Bushtits

☐ *__Black-capped Chickadee__, *Parus atricapillus.* Uncommon to fairly common resident in northern Ohio south from Lake Erie for about 70 miles. Rare to uncommon winter visitor downstate, except during invasion years when it sometimes becomes very common. *Max.:* 700, 21 December 1974 on the Cuyahoga Falls CBC. (SR/WR)

☐ *__Carolina Chickadee__, *Parus carolinensis.* Fairly common to common resident in the southern two-thirds of the state. Stragglers sometimes seen farther north. *Max.:* 1801, 29 December 1974 on the Cincinnati CBC. (R)

☐ __Boreal Chickadee__, *Parus Hudsonicus.* Casual winter visitor. Infrequent incursions result in a number of records, usually in November and December, but rarely as late as April. Most records from Lucas, Ottawa, Cuyhoga, and Lake counties.

☐ *__Tufted Titmouse__, *Parus bicolor.* Fairly common to common resident throughout Ohio. *Max.:* 887, 30 December 1973 on the Cincinnati CBC. (R)

Family Sittidae: Nuthatches

☐ *__Red-breasted Nuthatch__, *Sitta canadensis.* Rare and sometimes absent to common migrant and winter visitor. Nests rarely in Ashtabula, Lake, Cuyahoga, Lorain, and Lucas counties. *Max.:* 45, 23 April 1981 at Greenlawn Cemetery in Columbus (T). (ESM/SR/LFM/WR)

☐ *__White-breasted Nuthatch__, *Sitta carolinensis.* Uncommon to common resident in all 88 counties of Ohio. *Max.:* 109, 15 December 1979 on the Wooster CBC; and 161, 26 December 1971 on the Lakewood CBC.(R)

Red-breasted Nuthatch

Family Certhiidae: Creepers

☐ ***Brown Creeper**, *Certhia americana*. Uncommon to fairly common migrant and winter resident. In northern Ohio, nests rarely in Ashtabula, Lake, Portage, Columbiana, Geauga, and Cuyahoga counties—and evidence of nesting in Hocking County. *Max.:* 112, 26 December 1971 on the Cincinnati CBC; and 100, 27 December 1959 on the Buckeye Lake, Licking County CBC. (ESM/SR/LFM/WR)

Family Troglodytidae: Wrens

☐ **Rock Wren**, *Salpinctes obsoletus*. Accidental–hypothetical. One record: an individual 7–14 December 1963 at Edgewater Park in Cleveland (m. obs.).

☐ ***Carolina Wren**, *Thryothorus ludovicianus*. Mostly resident, but exhibits some migratory movement and considerable shifting of populations. Especially vulnerable to severe winters which sometimes eliminate it from large portions of its statewide breeding range. Recent hard winters have greatly reduced its numbers. *Max.:* 1801, 29 December 1974 on the Cincinnati CBC. (R)

☐ ***Bewick's Wren**, *Thryomanes bewickii*. Rare to very rare migrant and summer resident. Has been recorded nesting in 61 scattered counties, but is probably absent from many of them now. Slightly more common in southern Ohio. (ESM/SR/FM)

☐ ***House Wren**, *Troglodytes aedon*. Uncommon to common migrant and summer resident nesting throughout the state. Very rare winter vagrant. *Max.:* 200, 14 May 1949 at Lakeside, Ottawa County (Campbell). (SM/SR/FM)

☐ ***Winter Wren**, *Troglodytes troglodytes*. Rare to fairly common migrant. Nests rarely in Cuyahoga County and there is evidence to indicate nesting in Geauga and Lake counties. Rare in winter. *Max.:* 60, 18 April 1975 at Greenlawn Cemetery in Columbus (T). (ESM/SR/LFM)

☐ ***Sedge Wren**, *Cistothorus platensis*. Rare to uncommon migrant and erratic summer resident. Has nested in 39 counties, mostly in the northern two-thirds of the state. *Max.:* 25, 24 June 1930 in Spencer Township of Lucas County (Campbell). A few winter records. (SM/SR/FM)

☐ ***Marsh Wren**, *Cistothorus palustris*. Locally rare to fairly common migrant and summer resident known to breed in cattail marshes in 48 counties. Rare or absent nesting bird in the unglaciated counties. A few winter records. *Max.:* 150, 18 July 1936 and 22 May 1948 at Little Cedar Point Marsh (Campbell). (SM/SR/FM)

Family Muscicapidae: Old World Warblers, Gnatcatchers, Kinglets, and Thrushes

☐ **Golden-crowned Kinglet**, *Regulus satrapa*. Uncommon to very common migrant and rare to uncommon winter resident. *Max.:* 150, 4 October 1969 along the Cleveland lakefront (Klamm); 230, 1 October 1969 at Little Cedar Point, Lucas County (T), and 25,000 to 50,000 on 7 October 1954, passing over South Bass Island (M. Trautman). (ESM/LFM/WR)

☐ **Ruby-crowned Kinglet**, *Regulus calendula*. Uncommon to very common migrant and rare to uncommon winter resident. *Max.:* 120, 26 April 1959 at Greenlawn Cemetery in Columbus (T); and 120, 4 October 1969 along the Cleveland lakefront (Klamm). (ESM/LFM/WR)

☐ ***Blue-gray Gnatcatcher**, *Polioptila caerulea*. Uncommon to common migrant and summer resident, most numerous as a nesting bird in the unglaciated counties. *Max.:* 19, 30 April 1981 in the Clear Creek Valley, Hocking and Fairfield counties. (T). (ESM/SR/EFM)

☐ ***Eastern Bluebird**, *Sialia sialis*. Rare to common migrant with a considerable percentage of the population resident. Periodic fluctuations in numbers due to severe weather. Breeds in every county, but less numerous in western Ohio. *Max.:* over 100, 22 June 1969 in Highland and Adams counties (T); and 331, 26 December 1971 on the Cincinnati CBC. (ESM/SR/LFM/WR)

☐ **Townsend's Solitaire**, *Myadestes townsendi*. Accidental. Two records: an individual was present from 26 December 1938 to 14 January 1939 at the Boy Scout Reservation in Sylvania Township, Lucas County (Flickinger, Hiett, P. Jones, J. MacLean, J. Nessle), and another was found 24 May 1970 at Magee Marsh, Ottawa County (Van Camp), and collected on the 25th (M. Trautman).

☐ ***Veery**, *Catharus fuscescens*. Uncommon to fairly common migrant and breeding bird in 24 northern and northeastern counties, plus records in Montgomery, Hamilton, and Hocking counties. *Max.:* 43, 14 May 1981 at Greenlawn Cemetery (T).

☐ **Gray-cheeked Thrush**, *Catharus minimus*. Rare to uncommon migrant. Several winter records. *Max.:* 10, 13 May 1961 at Little Cedar Point (T), and seven, 14 May 1981 at Greenlawn Cemetery in Columbus (T). (SM/FM)

☐ **Swainson's Thrush**, *Catharus ustulatus*. Fairly common to very common migrant. Probably has nested in Lake County: a juvenile not long out of the nest was banded 2 August 1976 at Waite Hill (Flanigan). Several December records. *Max.:* over 300, 21 May 1939 at Cedar Point, Lucas County (E. S. Thomas); and 400, 14 May 1981 at Greenlawn Cemetery in Columbus (T). (SM/FM)

☐ ***Hermit Thrush**, *Catharus Guttatus*. Uncommon to fairly common migrant and very rare nesting bird in Ashtabula and Hocking counties. Also breeding evidence from Lorain, Ashland, and Cuyahoga counties. Rare in winter. *Max.:* 250, 29 April 1934, and 75, 14 October 1934 (Campbell), at Little Cedar Point; and 30, 14 April 1983 at Greenlawn Cemetery in Columbus (T). (ESM/SR/LFM/WR)

☐ ***Wood Thrush**, *Hylocichla mustelina*. Fairly common migrant and summer resident widespread throughout the state. Most common as a breeding bird in southern and eastern counties, and the Oak Openings in Lucas County. Rare winter straggler. *Max.:* 36, 25 May 1975 in Hocking County (T); and 26, 16 May 1981 at Greenlawn Cemetery in Columbus (T). (SM/SR/FM)

☐ **Varied Thrush**, *Ixoreus naevius*. Accidental. Eight recent winter occurrences commencing with the first Ohio record, an individual 18 December 1977 to 5 January 1978 at Mentor, Lake County (photographed by W. Klamm); another at Findley State Park, 21 December 1979 to 29 February 1980 (Champney *et al.*); one during the winter of 1979–80 at Cincinnati (m. obs.); one 10–29 February 1980 at Mansfield (McKee *et al.*); two records in the Cleveland area during the winter of 1980–81 (obs. u.); one at Lima in February 1981 (obs. u.); and one at Darbydale, Franklin County, January 1982 (P. Wood, J. Sheridan *et al.*).

☐ ***American Robin**, *Turdus migratorius*. Common to abundant migrant and widespread summer resident. Locally rare or absent to abundant in winter at roosts and where food is plentiful. Frequently migrates north in late February. *Max.:* 6000, winter of 1957–58 at Utica, Licking County (m. obs.); 4500, 1 January 1971 at a roost in Mohican State Forest recorded on the CBC; and 3000, winter of 1971–72 at Painesville (Strock). (ESM/SR/LFM/WR)

Family Mimidae: Mockingbirds and Thrashers

☐ ***Gray Catbird**, *Dumetella carolinensis*. Fairly common to common migrant and widespread summer resident. Sometimes found in winter. *Max.:* 60, 10 May 1958 at Greenlawn Cemetery in Columbus (T). (SM/SR/FM)

☐ ***Northern Mockingbird**, *Mimus polyglottos*. Uncommon to common resident and occasional migrant, most numerous in the southern two-thirds of Ohio. Rare to uncommon in northern counties. *Max.:* 416, 26 December 1971 on the Cincinnati CBC.(R)

☐ ***Brown Thrasher**, *Toxostoma rufum*. Uncommon to common migrant and summer resident nesting locally throughout Ohio. Rare in winter. *Max.:* 30, 18 April 1963 and 40, 30 April 1965 at Greenlawn Cemetery Columbus (T). (ESM/SR/FM)

Family Motacillidae: Wagtails and Pipits

☐ **Water Pipit**, *Anthus spinoletta*. Locally rare to very common migrant, and rare to uncommon winter resident. *Max.:* 400, 5 November 1959 at Utica, Licking County (C. Wagner); 218, 1 April 1975 in Delaware County (Counts); and 60, 19 December 1971 on the Kingston CBC. (ESM/LFM)

☐ **Sprague's Pipit**, *Anthus spragueii.* Casual spring and fall migrant. About a dozen records, half of them in the Cleveland area, plus Lucas, Ross, Butler, and Franklin counties. *Max.:* four to six, 23–26 April 1961 at Forest Hill Park, Cuyahoga County (m. obs.); and three, 25 May 1972 in downtown Cleveland (Leach).

Family Bombycillidae: Waxwings

☐ **Bohemian Waxwing**, *Bombycilla garrulus.* Casual vagrant in winter. Under 20 modern records for the following counties: Lake, Cuyahoga, Lucas, Ottawa, Wood, and Hamilton. *Max.:* 30, 8 March 1940 at Rocky River, Cuyahoga County (Bohme, Corry). (WR)

☐ ***Cedar Waxwing**, *Bombycilla cedrorum.* Uncommon to abundant, rather erratic migrant and widespread summer resident. Sometimes found in winter. *Max.:* 1000, 4–5 November 1939 at Waite Hill, Lake County (F. Sherwin); 716, 21 December 1974 on the Cuyahoga Falls CBC; and 400, 13 March 1968 along the Ross-Pickaway County Line Road (I. Kassoy). (I/SM/SR/FM/WR)

Family Laniidae: Shrikes

☐ **Northern Shrike**, *Lanius excubitor.* Rare winter visitor recorded in Cuyahoga, Lake, Ashtabula, Lucas, Harrison, Lorain, Seneca, Delaware, Licking, Ashland, Mercer, Mahoning, and Hamilton counties. *Max.:* eight, 25 December 1955 at different locations in Ashtabula County (Hicks).(WR)

☐ ***Loggerhead Shrike**, *Lanius ludovicianus.* Rare migrant, summer resident, and winter vagrant. Never numerous, but much reduced in numbers in recent years and is absent from much of its almost state-wide breeding range. (I/R)

Family Sturnidae: Starlings

☐ ***European Starling**, *Sturnus vulgaris.* Very common to very abundant migrant and resident. First successfully introduced into the United States in 1890, when 80 birds were released in Central Park, New York City. The first Ohio record was in January 1916 (Hicks). *Max.:* 150,000 on 12 March 1972 at Columbus (T); and 449,968, 18 December 1977 on the Dayton CBC. (SM/SR/FM/WR)

Family Vireonidae: Vireos

☐ ***White-eyed Vireo,** *Vireo griseus.* Uncommon to fairly common migrant and summer resident in 36 counties, most numerous in unglaciated parts of the state with nesting records extending north to Franklin, Licking, Coshocton, Tuscarawas, Harrison, and Jefferson counties. *Max.:* 14, 2 May 1970 in Hocking and Fairfield counties (T). (ESM/SR/FM)

☐ ***Bell's Vireo,** *Vireo bellii.* Rare migrant. About two dozen records, most from April 27 to mid-May. Two nesting records: June 1968 near Cincinnati (Wiseman *et al.*), and June 1980 to 1982, at Irwin Prairie, Lucas County (m. obs.). (SM/SR/FM)

☐ ***Solitary Vireo,** *Vireo solitarius.* Uncommon migrant. A few nesting records in Astabula County (Hicks) and one record at Barneby Center, Fairfield County. *Max.:* five at Greenlawn Cemetery, Columbus, 5 May 1971 (T). (ESM/SR/FM)

☐ ***Yellow-throated Vireo,** *Vireo flavifrons.* Uncommon migrant and widespread, but rather local, resident breeding in 79 counties. Less common in western and northwestern Ohio. *Max.:* seven, 14 August 1969 near Darbydale, Franklin County (T). (SM/SR/FM)

☐ ***Warbling Vireo,** *Vireo gilvus.* Uncommon to fairly common migrant and summer resident in every county, frequently nesting in cottonwoods and sycamores along streams and rivers. *Max.:* 36, 27 May 1974 along the Mohican River, Ashland County (T). (SM/SR/FM)

☐ **Philadelphia Vireo,** *Vireo philadelphicus.* Rare to uncommon migrant. *Max.:* six, 19 May 1973 at Greenlawn Cemetery in Columbus (T). (SM/FM)

☐ ***Red-eyed Vireo,** *Vireo olivaceus.* Fairly common to common migrant and widespread summer resident nesting throughout the state. *Max.:* 40, 21 May 1960 at Greenlawn Cemetery in Columbus (T); and 42, 31 August 1980 at Crane Creek State Park and Ottawa NWR (Counts, Alexander). (SM/SR/FM)

FAMILY EMBERIZIDAE: WOOD WARBLERS

Subfamily Parulinae

☐ ***Blue-winged Warbler**, *Vermivora pinus.* Uncommon migrant and fairly common widespread summer resident nesting locally in all but eight west-central counties. Most numerous in southern Ohio. *Max.:* 14, 5 June 1966 in Hocking County (T). (SM/SR/EFM)

☐ ***Golden-winged Warbler**, Vermivora chrysoptera.* Rare to uncommon migrant and rare nesting bird in 22 widely scattered counties, but most concentrated in southeastern Ohio. *Max.:* 15, 14 June 1933 in the Oak Openings, Lucas County (Campbell); three, 5 May 1965 at Greenlawn Cemetery in Columbus (T); and four, 3 May 1969 at Winous Point Marsh, Ottawa County (T). (SM/SR/FM)

☐ **Tennessee Warbler**, *Vermivora peregrina.* Uncommon to very common migrant. Early fall migrant: juveniles have been mist-netted and banded in northern Ohio as early as August 1 (Flanigan). *Max.:* 200, 24 May 1946 in Lucas County (Campbell); and 50, 17 May 1975 heard singing between Columbus and Ottawa County (T). (SM/FM)

☐ **Orange-crowned Warbler**, *Vermivora celata.* Rare to uncommon migrant. Some late fall and early December records. *Max.:* 32, 16 May 1948 at Put-in-Bay (M. Trautman); and a troupe of 10, 17 May 1976 at Crane Creek State Park (T). (SM/LFM)

☐ **Nashville Warbler**, *Vermivora ruficapilla.* Uncommon to common migrant. A few late fall records. *Max.:* 60, 9 May 1937 in Lucas County (Campbell); 40, 2 May 1970 at Greenlawn Cemetery in Columbus (T); and 150, 13 May 1961 at Little Cedar Point (T). (SM/FM)

☐ ***Northern Parula**, Parula americana.* Rare to uncommon migrant; summer resident in 19 widely scattered counties in southern and eastern Ohio, plus very locally in Richland, Ashland, Knox, and Holmes counties. *Max.:* six, 17 May 1975 in Hocking County (T). (SM/SR/FM)

☐ ***Yellow Warbler**, Dendroica petechia.* Uncommon to very common migrant and summer resident throughout Ohio, but breeding populations are reduced in many areas from previous years. Most numerous in unglaciated counties and, locally, in large marshes. *Max.:* 1500, 15 May 1948 at Bay Point, Ottawa County (Campbell). (SM/SR/EFM)

☐ ***Chestnut-sided Warbler**, Dendroica pensylvanica.* Uncommon to common migrant; rare to uncommon resident in 12 counties in northwest and northeast Ohio, plus records of single pairs nesting in the Clear Creek Valley, Fairfield County. *Max.:* 200, 13 May 1961 at Little Cedar Point, Lucas County (T). (SM/SR/FM)

☐ ***Magnolia Warbler**, Dendroica magnolia.* Uncommon to fairly common migrant; sometimes abundant in local concentrations along the western shores of Lake Erie. Rare nesting bird in Ashtabula, Geauga,

Lucas, and Hocking counties. *Max.:* 500, 13 May 1961 at Little Cedar Point (T). (SM/SR/FM)

☐ **Cape May Warbler**, *Dendroica tigrina*. Uncommon to common migrant. A few December records. *Max.:* 50, 13 May 1961 at Little Cedar Point (T). (SM/FM)

☐ ***Black-throated Blue Warbler**, *Dendroica caerulescens*. Rare to common migrant. Very rare nesting bird in Ashtabula and Geauga counties. *Max.:* a migratory flock of 200, 4 May 1936 on Little Mountain, Lake County (*fide* A. Williams). (SM/SR/FM)

☐ **Yellow-rumped Warbler**, *Dendroica coronata*. Common to abundant migrant. Frequently winters in modest numbers. Several records of Audubon's Warbler, the western form of the species, have been reported. *Max.:* 700, 30 September 1944 at Little Cedar Point (Campbell); 150, 27 April 1942 at Shaker Lake, Cuyahoga County (A. Williams); and 118, 23 December 1979 on the Columbus CBC. (ESM/LFM/WR)

☐ **Black-throated Gray Warbler**, *Dendroica nigrescens*. Casual western vagrant. Nine late April and May records of individual birds in Cuyahoga and Lake counties between 1920 and 1967; one, 15 November 1950 on the Ohio State University campus at Columbus (E. S. Thomas, G. Rea); one, 5 December 1969 in Athens (H. Smith); and one, 20 April 1980 at Lorain (Pogacnik).

☐ **Townsend's Warbler**, *Dendroica townsendi*. Accidental. One individual 7 April 1973, well documented, at Crane Creek State Park (E. Tramer, Van Camp *et al.*).

☐ ***Black-throated Green Warbler**, *Dendroica virens*. Uncommon to common migrant; uncommon to locally common resident in six southern counties (Hocking, Fairfield, Jackson, Lawrence, Scioto, and Adams), six northeastern counties (Lake, Cuyahoga, Geauga, Ashtabula, Mahoning, and Columbiana), plus Ashland and Knox counties. Ten to 19 pairs nested between 1933 and 1938 on Little Mountain, Lake County (B. Bole, Jr.). *Max.:* 200, 23 September 1944 in Lucas County (Campbell). (SM/SR/FM)

☐ ***Blackburnian Warbler**, *Dendroica fusca*. Uncommon to fairly common migrant; sometimes very common at concentration points along the shores of western Lake Erie. Rare nesting bird in Ashtabula, Lake, and Geauga counties. *Max.:* 100, 24 May 1947 in Lucas and Ottawa counties (Campbell); and 50, 13 May 1961 at Little Cedar Point (T). (SM/SR/FM)

□ ***Yellow-throated Warbler**, *Dendroica dominica.* Rare migrant; locally rare to uncommon breeding bird—usually in sycamores along streams—in 19 counties in southern, extreme southwestern and, rarely, in central Ohio. *Max.:* eight, 17 April 1970 at Tar Hollow State Park, Hocking County; and 20, 8 May 1971 in the Clear Creek Valley, Hocking and Fairfield counties (T). (SM/SR/EFM)

□ ***Pine Warbler**, *Dendroica pinus.* Rare to uncommon migrant. Nests rarely in Ashtabula, Lake, Ashland, and Knox counties; more commonly in Fairfield, Hocking, Jackson, and Scioto counties. A few winter records. *Max.:* about 20, 13 and 14 March 1977 at Cincinnati (Wiseman); and three, 19 April 1964 at Greenlawn Cemetery in Columbus (C. Dawson, E. S. Thomas). (ESM/SR/FM)

□ **Kirtland's Warbler**, *Dendroica kirtlandii.* The first known specimen of this species was collected 13 May 1851 on the grounds of the eminent naturalist Dr. Jared P. Kirtland in what is now Lakewood, Cuyahoga County. This very rare migrant, most often seen in May, has been observed about 15 times in Cuyahoga County, about 12 times in Lucas and Ottawa counties, and records are at hand for eight sightings in Franklin County. It has also been reported from Licking, Seneca, and Hamilton counties. Some fall records, all in the Rocky River Valley, Cuyahoga County, are: two, 7 October 1934; one, 2 September 1935; one, 8 September 1940, and two, 8 September 1946 (all reported by J. McQuown). (SM/FM)

□ ***Prairie Warbler**, *Dendroica discolor.* Rare to uncommon migrant; nests in 20 counties, mostly in southern and southeastern Ohio, but has also been reported nesting in Licking, Muskingham, and Holmes counties. *Max.:* 25, 22 June 1969 in Adams County (T); 24, 29 June 1969 in Hocking and Fairfield counties (T); and 8 pairs in June 1977 in Holmes County (D. Kline). (SM/SR/EFM)

□ **Palm Warbler**, *Dendroica palmarum.* Rare to common migrant. *Max.:* 200, 6 May 1934 in Lucas County (Campbell); and 20, 6 May 1961 in Columbus (T). Rare in winter. (SM/FM)

□ ***Bay-breasted Warbler**, *Dendroica castanea.* Uncommon to very common migrant, rather late in spring and more numerous in fall. *Max.:* 100, 24 May 1973 at Greenlawn Cemetery in Columbus (T); and 125, 21 September 1958 in Columbus (T). (LSM/FM)

□ **Blackpoll Warbler**, *Dendroica striata.* Uncommon to common late spring and fall migrant. *Max.:* 16, 24 May 1973 at Greenlawn Cemetery in Columbus (T); and 12, 25 May 1975 at Crane Creek State Park (m. obs.). (LSM/FM)

☐ ***Cerulean Warbler**, *Dendroica cerulea*. Uncommon to fairly common migrant, and rare to fairly common nesting bird in woods throughout Ohio. Less numerous in northwest and western parts of the state. Formerly more numerous in many areas. *Max.:* 18, 13 June 1970 in Fairfield and Hocking counties (T); and 15, 28 April 1974 at Crane Creek State Park (*fide* Campbell). (SM/SR/FM)

☐ ***Black-and-White Warbler**, *Mniotilta varia*. Uncommon to fairly common migrant. Fairly common nesting bird in Allegheny Plateau counties and very locally in other parts of Ohio. *Max.:* 25, 9 May 1937 at Little Cedar Point, Lucas County (Campbell). (SM/SR/FM)

☐ ***American Redstart**, *Setophaga ruticilla*. Uncommon to common migrant; summer resident in 69 counties, but absent or rare in southwestern counties and parts of western Ohio. *Max.:* 150, 13 May 1961 at Little Cedar Point (T). (SM/SR/FM)

☐ ***Prothonotary Warbler**, *Protonotaria citrea*. Rare migrant and rare to uncommon local nesting bird. Has nested in 34 scattered counties. Most numerous as a breeder at locations such as Crane Creek State Park, Lake St. Marys, Cranberry Marsh at Buckeye Lake, Killbuck State Wildlife Area, and Paint Creek. *Max.:* 25, 23 May 1981 at Cranberry Marsh (Counts). (SM/SR/EFM)

☐ ***Worm-eating Warbler**, *Helmitheros vermivorus*. Rather rare migrant in most of the state. Locally rare to uncommon summer resident in 44 counties in eastern and southern Ohio, most numerous in Hocking, Jackson, Scioto, Vinton, Athens, and Ross counties. *Max.:* 12, 6 May 1975 after a morning thunderstorm at Firestone Park, Summit County (Tveekrem); seven, 28 April 1974 at Crane Creek State Park (Campbell), and ten, 8 June 1958 in the Clear Creek Valley, Fairfield and Hocking counties (T). (SM/SR/FM)

☐ **Swainson's Warbler**, *Limnothlypis swainsonii*. Accidental. One collected 21 June 1947 in Lawrence County (Green), and the following sight records: one, 12 May 1963 at Huntington Reservation, Cuyahoga County (obs. u.); one, 18 May 1971 near Chardon, Geauga County (Spare); another near Chardon, 13 May 1972 (Martin); one, 12 May 1975 at Firestone Park, Summit County (Biscan), and one in late May 1976 at East Liverpool, Columbiana County (N. Laitsch).

☐ ***Ovenbird**, *Seiurus aurocapillus*. Uncommon to fairly common migrant, and rare to common resident nesting in every county. Most numerous in unglaciated regions of the state, northeastern Ohio and, locally, in northwestern Ohio. *Max.:* 40, 25 May 1975 in Fairfield and Hocking counties (T). (SM/SR/FM)

☐ *Northern Waterthrush*, *Seiurus noveboracensis*. Rare to uncommon migrant; locally rare nesting bird in Ashtabula, Trumbull, Lake, Geauga, Portage, and Huron counties. *Max.:* 10, 14 May 1971 in Ottawa and Lucas counties (T). (SM/SR/FM)

☐ *Louisiana Waterthrush*, *Seiurus motacilla*. Rare to uncommon migrant; uncommon to locally common nesting bird, except in much of western and northwestern Ohio. Most common in Hocking, Jackson, Vinton, Scioto, and Athens counties. *Max.:* 16, 7 June 1958 in Hocking County (T). (SM/SR/FM)

☐ *Kentucky Warbler*, *Oporornis formosus*. Rare to uncommon migrant, nesting in 44 counties of southern, eastern, and east-central Ohio, locally north to Ashland, Wayne, Stark, and Mahoning counties. Several breeding records from Ottawa and Lucas counties. *Max.:* 16, 8 June 1958 in Hocking and Fairfield counties (T). (SM/SR/FM)

☐ Connecticut Warbler, *Oporornis agilis*. Rare late spring and fall migrant. *Max.:* three, 6 October 1958 at Greenlawn Cemetery in Columbus (T); and from 15 to 25 daily between 22 and 25 May 1929 at Buckeye Lake, Licking County (M. Trautman). (LSM/FM)

☐ *Mourning Warbler*, *Oporornis philadelphia*. Rare to uncommon late spring and fall migrant. Very rare breeder in the Oak Openings of Lucas County, and evidence of nesting in Geauga County (B. Bole, Jr.). *Max.:* 15 to 50 daily between 22 and 25 May 1929 at Buckeye Lake, Licking County (M. Trautman); and five, 28 May 1974 at Greenlawn Cemetery in Columbus (T). (LSM/FM)

☐ *Common Yellowthroat*, *Geothlypis trichas*. Uncommon to common migrant and summer resident throughout the state. *Max.:* 300, 18 July 1936 in the Oak Openings of Lucas County (Campbell). An average of 52 pairs nest annually in a seven-mile stretch of the Clear Creek Valley, Fairfield and Hocking counties (T). Rare in winter. (SM/SR/FM)

☐ *Hooded Warbler*, *Wilsonia citrina*. Rare to uncommon migrant; uncommon to fairly common nesting bird in much of southern and southeastern Ohio with local concentrations in northeastern counties and a few in Lucas County. *Max.:* five, 22 April 1973 at Greenlawn Cemetery in Columbus (T). (SM/SR/EFM)

☐ Wilson's Warbler, *Wilsonia pusilla*. Rare to fairly common migrant. Several winter records. *Max.:* 50, 21 May 1939 near Little Cedar Point, Lucas County (Campbell). (SM/FM)

☐ ***Canada Warbler**, *Wilsonia canadensis*. Rare to uncommon migrant. Rare nesting bird in Hocking, Fairfield, Lucas, Ashtabula, and Geauga counties. *Max.:* 30, 23 May 1931 in Lucas County (Campbell); and 15, 18 May 1974 in Ottawa and Lucas counties (T). (SM/FM)

☐ **Painted Redstart**, *Myioborus picta*. Accidental. An individual was present from 15–22 November 1970 at the home of Dr. and Mrs. Joseph Hadden in Middleburg Heights, Cuyahoga County. Photographed and seen by many local birders.

☐ ***Yellow-breasted Chat**, *Icteria virens*. Rare to fairly common migrant; fairly common nesting bird in southern Ohio, less numerous north of central Ohio, and absent from seven northwestern counties. *Max.:* 48, 25 May 1975 in Hocking and Fairfield counties (T); and 20 to 200 daily from 4–20 May at Buckeye Lake before 1940 (M. Trautman). (SM/SR/EFM)

Subfamily Thraupiae: Tanagers

☐ ***Summer Tanager**, *Piranga rubra*. Rare to uncommon migrant; uncommon to fairly common summer resident in the southern half of the state, plus scattered nesting records in Cuyahoga, Summit, Ashland, Lucas, Wyandot, and Delaware counties. *Max.:* 10, 8 June 1958 in Hocking and Fairfield counties (T). (SM/SR/EFM)

☐ ***Scarlet Tanager**, *Piranga olivacea*. Uncommon to fairly common migrant and widespread summer resident nesting in every county. Most numerous in the unglaciated counties of southern and southeastern Ohio, and the rolling woodlands of the northeastern counties. *Max.:* 18, 24 May 1973 at Greenlawn Cemetery in Columbus (T). (SM/SR/FM)

☐ **Western Tanager**, *Piranga ludoviciana*. Accidental. One in the spring of 1962 near Yellow Springs, Greene County (D. Wheeler); one, 24 November 1962 at Mayfield Heights, Cuyahoga County (obs. u.); one from 1–28 December 1963 at a feeder in Mentor, Lake County (m. obs.); and another photographed there and seen by many birders from 21 December 1971 to 3 January 1972 (*fide* Fais).

Subfamily Cardinalinae

☐ ***Northern Cardinal**, *Cardinalis cardinalis*. Uncommon to very common and widespread resident, sometimes in large loose flocks of 50 or more birds in winter before spring dispersal. Less numerous in northern Ohio. *Max.:* 3775, 27 December 1970 on the Cincinnati CBC. (R)

☐ ***Rose-breasted Grosbeak**, *Pheucticus ludovicianus.* Uncommon to common migrant. Fairly common summer resident in 18 counties of northeastern Ohio, and nine counties in the northwestern part of the state. Scattered nesting records in Delaware, Licking, Franklin, Fairfield, and Hamilton counties. A few December records. *Max.:* 60, 6 May 1976, and 81, 13 May 1975, at Greenlawn Cemetery in Columbus (T). (SM/SR/FM)

☐ **Black-headed Grosbeak**, *Pheucticus melanocephalus.* Accidental western vagrant. At least six records: one, 24 April 1960 at Cleveland (B. Bole, Jr. *et al.*); one, 3 and 5 March 1965 at a feeding station in Lucas County (Wood, *fide* Campbell); one, 19 May 1974 in Lucas County (Campbell); one, 1 January to 5 April 1975, photographed at an Akron feeder (R. Graham, *fide* Szabo); one, 14 May 1975 in Columbus (T); and one from January to March 1976 at Cincinnati (M. Garvin, Wiseman).

☐ ***Blue Grosbeak**, *Guiraca caerulea.* Rare spring and summer vagrant; very rare nesting bird with records in Vinton, Adams, Meigs, and Hamilton counties. Non-breeding birds have been observed in 17 counties as far north as Lake Erie. Very unseasonal was an immature male visiting a feeder in Mentor, Lake County, from 3 March to 4 April 1962 (obs. u.).

☐ ***Indigo Bunting**, *Passerina cyanea.* Fairly common to very common migrant and widespread summer resident. Nests in every county. *Max.:* 300, 6 September 1941 in Lucas County (Campbell); 120, 25 May 1975 in Hocking County (T); and 238, 16 May 1981, migrating west along the Lake Erie shore in Ottawa County in flocks of up to 18 birds (T). (SM/SR/FM)

☐ ***Dickcissel**, *Spiza americana.* Erratic, rare to uncommon migrant and summer resident. Nests irregularly in the western half of the state with a few scattered records in central and northeastern Ohio. Less numerous than formerly. A considerable number of winter records, especially at feeders. *Max.:* 150, 2 June 1934 at Cedar Point Marsh, Ottawa County (Campbell); six, 5 July 1974, near Alum Creek Reservoir, Delaware County (T). (I/SR)

Subfamily Emberizine

☐ **Green-tailed Towhee**, *Pipilo chlorurus*. Accidental. Two records: one from December 1963 through January 1964 at a feeder in Columbus (G. Smith, E. Limes, J. Ray, R. Hunter), and one banded in September 1964 at Ashtabula (H. Nehl).

☐ ***Rufous-sided Towhee**, *Pipilo erythrophthalmus*. Uncommon to common migrant. Nests throughout the state in wooded areas; most common in unglaciated counties. Frequently seen in winter, especially in southern Ohio. *Max.:* 150, 2 May 1936 in the Oak Openings, Lucas County (Campbell); and 125, 17 April 1963 at Greenlawn Cemetery (T). (ESM/SR/LFM/WR)

☐ ***Bachman's Sparrow**, *Aimophila aestivalis*. Irregular, rare migrant and summer resident, greatly reduced in numbers during the past 30 years. Formerly nested in 37 counties, mostly in southern and southeastern Ohio with peripheral records as far north as Lucas and Ashland counties.

☐ **American Tree Sparrow**, *Spizella arborea*. Uncommon to locally very abundant winter resident. *Max.:* 2006, 29 December 1955 on the Delaware CBC. (WR)

☐ ***Chipping Sparrow**, *Spizella passerina*. Fairly common to common migrant and summer resident nesting in every county. Somewhat more plentiful in the unglaciated counties of southern and southeastern Ohio. Extremely rare in winter. *Max.:* 83, 9 May 1978 at Greenlawn Cemetery in Columbus (T). (ESM/SR/FM)

☐ **Clay-colored Sparrow**, *Spizella pallida*. Accidental. Six records on hand: one, 12 May 1940, collected at Put-in-Bay (C. Walker, M. Trautman); one, 16 May 1948 at Put-in-Bay (Mayfield, Flickinger); one, 25 April 1964, and one, 9 May 1965, in the Oak Openings, Lucas County (A. Claugus); one, 16 May 1976 at Mentor Marsh, Lake County (LePage, Newhous); and one, 27–30 April 1981 at Magee Marsh (Peterjohn).

☐ ***Field Sparrow**, *Spizella pusilla*. Uncommon to common migrant and summer resident nesting throughout Ohio. Frequently seen in winter, especially in southern Ohio. *Max.:* 50, 9 May 1978 at Greenlawn Cemetery in Columbus (T); and 193, 26 December 1971 on the Cincinnati CBC. (ESM/SR/LFM/WR)

Lark Sparrow

☐ **Black-chinned Sparrow**, *Spizella atrogularis*. Accidental–hypothetical. One record: an individual observed 25 April 1974 in company with Field Sparrows at Ottawa NWR (Campbell).

☐ ***Vesper Sparrow**, *Pooecetes gramineus*. Uncommon to fairly common migrant and widespread summer resident, somewhat more numerous in northern Ohio, but much less plentiful than before 1960. *Max.:* 50 to 500 daily between mid-September and mid-October—before 1940—in the Buckeye Lake area, Licking County (M. Trautman); and 30, 19 April 1965 in Pickaway County (T). (ESM/SR/FM)

☐ ***Lark Sparrow**, *Chondestes grammacus*. Rare migrant and uncommon summer resident. Nests sparingly in southern and southeastern Ohio and in the Oak Openings of Lucas County. Probably found most often in Adams County, but scarce everywhere and probably absent from many of the 45 counties where it has been reported nesting.

☐ **Black-throated Sparrow**, *Amphispiza bilineata*. Accidental. An individual was observed and photographed from 5 November to 6 December 1961 at Ashtabula (Perkins, Stump).

☐ **Lark Bunting**, *Calamospiza melanocorys*. Accidental. Several records: an individual picked up 6 September 1944 at South Euclid, Cuyahoga County (M. Skaggs); a singing male, 28 June 1970 south of Conneaut, Ashtabula County (Perkins, m. obs.); a male from January to 8 May 1971 at a feeder at Thurston, Licking County (D. Fisher), and a female 28 April 1962 in Columbus (T).

☐ *Savannah Sparrow*, *Passerculus sandwichensis*. Uncommon to very common migrant. Widespread summer resident in the northern half of the state with a few scattered records farther south, including Franklin, Fairfield, Madison, Montgomery, and Hamilton counties. Numerous winter records. *Max.:* 60, 22 September 1971 at Killdeer Plains Wildlife Area, Wyandot County (A. Claugus); and 150, 15 April 1956 in Pickaway County (T). (ESM/SR/FM)

☐ **Baird's Sparrow**, *Ammodramus bairdii*. Accidental–hypothetical. Two records: one, 22 April 1951 at Put-in-Bay, Ottawa County (M. Trautman); and one heard singing in tall rye grass from 11–17 May 1964 in Montgomery County (J. Mason, J. Hill, C. Horst).

☐ ***Grasshopper Sparrow**, *Ammodramus savannarum*. Somewhat irregular, uncommon to common migrant and widespread nesting bird throughout the agricultural areas of Ohio. *Max.:* 18, 7 June 1970 in Adams County (T). (SM/SR/FM)

☐ ***Henslow's Sparrow**, *Ammodramus henslowii*. Erratic, rare to uncommon migrant and summer resident nesting in 55 counties mostly in northern and central Ohio, but scattered instances south to Mor-

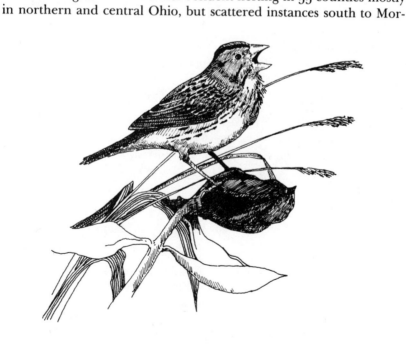

Henslow's Sparrow

gan, Athens, Jackson, and Clinton counties. Less numerous in recent years. *Max.:* 40 pairs in June 1977 in a large field in Holmes County (D. Kline). (sm/sr/fm)

☐ **LeConte's Sparrow**, *Ammodramus leconteii.* Very rare migrant, most records in April and May from Lucas to Lake County. One collected on 5 April 1880 in Hamilton County (Dury); six specimens collected in October 1936 in Clermont County, with additional birds at the same location the following spring (Goodpaster, Maslowski); and one collected in a sedgy swamp in Licking County, 23 November 1936 (Hicks). *Max.:* four, 8 August 1977 at Ottawa NWR (Van Camp *et al.*).

☐ **Sharp-tailed Sparrow**, *Ammodramus caudacutus.* Very rare migrant with most records from northern Ohio, especially the marshes of Lucas and Ottawa counties, and marshy edges and among the sand dunes of Lake Erie beaches in Cuyahoga County. Usually found 14–24 May and 14–30 September. *Max.:* 75 to 200, 30 September to 15 October 1964 in Winous Point Marsh, Ottawa County (M. Trautman, W. Goodpaster); two, 24 May 1974, at Killdeer Plains Wildlife Area (LeGrande); and two, 17 May 1980 at Mosquito Creek Lake (C. Johnson).

☐ **Fox Sparrow**, *Passerella iliaca.* Uncommon to common early spring and fall migrant. Numerous winter records, especially in southern Ohio. *Max.:* 43, 5 April 1976 at Greenlawn Cemetery in Columbus (T); and 21, 16 December 1979 on the Paint Creek CBC. (esm/lfm/wr)

☐ ***Song Sparrow**, *Melospiza melodia.* Fairly common to very common resident and migrant. Nests in every county. *Max.:* 215, 11 May 1963 in Ottawa and Lucas counties (T); and 1246, 28 December 1958 on the Cincinnati CBC. (r/esm/fm)

☐ **Lincoln's Sparrow**, *Melospiza lincolnii.* Rare to uncommon migrant. *Max.:* 20, 11 October 1936 at Little Cedar Point, Lucas County (Campbell). (sm/fm)

☐ ***Swamp Sparrow**, *Melospiza georgiana.* Uncommon to fairly common migrant and locally rare to uncommon nesting bird in 32 counties, mostly in northeastern Ohio, rarely in marshes and swales of Lucas and Ottawa counties. Numerous winter records. *Max.:* an unusual concentration of 532 birds, 5 October 1979 at Winous Point Marsh, Ottawa County (Pogacnik). (sm/fm/wr)

☐ ***White-throated Sparrow**, *Zonotrichia albicollis*. Uncommon to abundant migrant, rare to common winter resident—especially in southern Ohio—and a rare nesting bird in Ashtabula, Cuyahoga, Lorain, and Erie counties. *Max.:* 800, 6 May 1975 at Greenlawn Cemetery in Columbus (T); and 1058, 26 December 1977 on the Cincinnati CBC. (ESM/LFM/WR)

☐ **White-crowned Sparrow**, *Zonotrichia leucophrys*. Uncommon to common migrant. Sometimes locally numerous in winter. *Max.:* 72, 11 May 1974 in Lucas and Ottawa counties; and 126, 30 December 1956 on the Buckeye Lake CBC. (SM/FM/WR)

☐ **Harris' Sparrow**, *Zonotrichia querula*. Very rare western vagrant from October to May. Of 29 records since 1928, 18 were in northern Ohio; 11 from Columbus and farther south. *Max.:* four, 27 October 1957 at Metzger Marsh, Lucas County (Holt); and three, 26 December 1971 at a feeder in Lakewood, Cuyahoga County (CBC). (LFM/WR/SM)

☐ ***Dark-eyed Junco**, *Junco hyemalis*. Fairly common to very abundant migrant and winter visitor. Rare nesting bird in Ashtabula, Trumbull, Lake, Geauga, and Cuyahoga counties. Western "Oregon" Juncos and intergrades are sometimes observed. *Max.:* 2609, 29 December 1968 on the Cincinnati CBC. (LFM/WR/ESM/SR)

☐ **McCown's Longspur**, *Calcarius mccownii*. Accidental–hypothetical. One sight record of an individual 19 February 1928 near Newark Licking County (A. Claugus).

☐ **Lapland Longspur**, *Calcarius lapponicus*. Irregular, rare to infrequently very abundant winter visitor and migrant, more numerous in northern Ohio. *Max.:* 10,000 on 1 May 1949 in Lucas County (H. Mayfield); and 1176, 30 December 1961 on the Tiffin CBC. (LFM/WR/SM)

☐ **Smith's Longspur**, *Calcarius pictus*. Very rare, but sometimes occurs in sizable flocks during migration, mostly in central and southwestern Ohio, but occasionally in Cuyahoga County and other scattered locations. Most observations are in March and April. The first record for Ohio was a specimen collected 29 January 1888 near Ravena, Portage County (C. Streator). *Max.:* 100, 6 March 1971 in southwest Franklin County (E. S. Thomas, M. Trautman, T.); and 250, 15 April 1956 on the Ross-Pickaway County Line Road (D. Smith, I. Kassoy). (ESM/LFM)

☐ **Chestnut-collared Longspur**, *Calcarius ornatus*. Accidental–hypothetical. An individual in breeding plumage observed 15 May 1949 near Monclova, Lucas County (S. Holloway).

☐ **Snow Bunting**, *Plectrophenax nivalis*. Rare to locally abundant migrant and winter visitor, most numerous in northern Ohio. *Max.:* 5000, 25 October 1942 west of Toledo (Campbell); 2500, 22 February 1962 near Castalia, Erie County (O. Davies); and 5000, 26 January 1976 near Arlington, Hancock County (R. Phillips). (LFM/WR/ESM)

Subfamily Icterinae: Meadowlarks, Blackbirds, and Orioles

☐ *****Bobolink**, *Dolichonyx oryzivorus*. Rare to uncommon transient and summer resident having nested in most counties except in southern and southeastern Ohio. Local concentrations are sometimes found in migration and late summer. Greatly reduced in numbers since mid-century. *Max.:* 300, 25 August 1974 near the Alum Creek Reservoir, Delaware County (T); and between 1922 and 1934, Dr. Milton B. Trautman observed 600 to 2000 daily from 15 August to 15 September at Buckeye Lake, Licking County (Trautman, 380). (SM/SR/EFM)

☐ *****Red-winged Blackbird**, *Agelaius phoeniceus*. Common to very abundant migrant and widespread summer resident; rare in winter except near roosts when it is sometimes very numerous. *Max.:* 500,000 average daily 4–15 March 1975 during evening migratory flights along the Scioto River south of Columbus (T). (ESM/SR/LFM/WR)

☐ *****Eastern Meadowlark**, *Sturnella magna*. Fairly common to common migrant and widespread summer resident. Somewhat variable in numbers as a result of population losses in the northern part of its wintering range during severe weather. (ESM/SR/LFM/WR)

☐ *****Western Meadowlark**, *Sturnella neglecta*. Rare vagrant. Individuals have been reported from at least 16 counties and there are nesting records for Lucas, Wood, Henry, Defiance, Paulding and, possibly, Cuyahoga County.

☐ *****Yellow-headed Blackbird**, *Xanthocephalus xanthocephalus*. Rare vagrant, most often seen near Lake Erie, but scattered records throughout the state. A few individuals have nested intermittently in the marshes of Lucas and Ottawa counties for over 40 years. *Max.:* 25, 22 October 1947 in western Lucas County (Campbell). (ESM/SR/LFM)

Bobolink

☐ **Rusty Blackbird**, *Euphagus carolinus*. Rare to locally common migrant, sometimes abundant near roosts in winter. *Max.:* 5008, 16 December 1979 on the Buckeye Lake CBC. (EFM/LFM/WR)

☐ **Brewer's Blackbird**, *Euphagus cyanocephalus*. Rare migrant, possible winter visitor. Most often seen in small numbers near Lake Erie, but there have been a few instances of large numbers. *Max.:* estimated 100,000 at a roost October and November 1963 in Lorain (O. Davies).

☐ ***Common Grackle**, *Quiscalus quiscula*. Abundant migrant and very common summer resident. Sometimes numerous in winter near roosts. *Max.:* estimated 500,000 on 2 March 1975, migrating north along the Scioto River south of Columbus (T). (ESM/SR/LFM)

☐ ***Brown-headed Cowbird**, *Molothrus ater*. Common to very abundant migrant and summer resident. *Max.:* 25,000, 12 March 1972, migrating north along the Scioto River south of Columbus (T); and 50,000, 18 December 1977 on the Dayton CBC. (ESM/SR/LFM)

☐ ***Orchard Oriole**, *Icterus spurius*. Rare to uncommon migrant, nesting locally in over 50 scattered counties, most numerous in the eastern part of Ohio. *Max.:* 13, 20 June 1980 in Seneca County (Peterjohn); and 7, 7 June 1958 in Hocking County (T). (SM/SR/EFM)

☐ ***Northern Oriole**, *Icterus galbula*. Uncommon to fairly common migrant and widespread summer resident nesting in every part of the state. A few winter records. *Max.:* 100, 14 May 1948 at Lakeside, Ottawa County (Campbell); 50, 13 May 1961 at Little Cedar Point, Lucas County (T); and 52, 27 May 1974 along the Mohican River, Ashland County (T). (SM/SR/FM)

Family Fringillidae: Grosbeaks, Finches

☐ **Rosy Finch**, *Leucosticte arctoa*. Accidental–hypothetical. One at a feeder 5 April 1971 in Cuyahoga County, well documented (Hazen, *fide* Perkins).

☐ **Pine Grosbeak**, *Pinicola enucleator*. Very rare winter vagrant, most records from northern Ohio. Sightings beyond its normal range include one in the 1950s (no date) at Columbus (E. S. Thomas); one or two birds seen from 20 December 1951 to 26 January 1952 in Hamilton County (J. Zimmerman, W. Johannes, M. Bagel); three, 10 April 1966 in Delaware County (R. Ramey); and one, 5 February 1972 at Dawes Arboretum, Delaware County (B. Markham). *Max.:* a total of 400, including flocks of 100 and 60, 7 February 1962, in Akron and surrounding areas (J. Sheppard, M. Glassner). (WR)

☐ ***Purple Finch**, *Carpodacus purpureus*. Rare to common migrant; irregular winter resident, and rare to uncommon nesting bird. Breeds in Ashtabula, Lake, Cuyahoga, Trumbull, Mahoning, and Columbiana counties. Recent extensions of its breeding range have included records in Lucas, Seneca, Lorain, and Franklin counties. *Max.:* 186, 31 December 1956 on the O'Shaughnessy Reservoir CBC; and 250, 27 December 1959 near Monclova, Lucas County (Campbell). (ESM/SR/FM/WR)

☐ ***House Finch** *Carpodacus mexicanus*. The odyssey of this species' range expansion into Ohio begins on the west coast where it is native. In 1940, a shipment of illegally captured birds sent to dealers on the east coast was released on Long Island when the birds' protected status was discovered. Adapting to their new environment, they spread to New Jersey by 1949, Connecticut in 1957, and Washington, D.C., and Baltimore by 1962. In 1971, expanding populations had reached as far south as North Carolina, and other contingents were spearheading into Pennsylvania and western New York State.

The first bird to reach Ohio was recorded during the winter of 1962–63 at Holden Arboretum, Lake County, and by January 1964

Common Redpolls

there were two males present—and half a dozen other birds at nearby locations. Not many years later, House Finches were turning up in Dayton (1973), Columbus (1974), Mansfield (1976), Toledo (1978), and Cincinnati (1979). During the winter of 1980–81, 952 birds were tallied on 20 different CBCs, all in the eastern half of Ohio. (R)

☐ *Red Crossbill, *Loxia curvirostra.* Erratic, locally rare to fairly common winter visitor. A few nesting records from Cuyahoga County, and one record from Tar Hollow State Forest, Hocking County, in April 1973 (A. Staffan). *Max.:* 35, 31 December 1979 on the Grand Rapids–Waterville CBC; 30, 9 June 1976 at Mentor, Lake County (Jones); and 30 to 40, 10–15 June 1973 in Hocking County (Worth, Randle). (WR)

☐ White-winged Crossbill, *Loxia leucoptera.* Erratic, locally rare to fairly common winter visitor, most numerous in northern Ohio. *Max.:* 20 to 60 during the winter of 1971–72 at Waite Hill, Lake County (Sherwin); 20, 31 January 1976 at Columbus (C. Toops); and 12, 26 December 1977 on the Cincinnati CBC. (WR)

☐ Common Redpoll, *Carduelis flammea.* Irregular, rare winter visitor, more common in northern Ohio. *Max.:* 113, 27 November 1969 on the Cleveland waterfront (Klamm); 253, 28 December 1969 on the Youngstown CBC; 200, 7 January 1970 at Lorain (m. obs.); and 80 to

130, 19 January to 19 March 1970 at Columbus (m. obs.). (LFM/WR/ESM)

☐ **Hoary Redpoll**, *Carduelis hornemanni*. Accidental winter vagrant. Records include a specimen 16 March 1931 at Little Cedar Point, Lucas County (Hicks), and several sight records in Columbus from 19 December 1969 to 19 March 1970, associating with sizable flocks of Common Redpolls (E. S. Thomas, Rickley, Limes, Hengst, *et al.*).

☐ *****Pine Siskin**, *Carduelis pinus*. Rather erratic, rare to common migrant and winter visitor. Probably breeds sparingly in Ashtabula County. At Greenlawn Cemetery in Columbus, a nest with an incubating adult was found 14 April 1973 (M. Bolton, F. Bader, G. Trusty, W. Hamilton), and two others were found there 29 April and 6 May 1981 (T). (ESM/LFM/WR)

☐ *****American Goldfinch**, *Carduelis tristis*. Uncommon to abundant migrant and summer resident. Rather numerous in winter, especially at feeders. *Max.:* 2000, 1 May 1954 at Put-in-Bay (M. Trautman). (SM/SR/LFM/WR)

☐ **Evening Grosbeak**, *Coccothraustes vespertinus*. Irregular, very rare to locally common migrant and winter visitor. Most numerous in northern Ohio and the Allegheny Plateau counties. *Max.:* 125 in December 1961 and January 1962 at Rockbridge, Hocking County (C. Goslin); 325, 1 January 1972 on the Ashtabula CBC; and 348, 20 December 1975 on the Youngstown CBC. (WR/SM/LFM)

Family Passeridae: Weaver Finches

☐ *****House Sparrow**, *Passer domesticus*. Common to abundant year-round resident.

HYBRIDS

☐ **Brewster's Warbler**, *Vermivora leucobronchialis*. The dominant form of hybrid between the Golden-winged and Blue-winged warblers. Rare to uncommon in late April and May; frequently found in the Oak Openings, Lucas County, where it interbreeds with both Blue-winged and Golden-winged warblers.

☐ **Lawrence's Warbler**, *Vermivora lawrencei*. The recessive form of Golden-winged Warbler X Blue-winged Warbler hybrid. Very rare migrant and breeding bird. Scattered records from all over the state, but most often seen in northern Ohio, especially the Oak Openings of Lucas County.

EXOTICS AND POSSIBLE ESCAPES

Greater Flamingo, *Phoenicopterus ruber.*

Lesser White-fronted Goose, *Anser erythropus.*

Bar-headed Goose, *Anser indicus.*

Barnacle Goose, *Branta leucopsis.*

Egyptian Goose, *Alopochen aegyptiaca.*

Common Shelduck, *Tadorna tadorna.*

Ruddy Shelduck, *Casarca ferruginea.*

Chukar, *Alectoris chukar.*

Black Partridge, *Francolinus francolinus.*

Elliot's Pheasant, *Syrmaticus ellioti.*

Ringed Turtle-dove, *Streptopelia risoria.*

Canary-winged Parakeet, *Brotogeris versicolorus.*

Monk Parakeet, *Myiopsitta monachus.*

Yellow-headed Parrot, *Amazona ochrocephala.*

Troupial, *Icterus icterus.*

Altamira (Lichtenstein's) Oriole, *Icterus gularis.*

European Goldfinch, *Carduelis carduelis.*

Eurasian Tree Sparrow, *Passer montanus.*

Birding and
Natural History Organizations

There are many organizations the birder can join. Local birding clubs are scattered fairly evenly around Ohio, and there are a number of national organizations. Many of the local clubs are affiliated with the National Audubon Society and offer joint memberships.

National Organizations

The National Audubon Society
950 Third Avenue
New York, NY 10022
(212) 832-3200
Publishes: *Audubon Magazine* bimonthly; *American Birds,* bimonthly.

American Birding Association
P.O. Box 4335
Austin, TX 78765
(512) 474-4804
Publishes: *Birding* bimonthly.

American Ornithologists' Union
National Museum of Natural History
Smithsonian Institute
Washington, D.C.
(612) 373-5643
Publishes: *The Auk* quarterly.

Wilson Ornithological Society
c/o Josselyn Van Tyne Memorial
   Library
Museum of Zoology
Ann Arbor, MI 48104
Publishes: *The Wilson Bulletin* quarterly.

National Wildlife Federation
1412 16th Street NW
Washington, D.C. 20036
Publishes: *National Wildlife* bimonthly, *International Wildlife* bimonthly, and *Ranger Rick.*

OHIO ORGANIZATIONS

Akron/Summit County

Greater Akron Audubon Society
c/o Ann Biscan

797 N. Firestone Boulevard
Akron, OH 44306 (or)

Carol Tveekrem
621 Surfside Drive
Akron, OH 44319
Newsletter, meetings, field trips.

Birding Hotlines:
Jessie Belitsky (216) 644-4790
Carol Tveekrem (216) 644-5006
Fred Fricker (216) 836-2670
Ann Biscan (216) 773-3129
Emil Bacik (216) 351-6636
Sibering Nature Center (216) 836-2185

Ashtabula/Ashtabula County

Sam Wharram Nature Club
c/o Mrs. Charles Berry
2019 Dewey Road
Ashtabula, OH 44004 (or)

Capt. Paul J. Perkins
118 Grandview Avenue
Conneaut, OH 44030
Newsletter, meetings, field trips.

Birding Hotlines:
Paul Perkins (216) 599-7765
Howard & Marcella Meahl
   (216) 998-4338

Canton/Stark County

Canton Audubon Society
P.O. Box 68
Newsletter, meetings, field trips.

Birding Hotlines:
Nick Rini (216) 877-9013
Richard Evans (216) 478-1037
Robert Ball (216) 499-7814
Arnold Fritz (216) 833-2503

Cleveland/Cuyahoga County

Cleveland Audubon Society
2063 E. Fourth Street
Cleveland, OH 44115
(216) 861-5093
Bulletin, meetings, field trips.
Taped Rare Bird Alert: (216) 861-2447

Kirtland Bird Club
The Cleveland Museum of Natural
History
Wade Oval, University Circle
Cleveland, OH 44106
(216) 231-4600
Newsletter, meetings, field trips.
Taped Rare Bird Alert: (216) 696-8186

Cincinnati/Hamilton County

Cincinnati Bird Club
c/o Cincinnati Nature Center
4949 Tealtown Road
Milford, OH 45150
(513) 831-1711
Newsletter, field trips, meetings.

Birding Hotlines:
Art Wiseman (513) 481-4302
George Perbix (513) 561-4122
Dave Styer (513) 559-0224

Columbus/Franklin County

Columbus Audubon Society
1065 Kendale Road North
Columbus, OH 43220
(614) 451-4591
Newsletter, meetings, field trips.
Taped Rare Bird Alert: (614) 221-9736

Columbus Natural History Society
111 Richards Avenue
Columbus, OH 43214
(614) 263-2445
Meetings, field trips.

Wheaton Club
c/o James Stahl
1326 Schrock Road
Columbus, OH 43229
(614) 882-5084
Bulletin, meetings, field trips.

Dayton/Montgomery County

Dayton Audubon Society
Dayton Museum of Natural History
2629 Ridge Avenue
Dayton, OH 45414
Newsletter, meetings, field trips.

Birding Hotlines:
Roland Mercer (513) 836-2453
Dick Mills (513) 294-6850
Aullwood Audubon Center
(513) 890-7360

Fremont/Sandusky County

R. B. Hayes Audubon Society
P.O. Box 92
Fremont, OH 43420
Newsletter, meetings, field trips.

Birding Hotlines:
Jean Knoblaugh (419) 992-4475

Greenville/Darke County

Nature Trails Club
c/o Dr. & Mrs. David Cox
8017 Fisher Dangler Road
Greenville, OH 45331 (or)
Mr. & Mrs. Martin Fourman
Rural Route #2
Arcanum, OH 45304
Schedules, meetings, field trips.

Birding Hotline:
Martin & Thelma Fourman
(513) 692-5947

Licking County

Licking County Audubon Society
c/o Dawes Arboretum
State Route 13
Newark, OH 43055
Newsletter, meetings, field trips.

Birding Hotlines:
Fritz Griffith (614) 928-4939
Herman Kind (614) 654-0402

Lima/Allen County

Tri-Moraine Audubon Society
c/o Philip Hugo
1631 W. High
Lima, OH 45805 (or)
Mrs. Jackie Light
2850 Fort Amanda Road
Lima, OH 45808
Newsletter, meetings, field trips.

Birding Hotlines:
George Heffner (419) 222-4466
Harvey Hiebert (419) 358-2177

Mansfield/Richland County

Mohican Audubon Society
P.O. Box 3731

Mansfield, OH 44907
Newsletter, meetings, field trips.

Birding Hotlines:
Marion Mansfield (419) 756-0603
Bud Console (419) 529-5755

Marietta/Washington County

Marietta Audubon Club
c/o Mrs. Jerie Stewart
600 Masonic Park Road
Marietta, OH 45750 (or)
Rosalie Pitner
Rural Route #1, Mitchell Lane
Marietta, OH 45750
Schedule, meetings, field trips.

Birding Hotlines:
Jerie Stewart (614) 373-5030
Rosalie Pitner (614) 373-3620

Marion/Marion County

Burroughs Nature Club of Marion
c/o Mrs. Howard Iams
1247 Oakwood Road
Marion, OH 43302
Schedule, meetings, field trips.

Birding Hotline:
Hemmerly Flowers (614) 387-1163

Middletown/Butler County

Middletown Audubon Society, Inc.
P.O. Box 675
Middletown, OH 45042
Newsletter, meetings, field trips.

Birding Hotlines:
Hayward Ball (513) 777-3383
Bruce Peters, Jr. (513) 423-2596

Portsmouth/Scioto County

Shawnee Nature Club
P.O. Box 1432
Friendship, OH 45630
Schedule, meetings, field trips.

Birding Hotlines:
Harry & Elsie Knighton (614) 354-2018
Dave Todt (614) 858-6053
James & Virginia Nickel (614) 858-4320

Salem/Mahoning County

Salem Bird Study Club
c/o William C. Baker
559 Euclid Street
Salem, OH 44460 (or)

Mrs. Raymond Crewson
466 West Oregon Avenue
Sebring, OH 44672
Yearbook, meetings, field trips.

Birding Hotline:
Margaret & Bill Baker (216) 337-7593
Ray Crewson (216) 938-2564
Wanda & Howard Horst
(216) 549-2286

Sandusky/Erie County

Firelands Audubon Society
c/o J. G. Frost
1419 Erie Boulevard
Sandusky, OH 44870
Newsletter, meetings, field trips.

Birding Hotlines:
John Blakeman (419) 625-1091
J. Frost (419) 625-2580
J. Leighton (419) 734-3951

Springfield/Clark County

Clark County Audubon Society
c/o John Gallagher
23 South Center Street
Springfield, OH 45502
Newsletter, meetings, field trips.

Birding Hotlines:
Roger Gordon (513) 399-0114
Gus Stucker (513) 399-5474
Kevin McGowan (513) 323-4251

Steubenville/Jefferson County

Forest Audubon Society
c/o Clinton S. Banks
202 Wilma Avenue
Steubenville, OH 43952
Annual bulletin, meetings, field trips.

Birding Hotline:
Clinton Bank (614) 264-1595

Toledo/Lucas County

Toledo Naturalists' Association
c/o Myrtle Sarver
6011 North River Road
Waterville, OH 43566
(419) 878-4164
Bulletin, meetings, field trips.
Taped Rare Bird Alert: (419) 867-9765

Van Wert County

Upper Maumee Valley Naturalist's
Club

c/o Joseph Sheldon
520 East Main Street
Van Wert, OH 45891
Annual dinner meeting, CBC

Birding Hotlines:
Larry Rosner (419) 238-6075
Denton Stetler (419) 238-5260

Willoughby/Lake County

Burroughs Nature Club of Willoughby
c/o Greta Palliston, Jr.
4588 River Street
Willoughby, OH 44094 (or)
Richard Quigley
37550 Rogers Road
Willoughby, OH 44091
Newsletter, meetings, field trips.

Birding Hotlines:
Mary Huey (216) 951-8703
Carl Newhouse (216) 354-8750

Wooster/Wayne County

Wayne Nature Club
c/o Robert M. Bruce
1457 Cleveland Road
Wooster, OH 44691 (or)
Mr. & Mrs. James Atkinson
RFD #3
Wooster, OH 44691
Schedule, meetings, field trips.

Birding Hotlines:
Bob & Jeanne Bruce (216) 264-8535

Alden & Mary Schaffter
(216) 264-3155
Bob & Irene Sparr (216) 264-6791

Youngstown/Mahoning County

Grant M. Cook Bird Club
c/o Lyle D. Miller
5795 Mill Creek Boulevard
Youngstown, OH 44512 (or)
James Beeghly
43 Lee Run Road
Poland, OH 44514
Schedule, meetings, field trips.

Birding Hotlines:
Lyle Miller (216) 758-2879
Bill Bartolo (216) 758-3492
Randy Jones (216) 757-9225

Zanesville/Muskingham County

Zanesville Audubon Society
P.O. Box 2464
Zanesville, OH 43701
Newsletter, meetings, field trips.

Birding Hotlines:
Bob Bryant (614) 452-5972
Tom Kullman (614) 453-9014
Kenneth Gale (614) 452-7696

Tri-State/Ohio-W. Va.-Penn.

The Brooks Bird Club
707 Warwood Avenue
Wheeling, W. Va. 26003
Publication, meetings, field trips,
and annual Foray.

Taped Rare Bird Alerts

Cleveland   (216) 696-8186 (Kirtland Bird Club)
Cleveland   (216) 861-2447 (Cleveland Audubon Society)
Columbus   (614) 221-9736 (Columbus Audubon Society)
Toledo   (419) 867-9765 (Toledo Naturalists' Association)

Bibliography

American Birding Association
  1975 *Checklist: Birds of the Continental United States and Canada.* First Edition, Austin, TX.
American Ornithologists' Union
  1957 *Check-list of North American Birds.* 5th ed. (2nd printing). Baltimore, MD.
Arhib, Robert
  1979 The Blue List for 1980. *American Birds* 33:830–835.
Audubon Field Notes
  1947–1981 Bimonthly periodical, National Audubon Society, New York, NY.
Auk, The
  1923–1981 Bimonthly periodical, American Ornithologists' Union, Washington, D.C.
Balch, Lawrence G.
  1979 Identification of Groove-billed and Smooth-billed Anis. *Birding* 11:295–297.
*Bailey, David
  1975 *The Birds of Cedar Bog, Spring of 1975.* Nat. Hist. Dept., Ohio Historical Society, Vol. 4.
*Bent, A. C.
  1919–1958 *Life Histories of North American Birds.* United States National Museum, Bull. 107, 113, 121, 126, 130, 135, 142, 146, 162, 167, 170, 174, 176, 179, 191, 195, 196, 197, 203, and 211 (Also available in reprints from Dover, New York, NY).
*Bingaman, Ann
  1975 *Wahkeena Breeding Bird Census.* Nat. Hist. Dept., Ohio Historical Society, Vol. 4.
Bird Lore
  1921–1940 Bimonthly periodical, National Audubon Society, New York, NY.
*Blincoe, Benedict J.
  1967 *The Birds of Dayton and the Central Miami Valley.* Ohio Biological Survey, Biol. Notes #1 (Revised edition).
*Buchanan, Forest W.
  1980 *The Breeding Birds of Carroll and Northern Jefferson Counties, Ohio.* Ohio Biological Survey, Biol. Notes #12, Columbus, OH.
*Borror, Donald J.
  1950 A Check List of the Birds of Ohio with the migration dates for the birds of central Ohio. *Ohio Journal of Science* 50:1–32.
Braun, Lucy E.
  1961 *The Woody Plants of Ohio.* The Ohio State University Press, Columbus, OH.

Bull, John
    1975   *Birds of the New York Area.* Dover Press, New York, NY.
*Campbell, Louis W.
    1940   *Birds of Lucas County.* Toledo Museum of Science Bulletin #1.
*_____
    1968   *Birds of the Toledo Area.* The Toledo Blade Co.
Cedar Bog Symposium
    1973   Ohio Biological Survey, Circ. #4.
*Clark, Clarence F. and Sipe, James P.
    1970   *Birds of the Lake St. Marys Area.* Ohio Dept. Nat. Resources, Publ.
    #350.
*Cleveland Bird Calendar
    1950–1980   Kirtland Bird Club. Quarterly periodical. Cleveland, OH.
*Columbus Audubon Society Newsletter
    1960–1982   Columbus Audubon Society, monthly periodical, Sept.–
    May.
Courser, William D.
    1979   Continued Breeding Range Expansion of the Burrowing Owl in
    Florida. *American Birds* 33:143.
Davie, Oliver
    1882   *Naturalist's Manual.* Columbus, OH
_____
    1898   *Nests and Eggs of North American Birds.* 5th ed. McKay, Philadel-
    phia, PA.
*Dawson, William L.
    1903   *The Birds of Ohio.* Wheaton Publishing Co., Columbus, OH.
Geffen, Alice M.
    1978   *A Birdwatcher's Guide to the Eastern United States.* Barron's, Wood-
    bury, NY.
Godfrey, W. Earl
    1979   *The Birds of Canada.* National Museums of Canada, Ottawa,
    Canada.
Henninger, W. F.
    1909   A Preliminary List of the Birds of Middle and Southern Ohio.
    Wilson Bull. 14:77–93.
Hicks, Lawrence E.
    1928   Some interesting Ohio records. *Wilson Bull.* 41:43–44.
*_____
    1937   An Ohio Invasion of LeConte's Sparrows. *Auk* 54:545–46.
*_____
    1935   Distribution of the Breeding Birds of Ohio. *Ohio Biol. Surv. Bull.*
    32:125–90.
Hochbaum, H. Albert
    1955   *Travels and Traditions of Waterfowl.* University of Minnesota Press,
    Minneapolis.
Jones, Lynds
    1903   *The Birds of Ohio.* Ohio Acad. Sci. Spec. Paper #6.
Keller, Charles E., Shirley A., Timothy C.
    1979   *Indiana Birds and their Haunts.* Indiana University Press, Bloom-
    ington, IN.

*Kemsies, Emerson, and Randle, Worth
  1953   *Birds of Southwestern Ohio.* Edward Bros., Ann Arbor, MI.
Kirby, Edna L.
  1976   *Wahkeena Spring Flowers.* Nat. Hist. Dept., Ohio Historical Society, Vol. 5.
Mackenzie, John P. S.
  1977   *Birds in Peril.* Pagurian Press Limited, Toronto, Canada.
Lauro, Anthony J., and Spencer, Barbara J.
  1980   A method for separating juvenal and first-winter Ring-billed Gulls and Common Gulls. *American Birds* 34:111–117.
Lincoln, Frederick C.
  1950   *Migration of Birds.* U.S. Dept. Agr. Circ. 16.
Lowery, Jr., George H.
  1955   *Louisiana Birds.* Louisiana State University Press, Baton Rouge, La.
Matthiessen, Peter
  1959   *Wildlife in America.* Viking Press, New York, NY.
*McLaughlin, Vincent P.
  1979   Occurrence of Large-billed Tern (*Phaetusa simplex*) in Ohio. *American Birds* 33:727.
Melvin, Ruth W.
  1970   *A Guide to Ohio Outdoor Education Areas.* Ohio Dept. Nat. Resources and the Ohio Academy of Science. Columbus, OH.
*Newman, Donald L.
  1969   *A Field Book of Birds of the Cleveland Region.* Cleveland Museum of Natural History.
Oberholser, H. C.
  1896   A Preliminary List of the Birds of Wayne County, Ohio. Bull. of the Ohio Agr. Exp. Sta. Tech. Ser. 1:243–353.
Peterson, Roger Tory
  1961   *A Field Guide to Western Birds.* Houghton Mifflin, Boston, Mass.
Peterson, Roger Tory, Mountfort, Guy, and Hollum, P.A.D.
  1967   *A Field Guide to the Birds of Britain and Europe.* Houghton Mifflin, Boston, Mass.
Peterson, Roger Tory
  1980   *A Field Guide to the Birds East of the Rockies.* Houghton Mifflin, Boston, Mass.
Pettingill, Jr., Olin Sewall
  1962   *A Guide to Bird Finding East of the Mississippi.* 4th ed. Oxford University Press, New York, NY.
_____
  1970   *Ornithology in Laboratory and Field.* Burgess, Minneapolis, Minn.
*Redstart, The
  1957–1980   Quarterly publication, the Brooks Bird Club, Wheeling, W. Va.
Savaloja, Terry
  1981   Yellow Rail. *Birding* 13:80–85.
*Smith, H. G., Burnard, R. K., Good, E. E., and Keener, J. M.
  1973   Rare and Endangered Vertebrates of Ohio. *The Ohio Journal of Science* 73:257–271.

Tate, Jr., James
    1981   The Blue List for 1981. *American Birds* 35:3–10.
Terres, John K.
    1980   *The Audubon Society Encyclopedia of North American Birds.* Alfred A. Knopf, New York, NY.
Thomas, Edward S.
    1928   The Chickadees of Central Ohio. *Ohio State Museum Sci. Bull.* 1:76–77.
*_____
    1939–1981   Nature column, weekly. The *Columbus Sunday Dispatch.*
Thomson, A. L. (editor)
    1964   A New Dictionary of Birds. McGraw-Hill, New York, NY.
Thomson, Tom
    1974   *Checklist of the Birds of Ohio.* The Columbus Audubon Society.
*Trautman, Milton B.
    1940   *The Birds of Buckeye Lake, Ohio.* University of Michigan Museum of Zoology, Misc. Publ. No. 44.
*Trautman, Milton B., and Mary A.
    1968   Annotated List of the Birds of Ohio. *The Ohio Journal of Science* 68:257–332.
Trautman, Milton B.
    1979   Experiences and thoughts relative to Kirtland's Warbler. *The Jack Pine Warbler* 57:135–140.
Walker, Charles F.
    1928   The Seasons of Birds in Central Ohio. The Ohio State Museum Sci. Bull. 1:9–23.
*Wheaton Club Bulletin
    1956–1980   Annual publication of the Wheaton Club. Columbus, OH.
*Wheaton, J. M.
    1882   Report on the Birds of Ohio. *Geol. Surv. Ohio* 4:187–628.
*Williams, Arthur B.
    1950   *Birds of the Cleveland Region.* The Cleveland Museum of Natural History.
*Wilson Bulletin, The
    1925–1980   Quarterly publication of the Wilson Ornithological Society, Ann Arbor, MI.

Index to the Birds

Page numbers are grouped according to the three major divisions of the state: N denotes the northern tier of counties; WC, the west-central counties; and U, the unglaciated counties. Italicized page numbers refer to the annotated checklist of the birds. Species that are mentioned on nearly every page of the book are marked with an asterisk—the only page number given at asterisked entries is the italic one.

Site Index